Introduction to Autonomous Mobile Robots

Introduction to Autonomous Mobile Robots

Roland Siegwart and Illah R. Nourbakhsh

✳
A Bradford Book
The MIT Press
Cambridge, Massachusetts
London, England

This book was set in Times Roman by the authors using Adobe FrameMaker 7.0.
Printed and bound in the United States of America.

Library of Congress Cataloging-in-Publication Data

Siegwart, Roland.
  Introduction to autonomous mobile robots / Roland Siegwart and Illah Nourbakhsh.
    p. cm. — (Intelligent robotics and autonomous agents)
  "A Bradford book."
  Includes bibliographical references and index.
  ISBN 0-262-19502-X (hc : alk. paper)
  1. Mobile robots. 2. Autonomous robots. I. Nourbakhsh, Illah Reza, 1970– . II. Title. III. Series.

TJ211.415.S54 2004
629.8′92—dc22   2003059349

To Luzia and my children Janina, Malin and Yanik who give me their support and freedom to grow every day — RS

To my parents Susi and Yvo who opened my eyes — RS

To Marti who is my love and my inspiration — IRN

To my parents Fatemeh and Mahmoud who let me disassemble and investigate everything in our home — IRN

Slides and exercises that go with this book are available on:

http://www.mobilerobots.org

Contents

Acknowledgments

This book is the result of inspirations and contributions from many researchers and students at the Swiss Federal Institute of Technology Lausanne (EPFL), Carnegie Mellon University's Robotics Institute, Pittsburgh (CMU), and many others around the globe.

We would like to thank all the researchers in mobile robotics that make this field so rich and stimulating by sharing their goals and visions with the community. It is their work that enables us to collect the material for this book.

The most valuable and direct support and contribution for this book came from our past and current collaborators at EPFL and CMU. We would like to thank: Kai Arras for his contribution to uncertainty representation, feature extraction and Kalman filter localization; Matt Mason for his input on kinematics; Nicola Tomatis and Remy Blank for their support and assistance for the section on vision-based sensing; Al Rizzi for his guidance on feedback control; Roland Philippsen and Jan Persson for their contribution to obstacle avoidance; Gilles Caprari and Yves Piguet for their input and suggestions on motion control; Agostino Martinelli for his careful checking of some of the equations and Marco Lauria for offering his talent for some of the figures. Thanks also to Marti Louw for her efforts on the cover design.

This book was also inspired by other courses, especially by the lecture notes on mobile robotics at the Swiss Federal Institute of Technology, Zurich (ETHZ). Sincere thank goes to Gerhard Schweitzer, Martin Adams and Sjur Vestli. At the Robotics Institute special thanks go to Emily Hamner and Jean Harpley for collecting and organizing photo publication permissions. The material for this book has been used for lectures at EFPL and CMU since 1997. Thanks go to all the many hundreds of students that followed the lecture and contributed thought their corrections and comments.

It has been a pleasure to work with MIT Press, publisher of this book. Thanks to Ronald C. Arkin and the editorial board of the Intelligent Robotics and Autonomous Agents series for their careful and valuable review and to Robert Prior, Katherine Almeida, Sharon Deacon Warne, and Valerie Geary from MIT Press for their help in editing and finalizing the book.

Special thanks also to Marie-Jo Pellaud at EPFL for carefully correcting the text files and to our colleagues at the Swiss Federal Institute of Technology Lausanne and Carnegie Mellon University.

Preface

Mobile robotics is a young field. Its roots include many engineering and science disciplines, from mechanical, electrical and electronics engineering to computer, cognitive and social sciences. Each of these parent fields has its share of introductory textbooks that excite and inform prospective students, preparing them for future advanced coursework and research. Our objective in writing this textbook is to provide mobile robotics with such a preparatory guide.

This book presents an introduction to the fundamentals of mobile robotics, spanning the mechanical, motor, sensory, perceptual and cognitive layers that comprise our field of study. A collection of workshop proceedings and journal publications could present the new student with a snapshot of the state of the art in all aspects of mobile robotics. But here we aim to present a foundation — a formal introduction to the field. The formalism and analysis herein will prove useful even as the frontier of the state of the art advances due to the rapid progress in all of mobile robotics' sub-disciplines.

We hope that this book will empower both the undergraduate and graduate robotics student with the background knowledge and analytical tools they will need to evaluate and even critique mobile robot proposals and artifacts throughout their career. This textbook is suitable as a whole for introductory mobile robotics coursework at both the undergraduate and graduate level. Individual chapters such as those on Perception or Kinematics can be useful as overviews in more focused courses on specific sub-fields of robotics.

The origins of the this book bridge the Atlantic Ocean. The authors have taught courses on Mobile Robotics at the undergraduate and graduate level at Stanford University, ETH Zurich, Carnegie Mellon University and EPFL (Lausanne). Their combined set of curriculum details and lecture notes formed the earliest versions of this text. We have combined our individual notes, provided overall structure and then test-taught using this textbook for two additional years before settling on the current, published text.

For an overview of the organization of the book and summaries of individual chapters, refer to Section 1.2.

Finally, for the teacher and the student: we hope that this textbook proves to be a fruitful launching point for many careers in mobile robotics. That would be the ultimate reward.

1 Introduction

1.1 Introduction

Robotics has achieved its greatest success to date in the world of industrial manufacturing. Robot arms, or *manipulators*, comprise a 2 billion dollar industry. Bolted at its shoulder to a specific position in the assembly line, the robot arm can move with great speed and accuracy to perform repetitive tasks such as spot welding and painting (figure 1.1). In the electronics industry, manipulators place surface-mounted components with superhuman precision, making the portable telephone and laptop computer possible.

Yet, for all of their successes, these commercial robots suffer from a fundamental disadvantage: lack of mobility. A fixed manipulator has a limited range of motion that depends

Figure 1.1
Picture of auto assembly plant-spot welding robot of KUKA and a parallel robot Delta of SIG Demaurex SA (invented at EPFL [140]) during packaging of chocolates.

on where it is bolted down. In contrast, a mobile robot would be able to travel throughout the manufacturing plant, flexibly applying its talents wherever it is most effective.

This book focuses on the technology of mobility: how can a mobile robot move unsupervised through real-world environments to fulfill its tasks? The first challenge is locomotion itself. How should a mobile robot move, and what is it about a particular locomotion mechanism that makes it superior to alternative locomotion mechanisms?

Hostile environments such as Mars trigger even more unusual locomotion mechanisms (figure 1.2). In dangerous and inhospitable environments, even on Earth, such *teleoperated* systems have gained popularity (figures 1.3, 1.4, 1.5, 1.6). In these cases, the low-level complexities of the robot often make it impossible for a human operator to directly control its motions. The human performs localization and cognition activities, but relies on the robot's control scheme to provide motion control.

For example, Plustech's walking robot provides automatic leg coordination while the human operator chooses an overall direction of travel (figure 1.3). Figure 1.6 depicts an underwater vehicle that controls six propellers to autonomously stabilize the robot submarine in spite of underwater turbulence and water currents while the operator chooses position goals for the submarine to achieve.

Other commercial robots operate not where humans *cannot* go but rather share space with humans in human environments (figure 1.7). These robots are compelling not for reasons of mobility but because of their *autonomy*, and so their ability to maintain a sense of position and to navigate without human intervention is paramount.

Figure 1.2
The mobile robot Sojourner was used during the Pathfinder mission to explore Mars in summer 1997. It was almost completely teleoperated from Earth. However, some on-board sensors allowed for obstacle detection. (http://ranier.oact.hq.nasa.gov/telerobotics_page/telerobotics.shtm).
© NASA/JPL

Figure 1.3
Plustech developed the first application-driven walking robot. It is designed to move wood out of the forest. The leg coordination is automated, but navigation is still done by the human operator on the robot. (http://www.plustech.fi). © Plustech.

Figure 1.4
Airduct inspection robot featuring a pan-tilt camera with zoom and sensors for automatic inclination control, wall following, and intersection detection (http://asl.epfl.ch). © Sedirep / EPFL.

Figure 1.5
Picture of Pioneer, a robot designed to explore the Sarcophagus at Chernobyl. © Wide World Photos.

Figure 1.6
Picture of recovering MBARI's ALTEX AUV (autonomous underwater vehicle) onto the Icebreaker Healy following a dive beneath the Arctic ice. Todd Walsh © 2001 MBARI.

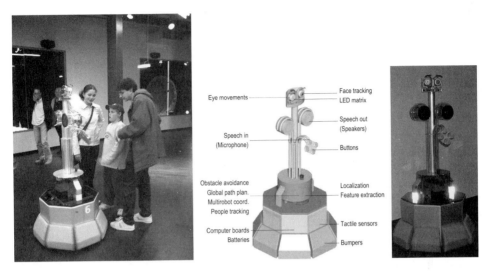

Figure 1.7
Tour-guide robots are able to interact and present exhibitions in an educational way [48, 118, 132, 143,]. Ten Roboxes have operated during 5 months at the Swiss exhibition EXPO.02, meeting hundreds of thousands of visitors. They were developed by EPFL [132] (http://robotics.epfl.ch) and commercialized by BlueBotics (http://www.bluebotics.ch).

Figure 1.8
Newest generation of the autonomous guided vehicle (AGV) of SWISSLOG used to transport motor blocks from one assembly station to another. It is guided by an electrical wire installed in the floor. There are thousands of AGVs transporting products in industry, warehouses, and even hospitals. © Swisslog.

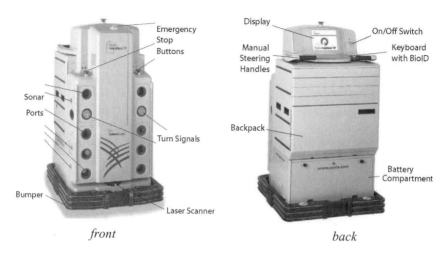

front   *back*

Figure 1.9
HELPMATE is a mobile robot used in hospitals for transportation tasks. It has various on-board sensors for autonomous navigation in the corridors. The main sensor for localization is a camera looking to the ceiling. It can detect the lamps on the ceiling as references, or landmarks (http://www.pyxis.com). © Pyxis Corp.

Figure 1.10
BR 700 industrial cleaning robot (left) and the RoboCleaner RC 3000 consumer robot developed and sold by Alfred Kärcher GmbH & Co., Germany. The navigation system of BR 700 is based on a very sophisticated sonar system and a gyro. The RoboCleaner RC 3000 covers badly soiled areas with a special driving strategy until it is really clean. Optical sensors measure the degree of pollution of the aspirated air (http://www.karcher.de). © Alfred Kärcher GmbH & Co.

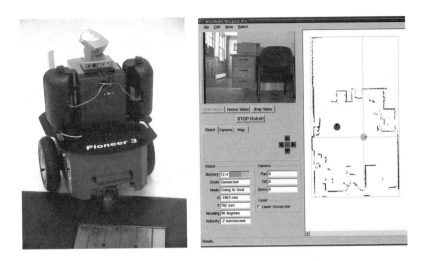

Figure 1.11
PIONEER is a modular mobile robot offering various options like a gripper or an on-board camera. It is equipped with a sophisticated navigation library developed at SRI, Stanford, CA (Reprinted with permission from ActivMedia Robotics, http://www.MobileRobots.com).

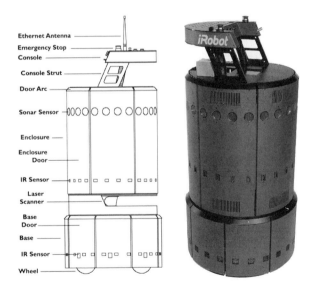

Ethernet Antenna
Emergency Stop
Console
Console Strut
Door Arc
Sonar Sensor
Enclosure
Enclosure Door
IR Sensor
Laser Scanner
Base Door
Base
IR Sensor
Wheel

Figure 1.12
B21 of iRobot is a sophisticated mobile robot with up to three Intel Pentium processors on board. It has a large variety of sensors for high-performance navigation tasks (http://www.irobot.com/rwi/). © iRobot Inc.

Figure 1.13
KHEPERA is a small mobile robot for research and education. It is only about 60 mm in diameter. Various additional modules such as cameras and grippers are available. More then 700 units had already been sold by the end of 1998. KHEPERA is manufactured and distributed by K-Team SA, Switzerland (http://www.k-team.com). © K-Team SA.

For example, AGV (autonomous guided vehicle) robots (figure 1.8) autonomously deliver parts between various assembly stations by following special electrical guidewires using a custom sensor. The Helpmate service robot transports food and medication throughout hospitals by tracking the position of ceiling lights, which are manually specified to the robot beforehand (figure 1.9). Several companies have developed autonomous cleaning robots, mainly for large buildings (figure 1.10). One such cleaning robot is in use at the Paris Metro. Other specialized cleaning robots take advantage of the regular geometric pattern of aisles in supermarkets to facilitate the localization and navigation tasks.

Research into high-level questions of cognition, localization, and navigation can be performed using standard research robot platforms that are tuned to the laboratory environment. This is one of the largest current markets for mobile robots. Various mobile robot platforms are available for programming, ranging in terms of size and terrain capability. The most popular research robots are those of ActivMedia Robotics, K-Team SA, and I-Robot (figures 1.11, 1.12, 1.13) and also very small robots like the Alice from EPFL (Swiss Federal Institute of Technology at Lausanne) (figure 1.14).

Although mobile robots have a broad set of applications and markets as summarized above, there is one fact that is true of virtually every successful mobile robot: its design involves the integration of many different bodies of knowledge. No mean feat, this makes mobile robotics as interdisciplinary a field as there can be. To solve locomotion problems, the mobile roboticist must understand mechanism and kinematics; dynamics and control theory. To create robust perceptual systems, the mobile roboticist must leverage the fields of signal analysis and specialized bodies of knowledge such as computer vision to properly employ a multitude of sensor technologies. Localization and navigation demand knowledge of computer algorithms, information theory, artificial intelligence, and probability theory.

Figure 1.15 depicts an abstract control scheme for mobile robot systems that we will use throughout this text. This figure identifies many of the main bodies of knowledge associated with mobile robotics.

This book provides an introduction to all aspects of mobile robotics, including software and hardware design considerations, related technologies, and algorithmic techniques. The intended audience is broad, including both undergraduate and graduate students in introductory mobile robotics courses, as well as individuals fascinated by the field. While not absolutely required, a familiarity with matrix algebra, calculus, probability theory, and computer programming will significantly enhance the reader's experience.

Mobile robotics is a large field, and this book focuses not on robotics in general, nor on mobile robot applications, but rather on mobility itself. From mechanism and perception to localization and navigation, this book focuses on the techniques and technologies that enable robust *mobility*.

Clearly, a useful, commercially viable mobile robot does more than just move. It polishes the supermarket floor, keeps guard in a factory, mows the golf course, provides tours in a museum, or provides guidance in a supermarket. The aspiring mobile roboticist will start with this book, but quickly graduate to course work and research specific to the desired application, integrating techniques from fields as disparate as human-robot interaction, computer vision, and speech understanding.

Figure 1.14
Alice is one of the smallest fully autonomous robots. It is approximately 2 x 2 x 2 cm, it has an autonomy of about 8 hours and uses infrared distance sensors, tactile whiskers, or even a small camera for navigation [54].

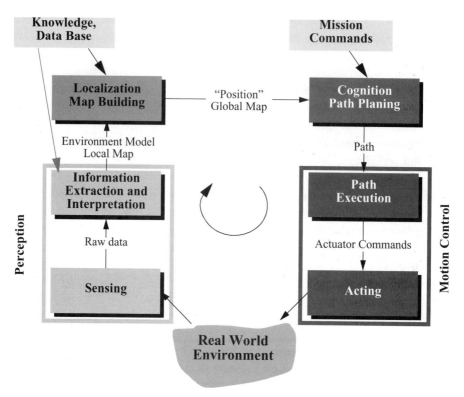

Figure 1.15
Reference control scheme for mobile robot systems used throughout this book.

1.2   An Overview of the Book

This book introduces the different aspects of a robot in modules, much like the modules shown in figure 1.15. Chapters 2 and 3 focus on the robot's low-level *locomotive ability*. Chapter 4 presents an in-depth view of *perception*. Then, Chapters 5 and 6 take us to the higher-level challenges of *localization* and even higher-level *cognition*, specifically the *ability to navigate robustly*. Each chapter builds upon previous chapters, and so the reader is encouraged to start at the beginning, even if their interest is primarily at the high level. Robotics is peculiar in that solutions to high-level challenges are most meaningful only in the context of a solid understanding of the low-level details of the system.

   Chapter 2, "Locomotion", begins with a survey of the most popular mechanisms that enable locomotion: wheels and legs. Numerous robotic examples demonstrate the particular talents of each form of locomotion. But designing a robot's locomotive system properly requires the ability to evaluate its overall motion capabilities quantitatively. Chapter 3, "Mobile Robot Kinematics", applies principles of kinematics to the whole robot, beginning with the kinematic contribution of each wheel and graduating to an analysis of robot maneuverability enabled by each mobility mechanism configuration.

The greatest single shortcoming in conventional mobile robotics is, without doubt, perception: mobile robots can travel across much of earth's man-made surfaces, but they cannot perceive the world nearly as well as humans and other animals. Chapter 4, "Perception", begins a discussion of this challenge by presenting a clear language for describing the performance envelope of mobile robot sensors. With this language in hand, chapter 4 goes on to present many of the off-the-shelf sensors available to the mobile roboticist, describing their basic principles of operation as well as their performance limitations. The most promising sensor for the future of mobile robotics is vision, and chapter 4 includes an overview of the theory of operation and the limitations of both charged coupled device (CCD) and complementary metal oxide semiconductor (CMOS) sensors.

But perception is more than sensing. Perception is also the *interpretation* of sensed data in meaningful ways. The second half of chapter 4 describes strategies for feature extraction that have been most useful in mobile robotics applications, including extraction of geometric shapes from range-based sensing data, as well as landmark and whole-image analysis using vision-based sensing.

Armed with locomotion mechanisms and outfitted with hardware and software for perception, the mobile robot can move and perceive the world. The first point at which mobility and sensing must meet is localization: mobile robots often need to maintain a sense of position. Chapter 5, "Mobile Robot Localization", describes approaches that obviate the need for direct localization, then delves into fundamental ingredients of successful localization strategies: belief representation and map representation. Case studies demonstrate various localization schemes, including both Markov localization and Kalman filter localization. The final part of chapter 5 is devoted to a discussion of the challenges and most promising techniques for mobile robots to autonomously map their surroundings.

Mobile robotics is so young a discipline that it lacks a standardized architecture. There is as yet no established robot operating system. But the question of architecture is of paramount importance when one chooses to address the higher-level competences of a mobile robot: how does a mobile robot navigate robustly from place to place, interpreting data, localizing and controlling its motion all the while? For this highest level of robot competence, which we term *navigation competence*, there are numerous mobile robots that showcase particular architectural strategies. Chapter 6, "Planning and Navigation", surveys the state of the art of robot navigation, showing that today's various techniques are quite similar, differing primarily in the manner in which they *decompose* the problem of robot control. But first, chapter 6 addresses two skills that a competent, navigating robot usually must demonstrate: obstacle avoidance and path planning.

There is far more to know about the cross-disciplinary field of mobile robotics than can be contained in a single book. We hope, though, that this broad introduction will place the reader in the context of mobile robotics' collective wisdom. This is only the beginning, but, with luck, the first robot you program or build will have only good things to say about you.

2 Locomotion

2.1 Introduction

A mobile robot needs locomotion mechanisms that enable it to move unbounded throughout its environment. But there are a large variety of possible ways to move, and so the selection of a robot's approach to locomotion is an important aspect of mobile robot design. In the laboratory, there are research robots that can walk, jump, run, slide, skate, swim, fly, and, of course, roll. Most of these locomotion mechanisms have been inspired by their biological counterparts (see figure 2.1).

There is, however, one exception: the actively powered wheel is a human invention that achieves extremely high efficiency on flat ground. This mechanism is not completely foreign to biological systems. Our bipedal walking system can be approximated by a rolling polygon, with sides equal in length d to the span of the step (figure 2.2). As the step size decreases, the polygon approaches a circle or wheel. But nature did not develop a fully rotating, actively powered joint, which is the technology necessary for wheeled locomotion.

Biological systems succeed in moving through a wide variety of harsh environments. Therefore it can be desirable to copy their selection of locomotion mechanisms. However, replicating nature in this regard is extremely difficult for several reasons. To begin with, mechanical complexity is easily achieved in biological systems through structural replication. Cell division, in combination with specialization, can readily produce a millipede with several hundred legs and several tens of thousands of individually sensed cilia. In man-made structures, each part must be fabricated individually, and so no such economies of scale exist. Additionally, the cell is a microscopic building block that enables extreme miniaturization. With very small size and weight, insects achieve a level of robustness that we have not been able to match with human fabrication techniques. Finally, the biological energy storage system and the muscular and hydraulic activation systems used by large animals and insects achieve torque, response time, and conversion efficiencies that far exceed similarly scaled man-made systems.

Type of motion	Resistance to motion	Basic kinematics of motion
Flow in a Channel 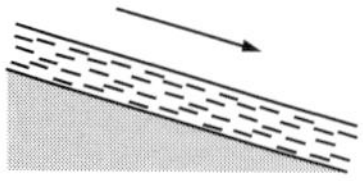	Hydrodynamic forces	Eddies 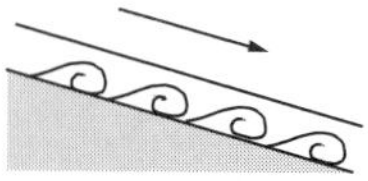
Crawl 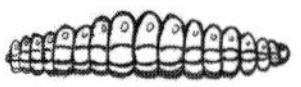	Friction forces	 Longitudinal vibration
Sliding 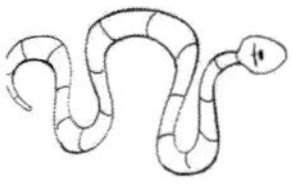	Friction forces	 Transverse vibration
Running 	Loss of kinetic energy	Oscillatory movement of a multi-link pendulum 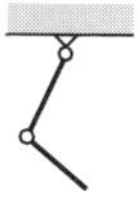
Jumping 	Loss of kinetic energy	Oscillatory movement of a multi-link pendulum 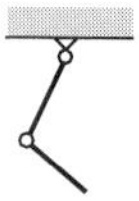
Walking 	Gravitational forces	Rolling of a polygon (see figure 2.2) 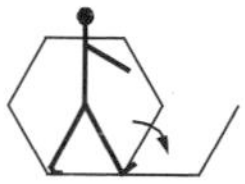

Figure 2.1
Locomotion mechanisms used in biological systems.

Owing to these limitations, mobile robots generally locomote either using wheeled mechanisms, a well-known human technology for vehicles, or using a small number of articulated legs, the simplest of the biological approaches to locomotion (see figure 2.2).

In general, legged locomotion requires higher degrees of freedom and therefore greater mechanical complexity than wheeled locomotion. Wheels, in addition to being simple, are extremely well suited to flat ground. As figure 2.3 depicts, on flat surfaces wheeled loco-motion is one to two orders of magnitude more efficient than legged locomotion. The rail-way is ideally engineered for wheeled locomotion because rolling friction is minimized on a hard and flat steel surface. But as the surface becomes soft, wheeled locomotion accumu-lates inefficiencies due to rolling friction whereas legged locomotion suffers much less because it consists only of point contacts with the ground. This is demonstrated in figure 2.3 by the dramatic loss of efficiency in the case of a tire on soft ground.

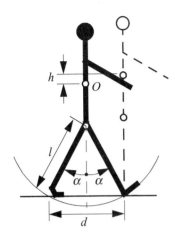

Figure 2.2
A biped walking system can be approximated by a rolling polygon, with sides equal in length d to the span of the step. As the step size decreases, the polygon approaches a circle or wheel with the radius l.

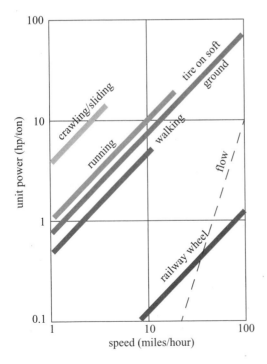

Figure 2.3
Specific power versus attainable speed of various locomotion mechanisms [33].

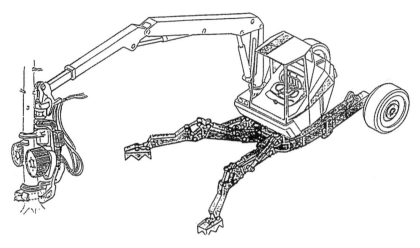

Figure 2.4
RoboTrac, a hybrid wheel-leg vehicle for rough terrain [130].

In effect, the efficiency of wheeled locomotion depends greatly on environmental qualities, particularly the flatness and hardness of the ground, while the efficiency of legged
locomotion depends on the leg mass and body mass, both of which the robot must support
at various points in a legged gait.

It is understandable therefore that nature favors legged locomotion, since locomotion
systems in nature must operate on rough and unstructured terrain. For example, in the case
of insects in a forest the vertical variation in ground height is often an order of magnitude
greater than the total height of the insect. By the same token, the human environment frequently consists of engineered, smooth surfaces, both indoors and outdoors. Therefore, it
is also understandable that virtually all industrial applications of mobile robotics utilize
some form of wheeled locomotion. Recently, for more natural outdoor environments, there
has been some progress toward hybrid and legged industrial robots such as the forestry
robot shown in figure 2.4.

In the section 2.1.1, we present general considerations that concern all forms of mobile
robot locomotion. Following this, in sections 2.2 and 2.3, we present overviews of legged
locomotion and wheeled locomotion techniques for mobile robots.

2.1.1 Key issues for locomotion

Locomotion is the complement of manipulation. In manipulation, the robot arm is fixed but
moves objects in the workspace by imparting force to them. In locomotion, the environment is fixed and the robot moves by imparting force to the environment. In both cases, the
scientific basis is the study of actuators that generate interaction forces, and mechanisms

that implement desired kinematic and dynamic properties. Locomotion and manipulation thus share the same core issues of stability, contact characteristics, and environmental type:

- stability
  - number and geometry of contact points
  - center of gravity
  - static/dynamic stability
  - inclination of terrain

- characteristics of contact
  - contact point/path size and shape
  - angle of contact
  - friction

- type of environment
  - structure
  - medium, (e.g. water, air, soft or hard ground)

A theoretical analysis of locomotion begins with mechanics and physics. From this starting point, we can formally define and analyze all manner of mobile robot locomotion systems. However, this book focuses on the mobile robot *navigation* problem, particularly stressing perception, localization, and cognition. Thus we will not delve deeply into the physical basis of locomotion. Nevertheless, the two remaining sections in this chapter present overviews of issues in legged locomotion [33] and wheeled locomotion. Then, chapter 3 presents a more detailed analysis of the kinematics and control of wheeled mobile robots.

2.2   Legged Mobile Robots

Legged locomotion is characterized by a series of point contacts between the robot and the ground. The key advantages include adaptability and maneuverability in rough terrain. Because only a set of point contacts is required, the quality of the ground between those points does not matter so long as the robot can maintain adequate ground clearance. In addition, a walking robot is capable of crossing a hole or chasm so long as its reach exceeds the width of the hole. A final advantage of legged locomotion is the potential to manipulate objects in the environment with great skill. An excellent insect example, the dung beetle, is capable of rolling a ball while locomoting by way of its dexterous front legs.

The main disadvantages of legged locomotion include power and mechanical complexity. The leg, which may include several degrees of freedom, must be capable of sustaining part of the robot's total weight, and in many robots must be capable of lifting and lowering the robot. Additionally, high maneuverability will only be achieved if the legs have a sufficient number of degrees of freedom to impart forces in a number of different directions.

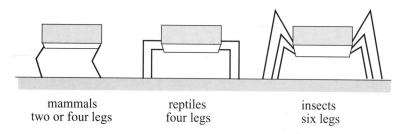

| mammals | reptiles | insects |
| two or four legs | four legs | six legs |

Figure 2.5
Arrangement of the legs of various animals.

2.2.1 Leg configurations and stability

Because legged robots are biologically inspired, it is instructive to examine biologically successful legged systems. A number of different leg configurations have been successful in a variety of organisms (figure 2.5). Large animals, such as mammals and reptiles, have four legs, whereas insects have six or more legs. In some mammals, the ability to walk on only two legs has been perfected. Especially in the case of humans, balance has progressed to the point that we can even jump with one leg[1]. This exceptional maneuverability comes at a price: much more complex active control to maintain balance.

In contrast, a creature with three legs can exhibit a static, stable pose provided that it can ensure that its center of gravity is within the tripod of ground contact. Static stability, demonstrated by a three-legged stool, means that balance is maintained with no need for motion. A small deviation from stability (e.g., gently pushing the stool) is passively corrected toward the stable pose when the upsetting force stops.

But a robot must be able to lift its legs in order to walk. In order to achieve static walking, a robot must have at least six legs. In such a configuration, it is possible to design a gait in which a statically stable tripod of legs is in contact with the ground at all times (figure 2.8).

Insects and spiders are immediately able to walk when born. For them, the problem of balance during walking is relatively simple. Mammals, with four legs, cannot achieve static walking, but are able to stand easily on four legs. Fauns, for example, spend several minutes attempting to stand before they are able to do so, then spend several more minutes learning to walk without falling. Humans, with two legs, cannot even stand in one place with static stability. Infants require months to stand and walk, and even longer to learn to jump, run, and stand on one leg.

---

1. In child development, one of the tests used to determine if the child is acquiring advanced locomotion skills is the ability to jump on one leg.

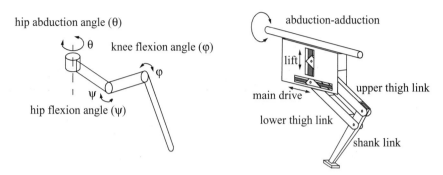

Figure 2.6
Two examples of legs with three degrees of freedom.

There is also the potential for great variety in the complexity of each individual leg. Once again, the biological world provides ample examples at both extremes. For instance, in the case of the caterpillar, each leg is extended using hydraulic pressure by constricting the body cavity and forcing an increase in pressure, and each leg is retracted longitudinally by relaxing the hydraulic pressure, then activating a single tensile muscle that pulls the leg in toward the body. Each leg has only a single degree of freedom, which is oriented longitudinally along the leg. Forward locomotion depends on the hydraulic pressure in the body, which extends the distance between pairs of legs. The caterpillar leg is therefore mechanically very simple, using a minimal number of extrinsic muscles to achieve complex overall locomotion.

At the other extreme, the human leg has more than seven major degrees of freedom, combined with further actuation at the toes. More than fifteen muscle groups actuate eight complex joints.

In the case of legged mobile robots, a minimum of two degrees of freedom is generally required to move a leg forward by lifting the leg and swinging it forward. More common is the addition of a third degree of freedom for more complex maneuvers, resulting in legs such as those shown in figure 2.6. Recent successes in the creation of bipedal walking robots have added a fourth degree of freedom at the ankle joint. The ankle enables more consistent ground contact by actuating the pose of the sole of the foot.

In general, adding degrees of freedom to a robot leg increases the maneuverability of the robot, both augmenting the range of terrains on which it can travel and the ability of the robot to travel with a variety of gaits. The primary disadvantages of additional joints and actuators are, of course, energy, control, and mass. Additional actuators require energy and control, and they also add to leg mass, further increasing power and load requirements on existing actuators.

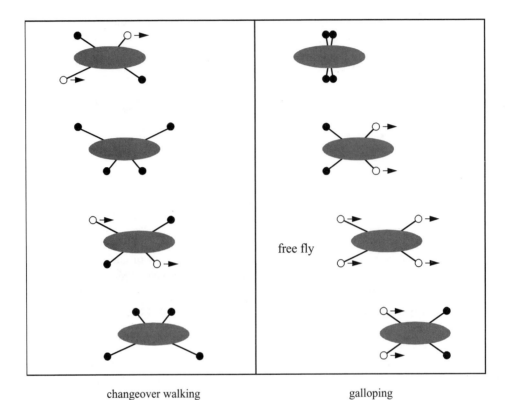

changeover walking   galloping

Figure 2.7
Two gaits with four legs. Because this robot has fewer than six legs, static walking is not generally possible.

In the case of a multilegged mobile robot, there is the issue of leg coordination for loco-motion, or gait control. The number of possible gaits depends on the number of legs [33]. The gait is a sequence of lift and release events for the individual legs. For a mobile robot with k legs, the total number of possible events N for a walking machine is

$$N = (2k-1)! \tag{2.1}$$

For a biped walker $k = 2$ legs, the number of possible events N is

$$N = (2k-1)! = 3! = 3 \cdot 2 \cdot 1 = 6 \tag{2.2}$$

The six different events are

1. lift right leg;

2. lift left leg;

3. release right leg;

4. release left leg;

5. lift both legs together;

6. release both legs together.

Of course, this quickly grows quite large. For example, a robot with six legs has far more gaits theoretically:

$$N = 11! = 39916800 \tag{2.3}$$

Figures 2.7 and 2.8 depict several four-legged gaits and the static six-legged tripod gait.

2.2.2 Examples of legged robot locomotion

Although there are no high-volume industrial applications to date, legged locomotion is an important area of long-term research. Several interesting designs are presented below, beginning with the one-legged robot and finishing with six-legged robots. For a very good overview of climbing and walking robots, see *http://www.uwe.ac.uk/clawar/*.

2.2.2.1 One leg

The minimum number of legs a legged robot can have is, of course, one. Minimizing the number of legs is beneficial for several reasons. Body mass is particularly important to walking machines, and the single leg minimizes cumulative leg mass. Leg coordination is required when a robot has several legs, but with one leg no such coordination is needed. Perhaps most importantly, the one-legged robot maximizes the basic advantage of legged locomotion: legs have single points of contact with the ground in lieu of an entire track, as with wheels. A single-legged robot requires only a sequence of single contacts, making it amenable to the roughest terrain. Furthermore, a hopping robot can dynamically cross a gap that is larger than its stride by taking a running start, whereas a multilegged walking robot that cannot run is limited to crossing gaps that are as large as its reach.

The major challenge in creating a single-legged robot is balance. For a robot with one leg, static walking is not only impossible but static stability when stationary is also impossible. The robot must actively balance itself by either changing its center of gravity or by imparting corrective forces. Thus, the successful single-legged robot must be dynamically stable.

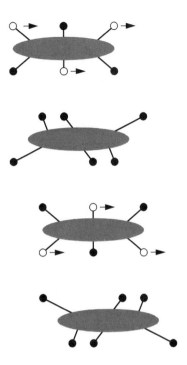

Figure 2.8
Static walking with six legs. A tripod formed by three legs always exists.

Figure 2.9 shows the Raibert hopper [28, 124], one of the most well-known single-legged hopping robots created. This robot makes continuous corrections to body attitude and to robot velocity by adjusting the leg angle with respect to the body. The actuation is hydraulic, including high-power longitudinal extension of the leg during stance to hop back into the air. Although powerful, these actuators require a large, off-board hydraulic pump to be connected to the robot at all times.

Figure 2.10 shows a more energy-efficient design developed more recently [46]. Instead of supplying power by means of an off-board hydraulic pump, the bow leg hopper is designed to capture the kinetic energy of the robot as it lands, using an efficient bow spring leg. This spring returns approximately 85% of the energy, meaning that stable hopping requires only the addition of 15% of the required energy on each hop. This robot, which is constrained along one axis by a boom, has demonstrated continuous hopping for 20 minutes using a single set of batteries carried on board the robot. As with the Raibert hopper, the bow leg hopper controls velocity by changing the angle of the leg to the body at the hip joint.

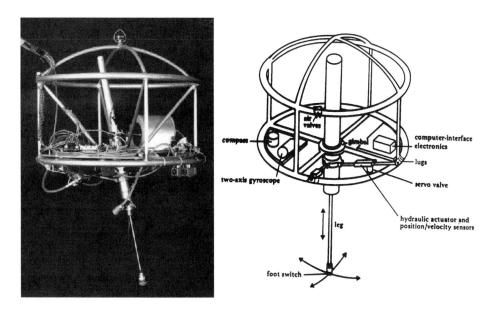

Figure 2.9
The Raibert hopper [28, 124]. Image courtesy of the LegLab and Marc Raibert. © 1983.

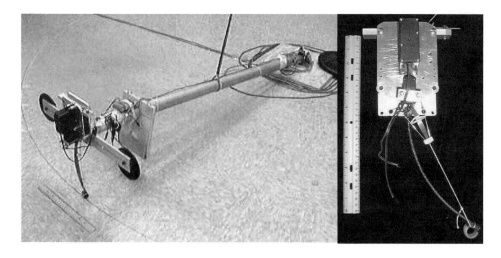

Figure 2.10
The 2D single bow leg hopper [46]. Image courtesy of H. Benjamin Brown and Garth Zeglin, CMU.

Specifications:

Weight:	7 kg
Height:	58 cm
Neck DOF:	4
Body DOF:	2
Arm DOF:	2 x 5
Legs DOF:	2 x 6
Five-finger Hands	

Figure 2.11
The Sony SDR-4X II, © 2003 Sony Corporation.

The paper of Ringrose [125] demonstrates the very important duality of mechanics and controls as applied to a single-legged hopping machine. Often clever mechanical design can perform the same operations as complex active control circuitry. In this robot, the physical shape of the foot is exactly the right curve so that when the robot lands without being perfectly vertical, the proper corrective force is provided from the impact, making the robot vertical by the next landing. This robot is dynamically stable, and is furthermore passive. The correction is provided by physical interactions between the robot and its environment, with no computer or any active control in the loop.

2.2.2.2 Two legs (biped)
A variety of successful bipedal robots have been demonstrated over the past ten years. Two legged robots have been shown to run, jump, travel up and down stairways, and even do aerial tricks such as somersaults. In the commercial sector, both Honda and Sony have made significant advances over the past decade that have enabled highly capable bipedal robots. Both companies designed small, powered joints that achieve power-to-weight performance unheard of in commercially available servomotors. These new "intelligent" servos provide not only strong actuation but also compliant actuation by means of torque sensing and closed-loop control.

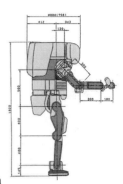

Specifications:

Maximum speed:	2 km/h
Autonomy:	15 min
Weight:	210 kg
Height:	1.82 m
Leg DOF:	2 x 6
Arm DOF:	2 x 7

Figure 2.12
The humanoid robot P2 from Honda, Japan. © Honda Motor Corporation.

The Sony Dream Robot, model SDR-4X II, is shown in figure 2.11. This current model is the result of research begun in 1997 with the basic objective of motion entertainment and communication entertainment (i.e., dancing and singing). This robot with thirty-eight degrees of freedom has seven microphones for fine localization of sound, image-based person recognition, on-board miniature stereo depth-map reconstruction, and limited speech recognition. Given the goal of fluid and entertaining motion, Sony spent considerable effort designing a motion prototyping application system to enable their engineers to script dances in a straightforward manner. Note that the SDR-4X II is relatively small, standing at 58 cm and weighing only 6.5 kg.

The Honda humanoid project has a significant history but, again, has tackled the very important engineering challenge of actuation. Figure 2.12 shows model *P2*, which is an immediate predecessor to the most recent Asimo model (advanced step in innovative mobility). Note from this picture that the Honda humanoid is much larger than the SDR-4X at 120 cm tall and 52 kg. This enables practical mobility in the human world of stairs and ledges while maintaining a nonthreatening size and posture. Perhaps the first robot to famously demonstrate biomimetic bipedal stair climbing and descending, these Honda humanoid series robots are being designed not for entertainment purposes but as human aids throughout society. Honda refers, for instance, to the height of Asimo as the minimum height which enables it to nonetheless manage operation of the human world, for instance, control of light switches.

Specifications:

Weight: 131 [kg]
Height: 1.88 [m]

DOF in total: 43
          Lower Limbs: 2 x 6
          Trunk: 3
          Arms: 2 x 10
          Neck: 4
          Eyes: 2 x 2

Figure 2.13
The humanoid robot WABIAN-RIII at Waseda University in Japan [75]. Image courtesy of Atsuo Takanishi, Waseda University.

An important feature of bipedal robots is their anthropomorphic shape. They can be built to have the same approximate dimensions as humans, and this makes them excellent vehicles for research in human-robot interaction. WABIAN is a robot built at Waseda Universities Japan (figure 2.13) for just such research [75]. WABIAN is designed to emulate human motion, and is even designed to dance like a human.

Bipedal robots can only be statically stable within some limits, and so robots such as P2 and WABIAN generally must perform continuous balance-correcting servoing even when standing still. Furthermore, each leg must have sufficient capacity to support the full weight of the robot. In the case of four-legged robots, the balance problem is facilitated along with the load requirements of each leg. An elegant design of a biped robot is the Spring Flamingo of MIT (figure 2.14). This robot inserts springs in series with the leg actuators to achieve a more elastic gait. Combined with "kneecaps" that limit knee joint angles, the Flamingo achieves surprisingly biomimetic motion.

2.2.2.3 Four legs (quadruped)
Although standing still on four legs is passively stable, walking remains challenging because to remain stable the robot's center of gravity must be actively shifted during the

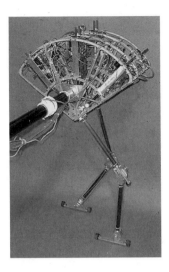

Figure 2.14
The Spring Flamingo developed at MIT [123]. Image courtesy of Jerry Pratt, MIT Leg Laboratory.

gait. Sony recently invested several million dollars to develop a four-legged robot called AIBO (figure 2.15). To create this robot, Sony produced both a new robot operating system that is near real-time and new geared servomotors that are of sufficiently high torque to support the robot, yet back drivable for safety. In addition to developing custom motors and software, Sony incorporated a color vision system that enables AIBO to chase a brightly colored ball. The robot is able to function for at most one hour before requiring recharging. Early sales of the robot have been very strong, with more than 60,000 units sold in the first year. Nevertheless, the number of motors and the technology investment behind this robot dog resulted in a very high price of approximately $1500.

Four-legged robots have the potential to serve as effective artifacts for research in human-robot interaction (figure 2.16). Humans can treat the Sony robot, for example, as a pet and might develop an emotional relationship similar to that between man and dog. Furthermore, Sony has designed AIBO's walking style and general behavior to emulate learning and maturation, resulting in dynamic behavior over time that is more interesting for the owner who can track the changing behavior. As the challenges of high energy storage and motor technology are solved, it is likely that quadruped robots much more capable than AIBO will become common throughout the human environment.

2.2.2.4 Six legs (hexapod)
Six-legged configurations have been extremely popular in mobile robotics because of their static stability during walking, thus reducing the control complexity (figures 2.17 and 1.3).

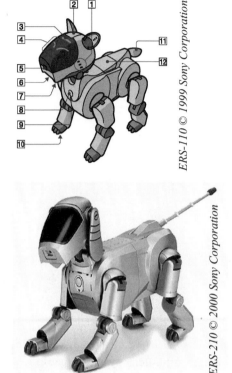

ERS-110 © 1999 Sony Corporation

ERS-210 © 2000 Sony Corporation

1   Stereo microphone: Allows AIBO to pick up surrounding sounds.
2   Head sensor: Senses when a person taps or pets AIBO on the head.
3   Mode indicator: Shows AIBO's operation mode.
4   Eye lights: These light up in blue-green or red to indicate AIBO's emotional state.
5   Color camera: Allows AIBO to search for objects and recognize them by color and movement.
6   Speaker: Emits various musical tones and sound effects.
7   Chin sensor: Senses when a person touches AIBO on the chin.
8   Pause button: Press to activate AIBO or to pause AIBO.
9   Chest light: Gives information about the status of the robot.
10 Paw sensors: Located on the bottom of each paw.
11 Tail light: Lights up blue or orange to show AIBO's emotional state.
12 Back sensor: Senses when a person touches AIBO on the back.

Figure 2.15
AIBO, the artificial dog from Sony, Japan.

In most cases, each leg has three degrees of freedom, including hip flexion, knee flexion, and hip abduction (see figure 2.6). Genghis is a commercially available hobby robot that has six legs, each of which has two degrees of freedom provided by hobby servos (figure 2.18). Such a robot, which consists only of hip flexion and hip abduction, has less maneuverability in rough terrain but performs quite well on flat ground. Because it consists of a straightforward arrangement of servomotors and straight legs, such robots can be readily built by a robot hobbyist.

Insects, which are arguably the most successful locomoting creatures on earth, excel at traversing all forms of terrain with six legs, even upside down. Currently, the gap between the capabilities of six-legged insects and artificial six-legged robots is still quite large. Interestingly, this is not due to a lack of sufficient numbers of degrees of freedom on the robots. Rather, insects combine a small number of active degrees of freedom with passive

Specifications:

Weight: 1   9 kg
Height: 0.25 m
DOF: 4 x 3

Figure 2.16
Titan VIII, a quadruped robot developed at Tokyo Institute of Technology.
(http://mozu.mes.titech.ac.jp/research/walk/). © Tokyo Institute of Technology.

Specifications:

Maximum speed: 0.5 m/s
Weight: 1   6 kg
Height: 0.3 m
Length: 0.7 m
No. of legs: 6
DOF in total: 6 x 3
Power consumption: 10 W

Figure 2.17
Lauron II, a hexapod platform developed at the University of Karlsruhe, Germany.
© University of Karlsruhe.

Figure 2.18
Genghis, one of the most famous walking robots from MIT, uses hobby servomotors as its actuators
(http://www.ai.mit.edu/projects/genghis). © MIT AI Lab.

structures, such as microscopic barbs and textured pads, that increase the gripping strength
of each leg significantly. Robotic research into such passive tip structures has only recently
begun. For example, a research group is attempting to re-create the complete mechanical
function of the cockroach leg [65].

It is clear from the above examples that legged robots have much progress to make
before they are competitive with their biological equivalents. Nevertheless, significant
gains have been realized recently, primarily due to advances in motor design. Creating
actuation systems that approach the efficiency of animal muscles remains far from the
reach of robotics, as does energy storage with the energy densities found in organic life
forms.

2.3   Wheeled Mobile Robots

The wheel has been by far the most popular locomotion mechanism in mobile robotics and
in man-made vehicles in general. It can achieve very good efficiencies, as demonstrated in
figure 2.3, and does so with a relatively simple mechanical implementation.

In addition, balance is not usually a research problem in wheeled robot designs, because
wheeled robots are almost always designed so that all wheels are in ground contact at all
times. Thus, three wheels are sufficient to guarantee stable balance, although, as we shall
see below, two-wheeled robots can also be stable. When more than three wheels are used,
a suspension system is required to allow all wheels to maintain ground contact when the
robot encounters uneven terrain.

Instead of worrying about balance, wheeled robot research tends to focus on the problems of traction and stability, maneuverability, and control: can the robot wheels provide

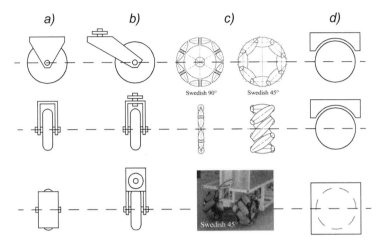

Figure 2.19
The four basic wheel types. (a) Standard wheel: two degrees of freedom; rotation around the (motorized) wheel axle and the contact point.(b) castor wheel: two degrees of freedom; rotation around an offset steering joint. (c) Swedish wheel: three degrees of freedom; rotation around the (motorized) wheel axle, around the rollers, and around the contact point. (d) Ball or spherical wheel: realization technically difficult.

sufficient traction and stability for the robot to cover all of the desired terrain, and does the robot's wheeled configuration enable sufficient control over the velocity of the robot?

2.3.1 Wheeled locomotion: the design space

As we shall see, there is a very large space of possible wheel configurations when one considers possible techniques for mobile robot locomotion. We begin by discussing the wheel in detail, as there are a number of different wheel types with specific strengths and weaknesses. Then, we examine complete wheel configurations that deliver particular forms of locomotion for a mobile robot.

2.3.1.1 Wheel design

There are four major wheel classes, as shown in figure 2.19. They differ widely in their kinematics, and therefore the choice of wheel type has a large effect on the overall kinematics of the mobile robot. The standard wheel and the castor wheel have a primary axis of rotation and are thus highly directional. To move in a different direction, the wheel must be steered first along a vertical axis. The key difference between these two wheels is that the standard wheel can accomplish this steering motion with no side effects, as the center of rotation passes through the contact patch with the ground, whereas the castor wheel rotates around an offset axis, causing a force to be imparted to the robot chassis during steering.

Figure 2.20
Navlab I, the first autonomous highway vehicle that steers and controls the throttle using vision and radar sensors [61]. Developed at CMU.

The Swedish wheel and the spherical wheel are both designs that are less constrained by directionality than the conventional standard wheel. The Swedish wheel functions as a normal wheel, but provides low resistance in another direction as well, sometimes perpendicular to the conventional direction, as in the Swedish 90, and sometimes at an intermediate angle, as in the Swedish 45. The small rollers attached around the circumference of the wheel are passive and the wheel's primary axis serves as the only actively powered joint. The key advantage of this design is that, although the wheel rotation is powered only along the one principal axis (through the axle), the wheel can kinematically move with very little friction along many possible trajectories, not just forward and backward.

The spherical wheel is a truly omnidirectional wheel, often designed so that it may be actively powered to spin along any direction. One mechanism for implementing this spherical design imitates the computer mouse, providing actively powered rollers that rest against the top surface of the sphere and impart rotational force.

Regardless of what wheel is used, in robots designed for all-terrain environments and in robots with more than three wheels, a suspension system is normally required to maintain wheel contact with the ground. One of the simplest approaches to suspension is to design flexibility into the wheel itself. For instance, in the case of some four-wheeled indoor robots that use castor wheels, manufacturers have applied a deformable tire of soft rubber to the wheel to create a primitive suspension. Of course, this limited solution cannot compete with a sophisticated suspension system in applications where the robot needs a more dynamic suspension for significantly non flat terrain.

2.3.1.2 Wheel geometry

The choice of wheel types for a mobile robot is strongly linked to the choice of wheel arrangement, or wheel geometry. The mobile robot designer must consider these two issues simultaneously when designing the locomoting mechanism of a wheeled robot. Why do wheel type and wheel geometry matter? Three fundamental characteristics of a robot are governed by these choices: maneuverability, controllability, and stability.

Unlike automobiles, which are largely designed for a highly standardized environment (the road network), mobile robots are designed for applications in a wide variety of situations. Automobiles all share similar wheel configurations because there is one region in the design space that maximizes maneuverability, controllability, and stability for their standard environment: the paved roadway. However, there is no single wheel configuration that maximizes these qualities for the variety of environments faced by different mobile robots. So you will see great variety in the wheel configurations of mobile robots. In fact, few robots use the Ackerman wheel configuration of the automobile because of its poor maneuverability, with the exception of mobile robots designed for the road system (figure 2.20).

Table 2.1 gives an overview of wheel configurations ordered by the number of wheels. This table shows both the selection of particular wheel types and their geometric configuration on the robot chassis. Note that some of the configurations shown are of little use in mobile robot applications. For instance, the two-wheeled bicycle arrangement has moderate maneuverability and poor controllability. Like a single-legged hopping machine, it can never stand still. Nevertheless, this table provides an indication of the large variety of wheel configurations that are possible in mobile robot design.

The number of variations in table 2.1 is quite large. However, there are important trends and groupings that can aid in comprehending the advantages and disadvantages of each configuration. Below, we identify some of the key trade-offs in terms of the three issues we identified earlier: stability, maneuverability, and controllability.

2.3.1.3 Stability

Surprisingly, the minimum number of wheels required for static stability is two. As shown above, a two-wheel differential-drive robot can achieve static stability if the center of mass is below the wheel axle. Cye is a commercial mobile robot that uses this wheel configuration (figure 2.21).

However, under ordinary circumstances such a solution requires wheel diameters that are impractically large. Dynamics can also cause a two-wheeled robot to strike the floor with a third point of contact, for instance, with sufficiently high motor torques from standstill. Conventionally, static stability requires a minimum of three wheels, with the additional caveat that the center of gravity must be contained within the triangle formed by the ground contact points of the wheels. Stability can be further improved by adding more wheels, although once the number of contact points exceeds three, the hyperstatic nature of the geometry will require some form of flexible suspension on uneven terrain.

Table 2.1
Wheel configurations for rolling vehicles

# of wheels	Arrangement	Description	Typical examples
2		One steering wheel in the front, one traction wheel in the rear	Bicycle, motorcycle
		Two-wheel differential drive with the center of mass (COM) below the axle	Cye personal robot
3		Two-wheel centered differential drive with a third point of contact	Nomad Scout, smartRob EPFL
		Two independently driven wheels in the rear/front, 1 unpowered omnidirectional wheel in the front/rear	Many indoor robots, including the EPFL robots Pygmalion and Alice
		Two connected traction wheels (differential) in rear, 1 steered free wheel in front	Piaggio minitrucks
		Two free wheels in rear, 1 steered traction wheel in front	Neptune (Carnegie Mellon University), Hero-1
		Three motorized Swedish or spherical wheels arranged in a triangle; omnidirectional movement is possible	Stanford wheel Tribolo EPFL, Palm Pilot Robot Kit (CMU)
		Three synchronously motorized and steered wheels; the orientation is not controllable	"Synchro drive" Denning MRV-2, Georgia Institute of Technology, I-Robot B24, Nomad 200

Table 2.1
Wheel configurations for rolling vehicles

# of wheels	Arrangement	Description	Typical examples
4		Two motorized wheels in the rear, 2 steered wheels in the front; steering has to be different for the 2 wheels to avoid slipping/skidding.	Car with rear-wheel drive
		Two motorized and steered wheels in the front, 2 free wheels in the rear; steering has to be different for the 2 wheels to avoid slipping/skidding.	Car with front-wheel drive
		Four steered and motorized wheels	Four-wheel drive, four-wheel steering Hyperion (CMU)
		Two traction wheels (differential) in rear/front, 2 omnidirectional wheels in the front/rear	Charlie (DMT-EPFL)
		Four omnidirectional wheels	Carnegie Mellon Uranus
		Two-wheel differential drive with 2 additional points of contact	EPFL Khepera, Hyperbot Chip
		Four motorized and steered castor wheels	Nomad XR4000

Table 2.1
Wheel configurations for rolling vehicles

# of wheels	Arrangement	Description	Typical examples
6		Two motorized and steered wheels aligned in center, 1 omnidirectional wheel at each corner	First
		Two traction wheels (differential) in center, 1 omnidirectional wheel at each corner	Terregator (Carnegie Mellon University)
Icons for the each wheel type are as follows:			
◯	unpowered omnidirectional wheel (spherical, castor, Swedish);		
▨	motorized Swedish wheel (Stanford wheel);		
▭	unpowered standard wheel;		
▬	motorized standard wheel;		
▬◯	motorized and steered castor wheel;		
⊟	steered standard wheel;		
⊟	connected wheels.		

2.3.1.4 Maneuverability

Some robots are omnidirectional, meaning that they can move at any time in any direction along the ground plane (x, y) regardless of the orientation of the robot around its vertical axis. This level of maneuverability requires wheels that can move in more than just one direction, and so omnidirectional robots usually employ Swedish or spherical wheels that are powered. A good example is Uranus, shown in figure 2.24. This robot uses four Swedish wheels to rotate and translate independently and without constraints.

Figure 2.21
Cye, a commercially available domestic robot that can vacuum and make deliveries in the home, is
built by Aethon Inc. (http://www.aethon.com). © Aethon Inc.

In general, the ground clearance of robots with Swedish and spherical wheels is somewhat limited due to the mechanical constraints of constructing omnidirectional wheels. An
interesting recent solution to the problem of omnidirectional navigation while solving this
ground-clearance problem is the four-castor wheel configuration in which each castor
wheel is actively steered and actively translated. In this configuration, the robot is truly
omnidirectional because, even if the castor wheels are facing a direction perpendicular to
the desired direction of travel, the robot can still move in the desired direction by steering
these wheels. Because the vertical axis is offset from the ground-contact path, the result of
this steering motion is robot motion.

In the research community, other classes of mobile robots are popular which achieve
high maneuverability, only slightly inferior to that of the omnidirectional configurations.
In such robots, motion in a particular direction may initially require a rotational motion.
With a circular chassis and an axis of rotation at the center of the robot, such a robot can
spin without changing its ground footprint. The most popular such robot is the two-wheel
differential-drive robot where the two wheels rotate around the center point of the robot.
One or two additional ground contact points may be used for stability, based on the application specifics.

In contrast to the above configurations, consider the Ackerman steering configuration
common in automobiles. Such a vehicle typically has a turning diameter that is larger than
the car. Furthermore, for such a vehicle to move sideways requires a parking maneuver consisting of repeated changes in direction forward and backward. Nevertheless, Ackerman
steering geometries have been especially popular in the hobby robotics market, where a
robot can be built by starting with a remote control racecar kit and adding sensing and
autonomy to the existing mechanism. In addition, the limited maneuverability of Ackerman

steering has an important advantage: its directionality and steering geometry provide it with very good lateral stability in high-speed turns.

2.3.1.5 Controllability

There is generally an inverse correlation between controllability and maneuverability. For example, the omnidirectional designs such as the four-castor wheel configuration require significant processing to convert desired rotational and translational velocities to individual wheel commands. Furthermore, such omnidirectional designs often have greater degrees of freedom at the wheel. For instance, the Swedish wheel has a set of free rollers along the wheel perimeter. These degrees of freedom cause an accumulation of slippage, tend to reduce dead-reckoning accuracy and increase the design complexity.

Controlling an omnidirectional robot for a specific direction of travel is also more diffi-cult and often less accurate when compared to less maneuverable designs. For example, an Ackerman steering vehicle can go straight simply by locking the steerable wheels and driv-ing the drive wheels. In a differential-drive vehicle, the two motors attached to the two wheels must be driven along exactly the same velocity profile, which can be challenging considering variations between wheels, motors, and environmental differences. With four-wheel omnidrive, such as the Uranus robot, which has four Swedish wheels, the problem is even harder because all four wheels must be driven at exactly the same speed for the robot to travel in a perfectly straight line.

In summary, there is no "ideal" drive configuration that simultaneously maximizes sta-bility, maneuverability, and controllability. Each mobile robot application places unique constraints on the robot design problem, and the designer's task is to choose the most appropriate drive configuration possible from among this space of compromises.

2.3.2 Wheeled locomotion: case studies

Below we describe four specific wheel configurations, in order to demonstrate concrete applications of the concepts discussed above to mobile robots built for real-world activities.

2.3.2.1 Synchro drive

The synchro drive configuration (figure 2.22) is a popular arrangement of wheels in indoor mobile robot applications. It is an interesting configuration because, although there are three driven and steered wheels, only two motors are used in total. The one translation motor sets the speed of all three wheels together, and the one steering motor spins all the wheels together about each of their individual vertical steering axes. But note that the wheels are being steered with respect to the robot chassis, and therefore there is no direct way of reorienting the robot chassis. In fact, the chassis orientation does drift over time due to uneven tire slippage, causing rotational dead-reckoning error.

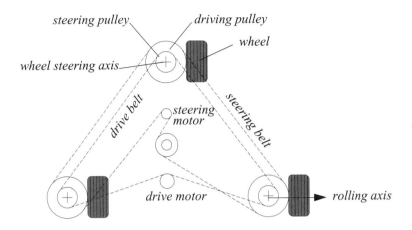

Figure 2.22
Synchro drive: The robot can move in any direction; however, the orientation of the chassis is not controllable.

Synchro drive is particularly advantageous in cases where omnidirectionality is sought. So long as each vertical steering axis is aligned with the contact path of each tire, the robot can always reorient its wheels and move along a new trajectory without changing its footprint. Of course, if the robot chassis has directionality and the designers intend to reorient the chassis purposefully, then synchro drive is only appropriate when combined with an independently rotating turret that attaches to the wheel chassis. Commercial research robots such as the Nomadics 150 or the RWI B21r have been sold with this configuration (figure 1.12).

In terms of dead reckoning, synchro drive systems are generally superior to true omnidirectional configurations but inferior to differential-drive and Ackerman steering systems. There are two main reasons for this. First and foremost, the translation motor generally drives the three wheels using a single belt. Because of to slop and backlash in the drive train, whenever the drive motor engages, the closest wheel begins spinning before the furthest wheel, causing a small change in the orientation of the chassis. With additional changes in motor speed, these small angular shifts accumulate to create a large error in orientation during dead reckoning. Second, the mobile robot has no direct control over the orientation of the chassis. Depending on the orientation of the chassis, the wheel thrust can be highly asymmetric, with two wheels on one side and the third wheel alone, or symmetric, with one wheel on each side and one wheel straight ahead or behind, as shown in figure 2.22. The asymmetric cases result in a variety of errors when tire-ground slippage can occur, again causing errors in dead reckoning of robot orientation.

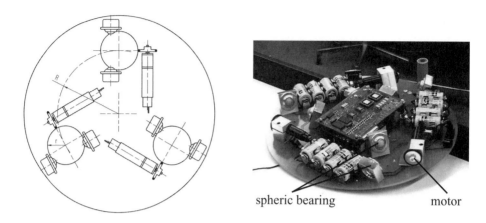

spheric bearing   motor

Figure 2.23
The Tribolo designed at EPFL (Swiss Federal Institute of Technology, Lausanne, Switzerland. Left: arrangement of spheric bearings and motors (bottom view). Right: Picture of the robot without the spherical wheels (bottom view).

2.3.2.2 Omnidirectional drive

As we will see later in section 3.4.2, omnidirectional movement is of great interest for complete maneuverability. Omnidirectional robots that are able to move in any direction (x, y, θ) at any time are also holonomic (see section 3.4.2). They can be realized by either using spherical, castor, or Swedish wheels. Three examples of such holonomic robots are presented below.

Omnidirectional locomotion with three spherical wheels. The omnidirectional robot depicted in figure 2.23 is based on three spherical wheels, each actuated by one motor. In this design, the spherical wheels are suspended by three contact points, two given by spherical bearings and one by a wheel connected to the motor axle. This concept provides excellent maneuverability and is simple in design. However, it is limited to flat surfaces and small loads, and it is quite difficult to find round wheels with high friction coefficients.

Omnidirectional locomotion with four Swedish wheels. The omnidirectional arrangement depicted in figure 2.24 has been used successfully on several research robots, including the Carnegie Mellon Uranus. This configuration consists of four Swedish 45-degree wheels, each driven by a separate motor. By varying the direction of rotation and relative speeds of the four wheels, the robot can be moved along any trajectory in the plane and, even more impressively, can simultaneously spin around its vertical axis.

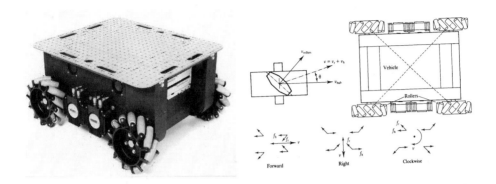

Figure 2.24
The Carnegie Mellon Uranus robot, an omnidirectional robot with four powered-swedish 45 wheels.

For example, when all four wheels spin "forward" or "backward" the robot as a whole moves in a straight line forward or backward, respectively. However, when one diagonal pair of wheels is spun in the same direction and the other diagonal pair is spun in the opposite direction, the robot moves laterally.

This four-wheel arrangement of Swedish wheels is not minimal in terms of control motors. Because there are only three degrees of freedom in the plane, one can build a three-wheel omnidirectional robot chassis using three Swedish 90-degree wheels as shown in table 2.1. However, existing examples such as Uranus have been designed with four wheels owing to capacity and stability considerations.

One application for which such omnidirectional designs are particularly amenable is mobile manipulation. In this case, it is desirable to reduce the degrees of freedom of the manipulator arm to save arm mass by using the mobile robot chassis motion for gross motion. As with humans, it would be ideal if the base could move omnidirectionally without greatly impacting the position of the manipulator tip, and a base such as Uranus can afford precisely such capabilities.

Omnidirectional locomotion with four castor wheels and eight motors. Another solution for omnidirectionality is to use castor wheels. This is done for the Nomad XR4000 from Nomadic Technologies (fig. 2.25), giving it excellent maneuverability. Unfortunately, Nomadic has ceased production of mobile robots.

The above three examples are drawn from table 2.1, but this is not an exhaustive list of all wheeled locomotion techniques. Hybrid approaches that combine legged and wheeled locomotion, or tracked and wheeled locomotion, can also offer particular advantages. Below are two unique designs created for specialized applications.

Figure 2.25
The Nomad XR4000 from Nomadic Technologies had an arrangement of four castor wheels for holo-nomic motion. All the castor wheels are driven and steered, thus requiring a precise synchronization and coordination to obtain a precise movement in x, y and θ.

2.3.2.3 Tracked slip/skid locomotion

In the wheel configurations discussed above, we have made the assumption that wheels are not allowed to skid against the surface. An alternative form of steering, termed slip/skid, may be used to reorient the robot by spinning wheels that are facing the same direction at different speeds or in opposite directions. The army tank operates this way, and the Nanokhod (figure 2.26) is an example of a mobile robot based on the same concept.

Robots that make use of tread have much larger ground contact patches, and this can significantly improve their maneuverability in loose terrain compared to conventional wheeled designs. However, due to this large ground contact patch, changing the orientation of the robot usually requires a skidding turn, wherein a large portion of the track must slide against the terrain.

The disadvantage of such configurations is coupled to the slip/skid steering. Because of the large amount of skidding during a turn, the exact center of rotation of the robot is hard to predict and the exact change in position and orientation is also subject to variations depending on the ground friction. Therefore, dead reckoning on such robots is highly inaccurate. This is the trade-off that is made in return for extremely good maneuverability and traction over rough and loose terrain. Furthermore, a slip/skid approach on a high-friction surface can quickly overcome the torque capabilities of the motors being used. In terms of power efficiency, this approach is reasonably efficient on loose terrain but extremely inefficient otherwise.

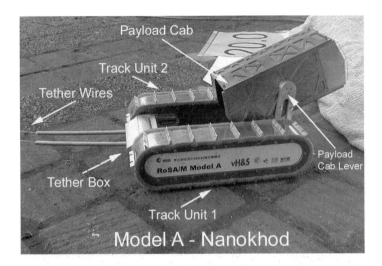

Figure 2.26
The microrover Nanokhod, developed by von Hoerner & Sulger GmbH and the Max Planck Institute, Mainz, for the European Space Agency (ESA), will probably go to Mars [138, 154].

2.3.2.4 Walking wheels

Walking robots might offer the best maneuverability in rough terrain. However, they are inefficient on flat ground and need sophisticated control. Hybrid solutions, combining the adaptability of legs with the efficiency of wheels, offer an interesting compromise. Solutions that passively adapt to the terrain are of particular interest for field and space robotics. The Sojourner robot of NASA/JPL (see figure 1.2) represents such a hybrid solution, able to overcome objects up to the size of the wheels. A more recent mobile robot design for similar applications has recently been produced by EPFL (figure 2.27). This robot, called Shrimp, has six motorized wheels and is capable of climbing objects up to two times its wheel diameter [97, 133]. This enables it to climb regular stairs though the robot is even smaller than the Sojourner. Using a rhombus configuration, the Shrimp has a steering wheel in the front and the rear, and two wheels arranged on a bogie on each side. The front wheel has a spring suspension to guarantee optimal ground contact of all wheels at any time. The steering of the rover is realized by synchronizing the steering of the front and rear wheels and the speed difference of the bogie wheels. This allows for high-precision maneuvers and turning on the spot with minimum slip/skid of the four center wheels. The use of parallel articulations for the front wheel and the bogies creates a virtual center of rotation at the level of the wheel axis. This ensures maximum stability and climbing abilities even for very low friction coefficients between the wheel and the ground.

Figure 2.27
Shrimp, an all-terrain robot with outstanding passive climbing abilities (EPFL [97, 133]).

The climbing ability of the Shrimp is extraordinary in comparison to most robots of similar mechanical complexity, owing much to the specific geometry and thereby the manner in which the center of mass (COM) of the robot shifts with respect to the wheels over time. In contrast, the Personal Rover demonstrates active COM shifting to climb ledges that are also several times the diameter of its wheels, as demonstrated in figure 2.28. A majority of the weight of the Personal Rover is borne at the upper end of its swinging boom. A dedicated motor drives the boom to change the front/rear weight distribution in order to facilitate step-climbing. Because this COM-shifting scheme is active, a control loop must explicitly decide how to move the boom during a climbing scenario. In this case the Personal Rover accomplished this closed-loop control by inferring terrain based on measurements of current flowing to each independently driven wheel [66].

As mobile robotics research matures we find ourselves able to design more intricate mechanical systems. At the same time, the control problems of inverse kinematics and dynamics are now so readily conquered that these complex mechanics can in general be controlled. So, in the near future, we can expect to see a great number of unique, hybrid mobile robots that draw together advantages from several of the underlying locomotion mechanisms that we have discussed in this chapter. They will each be technologically impressive, and each will be designed as the expert robot for its particular environmental niche.

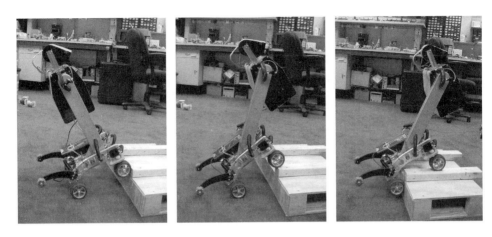

Figure 2.28
The Personal Rover, demonstrating ledge climbing using active center-of-mass shifting.

3 Mobile Robot Kinematics

3.1 Introduction

Kinematics is the most basic study of how mechanical systems behave. In mobile robotics, we need to understand the mechanical behavior of the robot both in order to design appropriate mobile robots for tasks and to understand how to create control software for an instance of mobile robot hardware.

Of course, mobile robots are not the first complex mechanical systems to require such analysis. Robot manipulators have been the subject of intensive study for more than thirty years. In some ways, manipulator robots are much more complex than early mobile robots: a standard welding robot may have five or more joints, whereas early mobile robots were simple differential-drive machines. In recent years, the robotics community has achieved a fairly complete understanding of the kinematics and even the dynamics (i.e., relating to force and mass) of robot manipulators [11, 32].

The mobile robotics community poses many of the same kinematic questions as the robot manipulator community. A manipulator robot's workspace is crucial because it defines the range of possible positions that can be achieved by its end effector relative to its fixture to the environment. A mobile robot's workspace is equally important because it defines the range of possible poses that the mobile robot can achieve in its environment. The robot arm's controllability defines the manner in which active engagement of motors can be used to move from pose to pose in the workspace. Similarly, a mobile robot's controllability defines possible paths and trajectories in its workspace. Robot dynamics places additional constraints on workspace and trajectory due to mass and force considerations. The mobile robot is also limited by dynamics; for instance, a high center of gravity limits the practical turning radius of a fast, car-like robot because of the danger of rolling.

But the chief difference between a mobile robot and a manipulator arm also introduces a significant challenge for *position estimation*. A manipulator has one end fixed to the environment. Measuring the position of an arm's end effector is simply a matter of understanding the kinematics of the robot and measuring the position of all intermediate joints. The manipulator's position is thus always computable by looking at current sensor data. But a mobile robot is a self-contained automaton that can wholly move with respect to its environment. There is no direct way to measure a mobile robot's position instantaneously. Instead, one must integrate the motion of the robot over time. Add to this the inaccuracies of *motion estimation* due to slippage and it is clear that measuring a mobile robot's position precisely is an extremely challenging task.

The process of understanding the motions of a robot begins with the process of describing the contribution each wheel provides for motion. Each wheel has a role in enabling the whole robot to move. By the same token, each wheel also imposes constraints on the robot's motion; for example, refusing to skid laterally. In the following section, we introduce notation that allows expression of robot motion in a global reference frame as well as the robot's local reference frame. Then, using this notation, we demonstrate the construction of simple forward kinematic models of motion, describing how the robot as a whole moves as a function of its geometry and individual wheel behavior. Next, we formally describe the kinematic constraints of individual wheels, and then combine these kinematic constraints to express the whole robot's kinematic constraints. With these tools, one can evaluate the paths and trajectories that define the robot's maneuverability.

3.2   Kinematic Models and Constraints

Deriving a model for the whole robot's motion is a bottom-up process. Each individual wheel contributes to the robot's motion and, at the same time, imposes constraints on robot motion. Wheels are tied together based on robot chassis geometry, and therefore their constraints combine to form constraints on the overall motion of the robot chassis. But the forces and constraints of each wheel must be expressed with respect to a clear and consistent reference frame. This is particularly important in mobile robotics because of its self-contained and mobile nature; a clear mapping between global and local frames of reference is required. We begin by defining these reference frames formally, then using the resulting formalism to annotate the kinematics of individual wheels and whole robots. Throughout this process we draw extensively on the notation and terminology presented in [52].

3.2.1   Representing robot position

Throughout this analysis we model the robot as a rigid body on wheels, operating on a horizontal plane. The total dimensionality of this robot chassis on the plane is three, two for position in the plane and one for orientation along the vertical axis, which is orthogonal to the plane. Of course, there are additional degrees of freedom and flexibility due to the wheel axles, wheel steering joints, and wheel castor joints. However by robot *chassis* we refer only to the rigid body of the robot, ignoring the joints and degrees of freedom internal to the robot and its wheels.

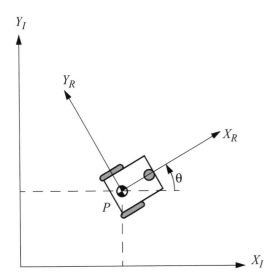

Figure 3.1
The global reference frame and the robot local reference frame.

In order to specify the position of the robot on the plane we establish a relationship between the global reference frame of the plane and the local reference frame of the robot, as in figure 3.1. The axes X_I and Y_I define an arbitrary inertial basis on the plane as the global reference frame from some origin O: $\{X_I, Y_I\}$. To specify the position of the robot, choose a point P on the robot chassis as its position reference point. The basis $\{X_R, Y_R\}$ defines two axes relative to P on the robot chassis and is thus the robot's local reference frame. The position of P in the global reference frame is specified by coordinates x and y, and the angular difference between the global and local reference frames is given by θ. We can describe the pose of the robot as a vector with these three elements. Note the use of the subscript I to clarify the basis of this pose as the global reference frame:

$$\xi_I = \begin{bmatrix} x \\ y \\ \theta \end{bmatrix} \tag{3.1}$$

To describe robot motion in terms of component motions, it will be necessary to map motion along the axes of the global reference frame to motion along the axes of the robot's local reference frame. Of course, the mapping is a function of the current pose of the robot. This mapping is accomplished using the *orthogonal rotation matrix:*

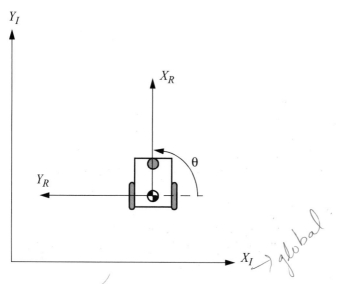

Figure 3.2
The mobile robot aligned with a global axis.

$$R(\theta) = \begin{bmatrix} \cos\theta & \sin\theta & 0 \\ -\sin\theta & \cos\theta & 0 \\ 0 & 0 & 1 \end{bmatrix} \qquad (3.2)$$

This matrix can be used to map motion in the global reference frame $\{X_I, Y_I\}$ to motion in terms of the local reference frame $\{X_R, Y_R\}$. This operation is denoted by $R(\theta)\dot{\xi}_I$ because the computation of this operation depends on the value of θ :

$$\dot{\xi}_R = R(\tfrac{\pi}{2})\dot{\xi}_I \qquad (3.3)$$

For example, consider the robot in figure 3.2. For this robot, because $\theta = \dfrac{\pi}{2}$ we can easily compute the instantaneous rotation matrix R:

$$R(\tfrac{\pi}{2}) = \begin{bmatrix} 0 & 1 & 0 \\ -1 & 0 & 0 \\ 0 & 0 & 1 \end{bmatrix} \qquad (3.4)$$

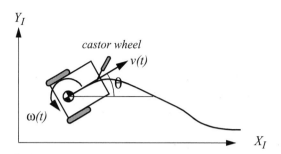

Figure 3.3
A differential-drive robot in its global reference frame.

Given some velocity ($\dot{x}, \dot{y}, \dot{\theta}$) in the global reference frame we can compute the components of motion along this robot's local axes X_R and Y_R. In this case, due to the specific angle of the robot, motion along X_R is equal to $\dot{y}$ and motion along Y_R is $-\dot{x}$:

$$\dot{\xi}_R = R(\frac{\pi}{2})\dot{\xi}_I = \begin{bmatrix} 0 & 1 & 0 \\ -1 & 0 & 0 \\ 0 & 0 & 1 \end{bmatrix} \begin{bmatrix} \dot{x} \\ \dot{y} \\ \dot{\theta} \end{bmatrix} = \begin{bmatrix} \dot{y} \\ -\dot{x} \\ \dot{\theta} \end{bmatrix} \qquad (3.5)$$

3.2.2 Forward kinematic models

In the simplest cases, the mapping described by equation (3.3) is sufficient to generate a formula that captures the forward kinematics of the mobile robot: how does the robot move, given its geometry and the speeds of its wheels? More formally, consider the example shown in figure 3.3.

This differential drive robot has two wheels, each with diameter r. Given a point P centered between the two drive wheels, each wheel is a distance l from P. Given r, l, θ, and the spinning speed of each wheel, $\dot{\phi}_1$ and $\dot{\phi}_2$, a forward kinematic model would predict the robot's overall speed in the global reference frame:

$$\dot{\xi}_I = \begin{bmatrix} \dot{x} \\ \dot{y} \\ \dot{\theta} \end{bmatrix} = f(l, r, \theta, \dot{\phi}_1, \dot{\phi}_2) \qquad (3.6)$$

From equation (3.3) we know that we can compute the robot's motion in the global reference frame from motion in its local reference frame: $\dot{\xi}_I = R(\theta)^{-1}\dot{\xi}_R$. Therefore, the strategy will be to first compute the contribution of each of the two wheels in the local reference frame, $\dot{\xi}_R$. For this example of a differential-drive chassis, this problem is particularly straightforward.

Suppose that the robot's local reference frame is aligned such that the robot moves forward along $+X_R$, as shown in figure 3.1. First consider the contribution of each wheel's spinning speed to the translation speed at P in the direction of $+X_R$. If one wheel spins while the other wheel contributes nothing and is stationary, since P is halfway between the two wheels, it will move instantaneously with half the speed: $x_{r1} = (1/2)r\dot{\varphi}_1$ and $x_{r2} = (1/2)r\dot{\varphi}_2$. In a differential drive robot, these two contributions can simply be added to calculate the x_R component of $\dot{\xi}_R$. Consider, for example, a differential robot in which each wheel spins with equal speed but in opposite directions. The result is a stationary, spinning robot. As expected, x_R will be zero in this case. The value of y_R is even simpler to calculate. Neither wheel can contribute to sideways motion in the robot's reference frame, and so y_R is always zero. Finally, we must compute the rotational component $\dot{\theta}_R$ of $\dot{\xi}_R$. Once again, the contributions of each wheel can be computed independently and just added. Consider the right wheel (we will call this wheel 1). Forward spin of this wheel results in *counterclockwise* rotation at point P. Recall that if wheel 1 spins alone, the robot pivots around wheel 2. The rotation velocity ω_1 at P can be computed because the wheel is instantaneously moving along the arc of a circle of radius $2l$:

$$\omega_1 = \frac{r\dot{\varphi}_1}{2l} \tag{3.7}$$

The same calculation applies to the left wheel, with the exception that forward spin results in *clockwise* rotation at point P:

$$\omega_2 = \frac{-r\dot{\varphi}_2}{2l} \tag{3.8}$$

Combining these individual formulas yields a kinematic model for the differential-drive example robot:

$$\dot{\xi}_I = R(\theta)^{-1} \begin{bmatrix} \dfrac{r\dot{\varphi}_1}{2} + \dfrac{r\dot{\varphi}_2}{2} \\ 0 \\ \dfrac{r\dot{\varphi}_1}{2l} + \dfrac{-r\dot{\varphi}_2}{2l} \end{bmatrix} \tag{3.9}$$

We can now use this kinematic model in an example. However, we must first compute $R(\theta)^{-1}$. In general, calculating the inverse of a matrix may be challenging. In this case, however, it is easy because it is simply a transform from $\dot{\xi}_R$ to $\dot{\xi}_I$ rather than vice versa:

$$
R(\theta)^{-1} = \begin{bmatrix} \cos\theta & -\sin\theta & 0 \\ \sin\theta & \cos\theta & 0 \\ 0 & 0 & 1 \end{bmatrix} \tag{3.10}
$$

Suppose that the robot is positioned such that $\theta = \pi/2$, $r = 1$, and $l = 1$. If the robot engages its wheels unevenly, with speeds $\dot{\varphi}_1 = 4$ and $\dot{\varphi}_2 = 2$, we can compute its velocity in the global reference frame:

$$
\dot{\xi}_I = \begin{bmatrix} \dot{x} \\ \dot{y} \\ \dot{\theta} \end{bmatrix} = \begin{bmatrix} 0 & -1 & 0 \\ 1 & 0 & 0 \\ 0 & 0 & 1 \end{bmatrix} \begin{bmatrix} 3 \\ 0 \\ 1 \end{bmatrix} = \begin{bmatrix} 0 \\ 3 \\ 1 \end{bmatrix} \tag{3.11}
$$

So this robot will move instantaneously along the y-axis of the global reference frame with speed 3 while rotating with speed 1. This approach to kinematic modeling can provide information about the motion of a robot given its component wheel speeds in straightforward cases. However, we wish to determine the space of possible motions for each robot chassis design. To do this, we must go further, describing formally the constraints on robot motion imposed by each wheel. Section 3.2.3 begins this process by describing constraints for various wheel types; the rest of this chapter provides tools for analyzing the characteristics and workspace of a robot given these constraints.

3.2.3 Wheel kinematic constraints

The first step to a kinematic model of the robot is to express constraints on the motions of individual wheels. Just as shown in section 3.2.2, the motions of individual wheels can later be combined to compute the motion of the robot as a whole. As discussed in chapter 2, there are four basic wheel types with widely varying kinematic properties. Therefore, we begin by presenting sets of constraints specific to each wheel type.

However, several important assumptions will simplify this presentation. We assume that the plane of the wheel always remains vertical and that there is in all cases one single point of contact between the wheel and the ground plane. Furthermore, we assume that there is no sliding at this single point of contact. That is, the wheel undergoes motion only under conditions of pure rolling and rotation about the vertical axis through the contact point. For a more thorough treatment of kinematics, including sliding contact, refer to [25].

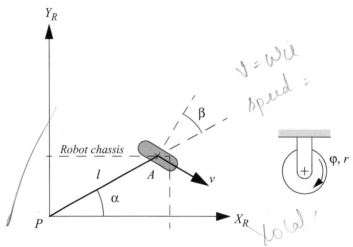

Figure 3.4
A fixed standard wheel and its parameters.

Under these assumptions, we present two constraints for every wheel type. The first constraint enforces the concept of rolling contact – that the wheel must roll when motion takes place in the appropriate direction. The second constraint enforces the concept of no lateral slippage – that the wheel must not slide orthogonal to the wheel plane.

3.2.3.1 Fixed standard wheel

The fixed standard wheel has no vertical axis of rotation for steering. Its angle to the chassis is thus fixed, and it is limited to motion back and forth along the wheel plane and rotation around its contact point with the ground plane. Figure 3.4 depicts a fixed standard wheel A and indicates its position pose relative to the robot's local reference frame $\{X_R, Y_R\}$. The position of A is expressed in polar coordinates by distance l and angle α. The angle of the wheel plane relative to the chassis is denoted by β, which is fixed since the fixed standard wheel is not steerable. The wheel, which has radius r, can spin over time, and so its rotational position around its horizontal axle is a function of time t: $\varphi(t)$.

The rolling constraint for this wheel enforces that all motion along the direction of the wheel plane must be accompanied by the appropriate amount of wheel spin so that there is pure rolling at the contact point:

$$\left[\sin(\alpha + \beta) \; -\cos(\alpha + \beta) \; (-l)\cos\beta\right] R(\theta)\dot{\xi}_I - r\dot{\varphi} = 0 \tag{3.12}$$

The first term of the sum denotes the total motion along the wheel plane. The three elements of the vector on the left represent mappings from each of $\dot{x}, \dot{y}, \dot{\theta}$ to their contributions for motion along the wheel plane. Note that the $R(\theta)\dot{\xi}_I$ term is used to transform the motion parameters $\dot{\xi}_I$ that are in the global reference frame $\{X_I, Y_I\}$ into motion parameters in the local reference frame $\{X_R, Y_R\}$ as shown in example equation (3.5). This is necessary because all other parameters in the equation, α, β, l, are in terms of the robot's local reference frame. This motion along the wheel plane must be equal, according to this constraint, to the motion accomplished by spinning the wheel, $r\dot{\varphi}$.

The sliding constraint for this wheel enforces that the component of the wheel's motion orthogonal to the wheel plane must be zero:

$$\left[\cos(\alpha+\beta)\ \sin(\alpha+\beta)\ l\sin\beta\right] R(\theta)\dot{\xi}_I = 0 \tag{3.13}$$

For example, suppose that wheel A is in a position such that $\{(\alpha = 0), (\beta = 0)\}$. This would place the contact point of the wheel on X_I with the plane of the wheel oriented parallel to Y_I. If $\theta = 0$, then the sliding constraint [equation (3.13)] reduces to

$$\begin{bmatrix} 1 & 0 & 0 \end{bmatrix} \begin{bmatrix} 1 & 0 & 0 \\ 0 & 1 & 0 \\ 0 & 0 & 1 \end{bmatrix} \begin{bmatrix} \dot{x} \\ \dot{y} \\ \dot{\theta} \end{bmatrix} = \begin{bmatrix} 1 & 0 & 0 \end{bmatrix} \begin{bmatrix} \dot{x} \\ \dot{y} \\ \dot{\theta} \end{bmatrix} = 0 \tag{3.14}$$

This constrains the component of motion along X_I to be zero and since X_I and X_R are parallel in this example, the wheel is constrained from sliding sideways, as expected.

3.2.3.2 Steered standard wheel

The steered standard wheel differs from the fixed standard wheel only in that there is an additional degree of freedom: the wheel may rotate around a vertical axis passing through the center of the wheel and the ground contact point. The equations of position for the steered standard wheel (figure 3.5) are identical to that of the fixed standard wheel shown in figure 3.4 with one exception. The orientation of the wheel to the robot chassis is no longer a single fixed value, β, but instead varies as a function of time: $\beta(t)$. The rolling and sliding constraints are

$$\left[\sin(\alpha+\beta)\ -\cos(\alpha+\beta)\ (-l)\cos\beta\right] R(\theta)\dot{\xi}_I - r\dot{\varphi} = 0 \tag{3.15}$$

$$\left[\cos(\alpha+\beta)\ \sin(\alpha+\beta)\ l\sin\beta\right] R(\theta)\dot{\xi}_I = 0 \tag{3.16}$$

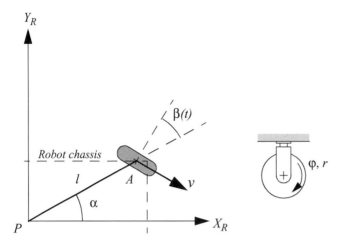

Figure 3.5
A steered standard wheel and its parameters.

These constraints are identical to those of the fixed standard wheel because, unlike $\dot{\phi}$, $\dot{\beta}$ does not have a direct impact on the instantaneous motion constraints of a robot. It is only by integrating over time that changes in steering angle can affect the mobility of a vehicle. This may seem subtle, but is a very important distinction between change in steering position, $\dot{\beta}$, and change in wheel spin, $\dot{\phi}$.

3.2.3.3 Castor wheel

Castor wheels are able to steer around a vertical axis. However, unlike the steered standard wheel, the vertical axis of rotation in a castor wheel does not pass through the ground contact point. Figure 3.6 depicts a castor wheel, demonstrating that formal specification of the castor wheel's position requires an additional parameter.

The wheel contact point is now at position B, which is connected by a rigid rod AB of fixed length d to point A fixes the location of the vertical axis about which B steers, and this point A has a position specified in the robot's reference frame, as in figure 3.6. We assume that the plane of the wheel is aligned with AB at all times. Similar to the steered standard wheel, the castor wheel has two parameters that vary as a function of time. $\phi(t)$ represents the wheel spin over time as before. $\beta(t)$ denotes the steering angle and orientation of AB over time.

For the castor wheel, the rolling constraint is identical to equation (3.15) because the offset axis plays no role during motion that is aligned with the wheel plane:

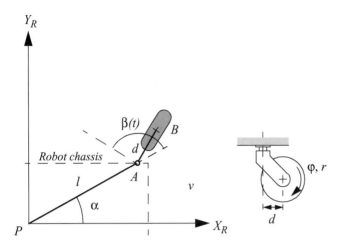

Figure 3.6
A castor wheel and its parameters.

$$\left[\sin(\alpha + \beta) \ -\cos(\alpha + \beta) \ (-l)\cos\beta\right]R(\theta)\dot{\xi}_I - r\dot{\varphi} \ = \ 0 \tag{3.17}$$

The castor geometry does, however, have significant impact on the sliding constraint. The critical issue is that the lateral force on the wheel occurs at point A because this is the attachment point of the wheel to the chassis. Because of the offset ground contact point relative to A, the constraint that there be zero lateral movement would be wrong. Instead, the constraint is much like a rolling constraint, in that appropriate rotation of the vertical axis must take place:

$$\left[\cos(\alpha + \beta) \ \sin(\alpha + \beta) \ d + l\sin\beta\right]R(\theta)\dot{\xi}_I + d\dot{\beta} \ = \ 0 \tag{3.18}$$

In equation (3.18), any motion orthogonal to the wheel plane must be balanced by an equivalent and opposite amount of castor steering motion. This result is critical to the success of castor wheels because by setting the value of $\dot{\beta}$ any arbitrary lateral motion can be acceptable. In a steered standard wheel, the steering action does not by itself cause a movement of the robot chassis. But in a castor wheel the steering action itself moves the robot chassis because of the offset between the ground contact point and the vertical axis of rotation.

Figure 3.7
Office chair with five castor wheels.

More concisely, it can be surmised from equations (3.17) and (3.18) that, given *any* robot chassis motion $\dot{\xi}_I$, there exists some value for spin speed $\dot{\varphi}$ and steering speed $\dot{\beta}$ such that the constraints are met. Therefore, a robot with only castor wheels can move with any velocity in the space of possible robot motions. We term such systems *omnidirectional*.

A real-world example of such a system is the five-castor wheel office chair shown in figure 3.7. Assuming that all joints are able to move freely, you may select any motion vector on the plane for the chair and push it by hand. Its castor wheels will spin and steer as needed to achieve that motion without contact point sliding. By the same token, if each of the chair's castor wheels housed two motors, one for spinning and one for steering, then a control system would be able to move the chair along any trajectory in the plane. Thus, although the kinematics of castor wheels is somewhat complex, such wheels do not impose any real constraints on the kinematics of a robot chassis.

3.2.3.4 Swedish wheel
Swedish wheels have no vertical axis of rotation, yet are able to move *omnidirectionally* like the castor wheel. This is possible by adding a degree of freedom to the fixed standard wheel. Swedish wheels consist of a fixed standard wheel with rollers attached to the wheel perimeter with axes that are antiparallel to the main axis of the fixed wheel component. The exact angle γ between the roller axes and the main axis can vary, as shown in figure 3.8.

For example, given a Swedish 45-degree wheel, the motion vectors of the principal axis and the roller axes can be drawn as in figure 3.8. Since each axis can spin clockwise or counterclockwise, one can combine any vector along one axis with any vector along the other axis. These two axes are not necessarily independent (except in the case of the Swedish 90-degree wheel); however, it is visually clear that any desired direction of motion is achievable by choosing the appropriate two vectors.

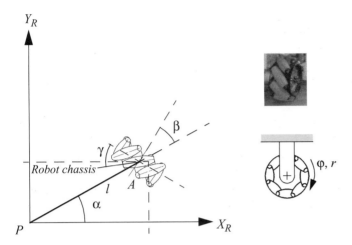

Figure 3.8
A Swedish wheel and its parameters.

The pose of a Swedish wheel is expressed exactly as in a fixed standard wheel, with the addition of a term, γ, representing the angle between the main wheel plane and the axis of rotation of the small circumferential rollers. This is depicted in figure 3.8 within the robot's reference frame.

Formulating the constraint for a Swedish wheel requires some subtlety. The instantaneous constraint is due to the specific orientation of the small rollers. The axis around which these rollers spin is a zero component of velocity at the contact point. That is, moving in that direction without spinning the main axis is not possible without sliding. The motion constraint that is derived looks identical to the rolling constraint for the fixed standard wheel in equation (3.12) except that the formula is modified by adding γ such that the effective direction along which the rolling constraint holds is along this zero component rather than along the wheel plane:

$$\left[\sin(\alpha + \beta + \gamma) \ -\cos(\alpha + \beta + \gamma) \ (-l)\cos(\beta + \gamma)\right] R(\theta)\dot{\xi}_I - r\dot{\varphi}\cos\gamma = 0 \qquad (3.19)$$

Orthogonal to this direction the motion is not constrained because of the free rotation $\dot{\varphi}_{sw}$ of the small rollers.

$$\left[\cos(\alpha + \beta + \gamma) \ \sin(\alpha + \beta + \gamma) \ l\sin(\beta + \gamma)\right] R(\theta)\dot{\xi}_I - r\dot{\varphi}\sin\gamma - r_{sw}\dot{\varphi}_{sw} = 0 \quad (3.20)$$

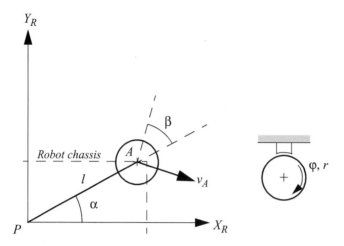

Figure 3.9
A spherical wheel and its parameters.

The behavior of this constraint and thereby the Swedish wheel changes dramatically as the value γ varies. Consider $\gamma = 0$. This represents the swedish 90-degree wheel. In this case, the zero component of velocity is in line with the wheel plane and so equation (3.19) reduces exactly to equation (3.12), the fixed standard wheel rolling constraint. But because of the rollers, there is no sliding constraint orthogonal to the wheel plane [see equation (3.20)]. By varying the value of $\dot{\varphi}$, any desired motion vector can be made to satisfy equation (3.19) and therefore the wheel is omnidirectional. In fact, this special case of the Swedish design results in fully decoupled motion, in that the rollers and the main wheel provide orthogonal directions of motion.

At the other extreme, consider $\gamma = \pi/2$. In this case, the rollers have axes of rotation that are parallel to the main wheel axis of rotation. Interestingly, if this value is substituted for γ in equation (3.19) the result is the fixed standard wheel sliding constraint, equation (3.13). In other words, the rollers provide no benefit in terms of lateral freedom of motion since they are simply aligned with the main wheel. However, in this case the main wheel never needs to spin and therefore the rolling constraint disappears. This is a degenerate form of the Swedish wheel and therefore we assume in the remainder of this chapter that $\gamma \neq \pi/2$.

3.2.3.5 Spherical wheel

The final wheel type, a ball or spherical wheel, places no direct constraints on motion (figure 3.9). Such a mechanism has no principal axis of rotation, and therefore no appropriate rolling or sliding constraints exist. As with castor wheels and Swedish wheels, the spherical wheel is clearly omnidirectional and places no constraints on the robot chassis kinematics. Therefore equation (3.21) simply describes the roll rate of the ball in the direction of motion v_A of point A of the robot.

$$\left[\sin(\alpha + \beta) \ -\cos(\alpha + \beta) \ (-l)\cos\beta\right] R(\theta)\dot{\xi}_I - r\dot{\varphi} = 0 \tag{3.21}$$

By definition the wheel rotation orthogonal to this direction is zero.

$$\left[\cos(\alpha + \beta) \ \sin(\alpha + \beta) \ l\sin\beta\right] R(\theta)\dot{\xi}_I = 0 \tag{3.22}$$

As can be seen, the equations for the spherical wheel are exactly the same as for the fixed standard wheel. However, the interpretation of equation (3.22) is different. The omnidirectional spherical wheel can have any arbitrary direction of movement, where the motion direction given by β is a free variable deduced from equation (3.22). Consider the case that the robot is in pure translation in the direction of Y_R. Then equation (3.22) reduces to $\sin(\alpha + \beta) = 0$, thus $\beta = -\alpha$, which makes sense for this special case.

3.2.4 Robot kinematic constraints

Given a mobile robot with M wheels we can now compute the kinematic constraints of the robot chassis. The key idea is that each wheel imposes zero or more constraints on robot motion, and so the process is simply one of appropriately combining all of the kinematic constraints arising from all of the wheels based on the placement of those wheels on the robot chassis.

We have categorized all wheels into five categories: (1) fixed and (2)steerable standard wheels, (3) castor wheels, (4) Swedish wheels, and (5) spherical wheels. But note from the wheel kinematic constraints in equations (3.17), (3.18), and (3.19) that the castor wheel, Swedish wheel, and spherical wheel impose *no* kinematic constraints on the robot chassis, since $\dot{\xi}_I$ can range freely in all of these cases owing to the internal wheel degrees of freedom.

Therefore only fixed standard wheels and steerable standard wheels have impact on robot chassis kinematics and therefore require consideration when computing the robot's kinematic constraints. Suppose that the robot has a total of N standard wheels, comprising N_f fixed standard wheels and N_s steerable standard wheels. We use $\beta_s(t)$ to denote the variable steering angles of the N_s steerable standard wheels. In contrast, β_f refers to the orientation of the N_f fixed standard wheels as depicted in figure 3.4. In the case of wheel spin, both the fixed and steerable wheels have rotational positions around the horizontal axle that vary as a function of time. We denote the fixed and steerable cases separately as $\varphi_f(t)$ and $\varphi_s(t)$, and use $\varphi(t)$ as an aggregate matrix that combines both values:

$$\varphi(t) = \begin{bmatrix} \varphi_f(t) \\ \varphi_s(t) \end{bmatrix} \tag{3.23}$$

The rolling constraints of all wheels can now be collected in a single expression:

$$J_1(\beta_s)R(\theta)\dot{\xi}_I - J_2\dot{\varphi} = 0 \tag{3.24}$$

This expression bears a strong resemblance to the rolling constraint of a single wheel, but substitutes matrices in lieu of single values, thus taking into account all wheels. J_2 is a constant diagonal $N \times N$ matrix whose entries are radii r of all standard wheels. $J_1(\beta_s)$ denotes a matrix with projections for all wheels to their motions along their individual wheel planes:

$$J_1(\beta_s) = \begin{bmatrix} J_{1f} \\ J_{1s}(\beta_s) \end{bmatrix} \tag{3.25}$$

Note that $J_1(\beta_s)$ is only a function of β_s and not β_f. This is because the orientations of steerable standard wheels vary as a function of time, whereas the orientations of fixed standard wheels are constant. J_{1f} is therefore a constant matrix of projections for all fixed standard wheels. It has size ($N_f \times 3$), with each row consisting of the three terms in the three-matrix from equation (3.12) for each fixed standard wheel. $J_{1s}(\beta_s)$ is a matrix of size ($N_s \times 3$), with each row consisting of the three terms in the three-matrix from equation (3.15) for each steerable standard wheel.

In summary, equation (3.24) represents the constraint that all standard wheels must spin around their horizontal axis an appropriate amount based on their motions along the wheel plane so that rolling occurs at the ground contact point.

We use the same technique to collect the sliding constraints of all standard wheels into a single expression with the same structure as equations (3.13) and (3.16):

$$C_1(\beta_s)R(\theta)\dot{\xi}_I = 0 \tag{3.26}$$

$$C_1(\beta_s) = \begin{bmatrix} C_{1f} \\ C_{1s}(\beta_s) \end{bmatrix} \tag{3.27}$$

C_{1f} and C_{1s} are ($N_f \times 3$) and ($N_s \times 3$) matrices whose rows are the three terms in the three-matrix of equations (3.13) and (3.16) for all fixed and steerable standard wheels. Thus equation (3.26) is a constraint over all standard wheels that their components of motion orthogonal to their wheel planes must be zero. This sliding constraint over all standard wheels has the most significant impact on defining the overall maneuverability of the robot chassis, as explained in the next section.

3.2.5 Examples: robot kinematic models and constraints

In section 3.2.2 we presented a forward kinematic solution for $\dot{\xi}_I$ in the case of a simple differential-drive robot by combining each wheel's contribution to robot motion. We can now use the tools presented above to construct the same kinematic expression by direct application of the rolling constraints for every wheel type. We proceed with this technique applied again to the differential drive robot, enabling verification of the method as compared to the results of section 3.2.2. Then we proceed to the case of the three-wheeled omnidirectional robot.

3.2.5.1 A differential-drive robot example

First, refer to equations (3.24) and (3.26). These equations relate robot motion to the rolling and sliding constraints $J_1(\beta_s)$ and $C_1(\beta_s)$, and the wheel spin speed of the robot's wheels, $\dot{\phi}$. Fusing these two equations yields the following expression:

$$\begin{bmatrix} J_1(\beta_s) \\ C_1(\beta_s) \end{bmatrix} R(\theta)\dot{\xi}_I = \begin{bmatrix} J_2\phi \\ 0 \end{bmatrix} \tag{3.28}$$

Once again, consider the differential drive robot in figure 3.3. We will construct $J_1(\beta_s)$ and $C_1(\beta_s)$ directly from the rolling constraints of each wheel. The castor is unpowered and is free to move in any direction, so we ignore this third point of contact altogether. The two remaining drive wheels are not steerable, and therefore $J_1(\beta_s)$ and $C_1(\beta_s)$ simplify to J_{1f} and C_{1f} respectively. To employ the fixed standard wheel's rolling constraint formula, equation (3.12), we must first identify each wheel's values for α and β. Suppose that the robot's local reference frame is aligned such that the robot moves forward along $+X_R$, as shown in figure 3.1. In this case, for the right wheel $\alpha = -\pi/2$, $\beta = \pi$, and for the left wheel, $\alpha = \pi/2$, $\beta = 0$. Note the value of β for the right wheel is necessary to ensure that positive spin causes motion in the $+X_R$ direction (figure 3.4). Now we can compute the J_{1f} and C_{1f} matrix using the matrix terms from equations (3.12) and (3.13). Because the two fixed standard wheels are parallel, equation (3.13) results in only one independent equation, and equation (3.28) gives

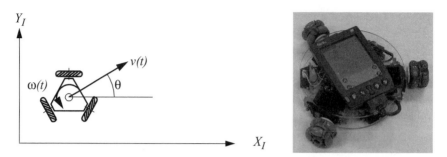

Figure 3.10
A three-wheel omnidrive robot developed by Carnegie Mellon University (www.cs.cmu.edu/~pprk).

$$\begin{bmatrix} \begin{bmatrix} 1 & 0 & l \\ 1 & 0 & -l \end{bmatrix} \\ \begin{bmatrix} 0 & 1 & 0 \end{bmatrix} \end{bmatrix} R(\theta)\dot{\xi}_I = \begin{bmatrix} J_2\dot{\varphi} \\ 0 \end{bmatrix} \tag{3.29}$$

Inverting equation (3.29) yields the kinematic equation specific to our differential drive robot:

$$\dot{\xi}_I = R(\theta)^{-1} \begin{bmatrix} 1 & 0 & l \\ 1 & 0 & -l \\ 0 & 1 & 0 \end{bmatrix}^{-1} \begin{bmatrix} J_2\dot{\varphi} \\ 0 \end{bmatrix} = R(\theta)^{-1} \begin{bmatrix} \frac{1}{2} & \frac{1}{2} & 0 \\ 0 & 0 & 1 \\ \frac{1}{2l} & -\frac{1}{2l} & 0 \end{bmatrix} \begin{bmatrix} J_2\dot{\varphi} \\ 0 \end{bmatrix} \tag{3.30}$$

This demonstrates that, for the simple differential-drive case, the combination of wheel rolling and sliding constraints describes the kinematic behavior, based on our manual calculation in section 3.2.2.

3.2.5.2 An omnidirectional robot example

Consider the omniwheel robot shown in figure 3.10. This robot has three Swedish 90-degree wheels, arranged radially symmetrically, with the rollers perpendicular to each main wheel.

First we must impose a specific local reference frame upon the robot. We do so by choosing point P at the center of the robot, then aligning the robot with the local reference

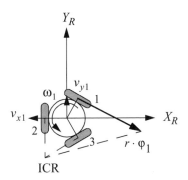

Figure 3.11
The local reference frame plus detailed parameters for wheel 1.

frame such that X_R is colinear with the axis of wheel 2. Figure 3.11 shows the robot and its local reference frame arranged in this manner.

We assume that the distance between each wheel and P is l, and that all three wheels have the same radius, r. Once again, the value of $\dot{\xi}_I$ can be computed as a combination of the rolling constraints of the robot's three omnidirectional wheels, as in equation (3.28). As with the differential- drive robot, since this robot has no steerable wheels, $J_1(\beta_s)$ simplifies to J_{1f}:

$$\dot{\xi}_I = R(\theta)^{-1} J_{1f}^{-1} J_2 \dot{\phi} \tag{3.31}$$

We calculate J_{1f} using the matrix elements of the rolling constraints for the Swedish wheel, given by equation (3.19). But to use these values, we must establish the values α, β, γ for each wheel. Referring to figure (3.8), we can see that $\gamma = 0$ for the Swedish 90-degree wheel. Note that this immediately simplifies equation (3.19) to equation (3.12), the rolling constraints of a fixed standard wheel. Given our particular placement of the local reference frame, the value of α for each wheel is easily computed: $(\alpha_1 = \pi/3)$, $(\alpha_2 = \pi)$, $(\alpha_3 = -\pi/3)$. Furthermore, $\beta = 0$ for all wheels because the wheels are tangent to the robot's circular body. Constructing and simplifying J_{1f} using equation (3.12) yields

$$
J_{1f} = \begin{bmatrix} \sin\frac{\pi}{3} & -\cos\frac{\pi}{3} & -l \\ 0 & -\cos\pi & -l \\ \sin-\frac{\pi}{3} & -\cos-\frac{\pi}{3} & -l \end{bmatrix} = \begin{bmatrix} \frac{\sqrt{3}}{2} & -\frac{1}{2} & -l \\ 0 & 1 & -l \\ -\frac{\sqrt{3}}{2} & -\frac{1}{2} & -l \end{bmatrix} \tag{3.32}
$$

Once again, computing the value of $\dot{\xi}_I$ requires calculating the inverse, J_{1f}^{-1}, as needed in equation (3.31). One approach would be to apply rote methods for calculating the inverse of a 3 x 3 square matrix. A second approach would be to compute the contribution of each Swedish wheel to chassis motion, as shown in section 3.2.2. We leave this process as an exercise for the enthusiast. Once the inverse is obtained, $\dot{\xi}_I$ can be isolated:

$$
\dot{\xi}_I = R(\theta)^{-1} \begin{bmatrix} \frac{1}{\sqrt{3}} & 0 & -\frac{1}{\sqrt{3}} \\ -\frac{1}{3} & \frac{2}{3} & -\frac{1}{3} \\ -\frac{1}{3l} & -\frac{1}{3l} & -\frac{1}{3l} \end{bmatrix} J_2 \dot{\varphi} \tag{3.33}
$$

Consider a specific omnidrive chassis with $l = 1$ and $r = 1$ for all wheels. The robot's local reference frame and global reference frame are aligned, so that $\theta = 0$. If wheels 1, 2, and 3 spin at speeds $(\varphi_1 = 4)$, $(\varphi_2 = 1)$, $(\varphi_3 = 2)$, what is the resulting motion of the whole robot? Using the equation above, the answer can be calculated readily:

$$
\dot{\xi}_I = \begin{bmatrix} \dot{x} \\ \dot{y} \\ \dot{\theta} \end{bmatrix} = \begin{bmatrix} 1 & 0 & 0 \\ 0 & 1 & 0 \\ 0 & 0 & 1 \end{bmatrix} \begin{bmatrix} \frac{1}{\sqrt{3}} & 0 & -\frac{1}{\sqrt{3}} \\ -\frac{1}{3} & \frac{2}{3} & -\frac{1}{3} \\ -\frac{1}{3} & -\frac{1}{3} & -\frac{1}{3} \end{bmatrix} \begin{bmatrix} 1 & 0 & 0 \\ 0 & 1 & 0 \\ 0 & 0 & 1 \end{bmatrix} \begin{bmatrix} 4 \\ 1 \\ 2 \end{bmatrix} = \begin{bmatrix} \frac{2}{\sqrt{3}} \\ -\frac{4}{3} \\ -\frac{7}{3} \end{bmatrix} \tag{3.34}
$$

So this robot will move instantaneously along the x-axis with positive speed and along the y axis with negative speed while rotating clockwise. We can see from the above examples that robot motion can be predicted by combining the rolling constraints of individual wheels.

The sliding constraints comprising $C_1(\beta_s)$ can be used to go even further, enabling us to evaluate the maneuverability and workspace of the robot rather than just its predicted motion. Next, we examine methods for using the sliding constraints, sometimes in conjunction with rolling constraints, to generate powerful analyses of the maneuverability of a robot chassis.

3.3 Mobile Robot Maneuverability

The kinematic mobility of a robot chassis is its ability to directly move in the environment. The basic constraint limiting mobility is the rule that every wheel must satisfy its sliding constraint. Therefore, we can formally derive robot mobility by starting from equation (3.26).

In addition to instantaneous kinematic motion, a mobile robot is able to further manipulate its position, over time, by steering steerable wheels. As we will see in section 3.3.3, the overall maneuverability of a robot is thus a combination of the mobility available based on the kinematic sliding constraints of the standard wheels, plus the additional freedom contributed by steering and spinning the steerable standard wheels.

3.3.1 Degree of mobility

Equation (3.26) imposes the constraint that every wheel must avoid any lateral slip. Of course, this holds separately for each and every wheel, and so it is possible to specify this constraint separately for fixed and for steerable standard wheels:

$$C_{1f}R(\theta)\dot{\xi}_I = 0 \tag{3.35}$$

$$C_{1s}(\beta_s)R(\theta)\dot{\xi}_I = 0 \tag{3.36}$$

For both of these constraints to be satisfied, the motion vector $R(\theta)\dot{\xi}_I$ must belong to the *null space* of the projection matrix $C_1(\beta_s)$, which is simply a combination of C_{1f} and C_{1s}. Mathematically, the null space of $C_1(\beta_s)$ is the space N such that for any vector n in N, $C_1(\beta_s)n = 0$. If the kinematic constraints are to be honored, then the motion of the robot must always be within this space N. The kinematic constraints [equations (3.35) and (3.36)] can also be demonstrated geometrically using the concept of a robot's *instantaneous center of rotation (ICR)*.

Consider a single standard wheel. It is forced by the sliding constraint to have zero lateral motion. This can be shown geometrically by drawing a *zero motion line* through its horizontal axis, perpendicular to the wheel plane (figure 3.12). At any given instant, wheel motion along the zero motion line must be zero. In other words, the wheel must be moving

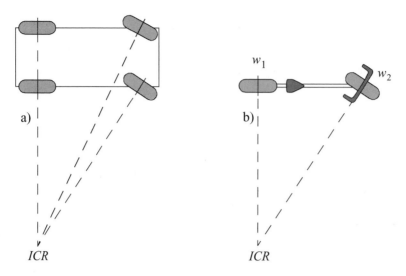

Figure 3.12
(a) Four-wheel with car-like Ackerman steering. (b) bicycle.

instantaneously along some circle of radius R such that the center of that circle is located on the zero motion line. This center point, called the instantaneous center of rotation, may lie anywhere along the zero motion line. When R is at infinity, the wheel moves in a straight line.

A robot such as the Ackerman vehicle in figure 3.12a can have several wheels, but must always have a single ICR. Because all of its zero motion lines meet at a single point, there is a single solution for robot motion, placing the ICR at this meet point.

This ICR geometric construction demonstrates how robot mobility is a function of the number of constraints on the robot's motion, not the number of wheels. In figure 3.12b, the bicycle shown has two wheels, w_1 and w_2. Each wheel contributes a constraint, or a zero motion line. Taken together the two constraints result in a single point as the only remaining solution for the ICR. This is because the two constraints are independent, and thus each further constrains overall robot motion.

But in the case of the differential drive robot in figure 3.13a, the two wheels are aligned along the same horizontal axis. Therefore, the ICR is constrained to lie along a line, not at a specific point. In fact, the second wheel imposes no additional kinematic constraints on robot motion since its zero motion line is identical to that of the first wheel. Thus, although the bicycle and differential-drive chassis have the same number of nonomnidirectional wheels, the former has two independent kinematic constraints while the latter has only one.

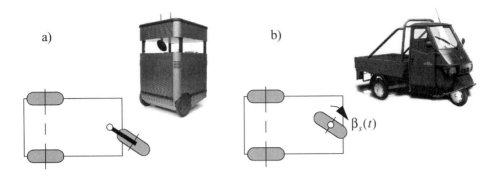

Figure 3.13
(a) Differential drive robot with two individually motorized wheels and a castor wheel, e.g., the Pygmalion robot at EPFL. (b) Tricycle with two fixed standard wheels and one steered standard wheel, e.g. Piaggio minitransporter.

The Ackerman vehicle of figure 3.12a demonstrates another way in which a wheel may be unable to contribute an independent constraint to the robot kinematics. This vehicle has two steerable standard wheels. Given the instantaneous position of just one of these steerable wheels and the position of the fixed rear wheels, there is only a single solution for the ICR. The position of the second steerable wheel is absolutely constrained by the ICR. Therefore, it offers no independent constraints to robot motion.

Robot chassis kinematics is therefore a function of the set of *independent* constraints arising from all standard wheels. The mathematical interpretation of independence is related to the *rank* of a matrix. Recall that the rank of a matrix is the smallest number of independent rows or columns. Equation (3.26) represents all sliding constraints imposed by the wheels of the mobile robot. Therefore $rank\left[C_1(\beta_s)\right]$ is the number of independent constraints.

The greater the number of independent constraints, and therefore the greater the rank of $C_1(\beta_s)$, the more constrained is the mobility of the robot. For example, consider a robot with a single fixed standard wheel. Remember that we consider only standard wheels. This robot may be a unicycle or it may have several Swedish wheels; however, it has exactly one fixed standard wheel. The wheel is at a position specified by parameters α, β, l relative to the robot's local reference frame. $C_1(\beta_s)$ is comprised of C_{1f} and C_{1s}. However, since there are no steerable standard wheels C_{1s} is empty and therefore $C_1(\beta_s)$ contains only C_{1f}. Because there is one fixed standard wheel, this matrix has a rank of one and therefore this robot has a single independent constrain on mobility:

$$C_1(\beta_s) = C_{1f} = \left[\cos(\alpha + \beta) \ \sin(\alpha + \beta) \ l\sin\beta\right] \tag{3.37}$$

Now let us add an additional fixed standard wheel to create a differential-drive robot by constraining the second wheel to be aligned with the same horizontal axis as the original wheel. Without loss of generality, we can place point P at the midpoint between the centers of the two wheels. Given α_1, β_1, l_1 for wheel w_1 and α_2, β_2, l_2 for wheel w_2, it holds geometrically that $\{(l_1 = l_2), (\beta_1 = \beta_2 = 0), (\alpha_1 + \pi = \alpha_2)\}$. Therefore, in this case, the matrix $C_1(\beta_s)$ has two constraints but a rank of one:

$$C_1(\beta_s) = C_{1f} = \begin{bmatrix} \cos(\alpha_1) & \sin(\alpha_1) & 0 \\ \cos(\alpha_1 + \pi) & \sin(\alpha_1 + \pi) & 0 \end{bmatrix} \tag{3.38}$$

Alternatively, consider the case when w_2 is placed in the wheel plane of w_1 but with the same orientation, as in a bicycle with the steering locked in the forward position. We again place point P between the two wheel centers, and orient the wheels such that they lie on axis x_1. This geometry implies that $\{(l_1 = l_2), (\beta_1 = \beta_2 = \pi/2), (\alpha_1 = 0), (\alpha_2 = \pi)\}$ and, therefore, the matrix $C_1(\beta_s)$ retains two independent constraints and has a rank of two:

$$C_1(\beta_s) = C_{1f} = \begin{bmatrix} \cos(\pi/2) & \sin(\pi/2) & l_1\sin(\pi/2) \\ \cos(3\pi/2) & \sin(3\pi/2) & l_1\sin(\pi/2) \end{bmatrix} = \begin{bmatrix} 0 & 1 & l_1 \\ 0 & -1 & l_1 \end{bmatrix} \tag{3.39}$$

In general, if $rank[C_{1f}] > 1$ then the vehicle can, at best, only travel along a circle or along a straight line. This configuration means that the robot has two or more independent constraints due to fixed standard wheels that do not share the same horizontal axis of rotation. Because such configurations have only a degenerate form of mobility in the plane, we do not consider them in the remainder of this chapter. Note, however, that some degenerate configurations such as the four-wheeled slip/skid steering system are useful in certain environments, such as on loose soil and sand, even though they fail to satisfy sliding constraints. Not surprisingly, the price that must be paid for such violations of the sliding constraints is that dead reckoning based on odometry becomes less accurate and power efficiency is reduced dramatically.

In general, a robot will have zero or more fixed standard wheels and zero or more steerable standard wheels. We can therefore identify the possible range of rank values for any robot: $0 \leq rank[C_1(\beta_s)] \leq 3$. Consider the case $rank[C_1(\beta_s)] = 0$. This is only possible if there are zero independent kinematic constraints in $C_1(\beta_s)$. In this case there are neither fixed nor steerable standard wheels attached to the robot frame: $N_f = N_s = 0$.

Consider the other extreme, $rank[C_1(\beta_s)] = 3$. This is the maximum possible rank since the kinematic constraints are specified along three degrees of freedom (i.e., the constraint matrix is three columns wide). Therefore, there cannot be more than three independent constraints. In fact, when $rank\left[C_1(\beta_s)\right] = 3$, then the robot is completely constrained in all directions and is, therefore, degenerate since motion in the plane is totally impossible.

Now we are ready to formally define a robot's *degree of mobility* δ_m:

$$\delta_m = dimN\left[C_1(\beta_s)\right] = 3 - rank\left[C_1(\beta_s)\right] \tag{3.40}$$

The dimensionality of the null space ($dimN$) of matrix $C_1(\beta_s)$ is a measure of the number of degrees of freedom of the robot chassis that can be immediately manipulated through changes in wheel velocity. It is logical therefore that δ_m must range between 0 and 3.

Consider an ordinary differential-drive chassis. On such a robot there are two fixed standard wheels sharing a common horizontal axis. As discussed above, the second wheel adds no independent kinematic constraints to the system. Therefore, $rank\left[C_1(\beta_s)\right] = 1$ and $\delta_m = 2$. This fits with intuition: a differential drive robot can control both the rate of its change in orientation and its forward/reverse speed, *simply by manipulating wheel velocities*. In other words, its *ICR* is constrained to lie on the infinite line extending from its wheels' horizontal axles.

In contrast, consider a bicycle chassis. This configuration consists of one fixed standard wheel and one steerable standard wheel. In this case, each wheel contributes an independent sliding constraint to $C_1(\beta_s)$. Therefore, $\delta_m = 1$. Note that the bicycle has the same total number of nonomidirectional wheels as the differential-drive chassis, and indeed one of its wheels is steerable. Yet it has one less degree of mobility. Upon reflection this is appropriate. A bicycle only has control over its forward/reverse speed by direct manipulation of wheel velocities. Only by steering can the bicycle change its *ICR*.

As expected, based on equation (3.40) any robot consisting only of omnidirectional wheels such as Swedish or spherical wheels will have the maximum mobility, $\delta_m = 3$. Such a robot can directly manipulate all three degrees of freedom.

3.3.2 Degree of steerability

The degree of mobility defined above quantifies the degrees of controllable freedom based on changes to wheel velocity. Steering can also have an eventual impact on a robot chassis pose ξ, although the impact is indirect because after changing the angle of a steerable standard wheel, the robot must move for the change in steering angle to have impact on pose.

As with mobility, we care about the number of independently controllable steering parameters when defining the *degree of steerability* δ_s:

$$\delta_s = rank\left[C_{1s}(\beta_s)\right] \tag{3.41}$$

Recall that in the case of mobility, an increase in the rank of $C_1(\beta_s)$ implied more kinematic constraints and thus a less mobile system. In the case of steerability, an increase in the rank of $C_{1s}(\beta_s)$ implies more degrees of steering freedom and thus greater eventual maneuverability. Since $C_1(\beta_s)$ includes $C_{1s}(\beta_s)$, this means that a steered standard wheel can both decrease mobility and increase steerability: its particular orientation at any instant imposes a kinematic constraint, but its ability to change that orientation can lead to additional trajectories.

The range of δ_s can be specified: $0 \leq \delta_s \leq 2$. The case $\delta_s = 0$ implies that the robot has no steerable standard wheels, $N_s = 0$. The case $\delta_s = 1$ is most common when a robot configuration includes one or more steerable standard wheels.

For example, consider an ordinary automobile. In this case $N_f = 2$ and $N_s = 2$. But the fixed wheels share a common axle and so $rank\left[C_{1f}\right] = 1$. The fixed wheels and any one of the steerable wheels constrain the ICR to be a point along the line extending from the rear axle. Therefore, the second steerable wheel cannot impose any independent kinematic constraint and so $rank\left[C_{1s}(\beta_s)\right] = 1$. In this case $\delta_m = 1$ and $\delta_s = 1$.

The case $\delta_s = 2$ is only possible in robots with no fixed standard wheels: $N_f = 0$. Under these circumstances, it is possible to create a chassis with two separate steerable standard wheels, like a pseudobicycle (or the two-steer) in which both wheels are steerable. Then, orienting one wheel constrains the ICR to a line while the second wheel can constrain the ICR to any point along that line. Interestingly, this means that the $\delta_s = 2$ implies that the robot can place its ICR anywhere on the ground plane.

3.3.3 Robot maneuverability

The overall degrees of freedom that a robot can manipulate, called the *degree of maneuverability* δ_M, can be readily defined in terms of mobility and steerability:

$$\delta_M = \delta_m + \delta_s \qquad\qquad (3.42)$$

Therefore maneuverability includes both the degrees of freedom that the robot manipulates directly through wheel velocity and the degrees of freedom that it indirectly manipulates by changing the steering configuration and moving. Based on the investigations of the previous sections, one can draw the basic types of wheel configurations. They are depicted in figure 3.14

Note that two robots with the same δ_M are not necessarily equivalent. For example, differential drive and tricycle geometries (figure 3.13) have equal maneuverability $\delta_M = 2$. In differential drive all maneuverability is the result of direct mobility because $\delta_m = 2$ and $\delta_s = 0$. In the case of a tricycle the maneuverability results from steering also: $\delta_m = 1$ and $\delta_s = 1$. Neither of these configurations allows the ICR to range anywhere on the plane. In both cases, the ICR must lie on a predefined line with respect to the robot refer-

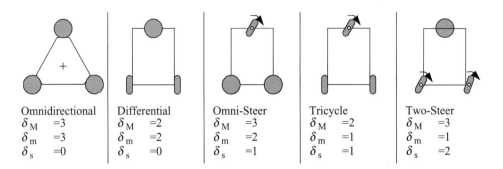

Omnidirectional	Differential	Omni-Steer	Tricycle	Two-Steer
δ_M =3	δ_M =2	δ_M =3	δ_M =2	δ_M =3
δ_m =3	δ_m =2	δ_m =2	δ_m =1	δ_m =1
δ_s =0	δ_s =0	δ_s =1	δ_s =1	δ_s =2

Figure 3.14
The five basic types of three-wheel configurations. The spherical wheels can be replaced by castor or Swedish wheels without influencing maneuverability. More configurations with various numbers of wheels are found in chapter 2.

ence frame. In the case of differential drive, this line extends from the common axle of the two fixed standard wheels, with the differential wheel velocities setting the *ICR* point on this line. In a tricycle, this line extends from the shared common axle of the fixed wheels, with the steerable wheel setting the *ICR* point along this line.

More generally, for any robot with $\delta_M = 2$ the *ICR* is always constrained to lie on a line and for any robot with $\delta_M = 3$ the *ICR* can be set to any point on the plane.

One final example will demonstrate the use of the tools we have developed above. One common robot configuration for indoor mobile robotics research is the *synchro drive* configuration (figure 2.22). Such a robot has two motors and three wheels that are locked together. One motor provides power for spinning all three wheels while the second motor provides power for steering all three wheels. In a three-wheeled synchro drive robot $N_f = 0$ and $N_s = 3$. Therefore $rank\left[C_{1s}(\beta_s)\right]$ can be used to determine both δ_m and δ_s. The three wheels do not share a common axle, therefore two of the three contribute independent sliding constraints. The third must be dependent on these two constraints for motion to be possible. Therefore $rank\left[C_{1s}(\beta_s)\right] = 2$ and $\delta_m = 1$. This is intuitively correct. A synchro drive robot with the steering frozen manipulates only one degree of freedom, consisting of traveling back and forth on a straight line.

However an interesting complication occurs when considering δ_s. Based on equation (3.41) the robot should have $\delta_s = 2$. Indeed, for a three-wheel-steering robot with the geometric configuration of a synchro drive robot this would be correct. However, we have additional information: in a synchro drive configuration a single motor steers all three wheels using a belt drive. Therefore, although ideally, if the wheels were independently steerable, then the system would achieve $\delta_s = 2$, in the case of synchro drive the drive system further constrains the kinematics such that in reality $\delta_s = 1$. Finally, we can compute maneuverability based on these values: $\delta_M = 2$ for a synchro drive robot.

This result implies that a synchro drive robot can only manipulate, in total, two degrees of freedom. In fact, if the reader reflects on the wheel configuration of a synchro drive robot it will become apparent that there is no way for the chassis orientation to change. Only the $x - y$ position of the chassis can be manipulated and so, indeed, a synchro drive robot has only two degrees of freedom, in agreement with our mathematical conclusion.

3.4   Mobile Robot Workspace

For a robot, maneuverability is equivalent to its control degrees of freedom. But the robot is situated in some environment, and the next question is to situate our analysis in the environment. We care about the ways in which the robot can use its control degrees of freedom to position itself in the environment. For instance, consider the Ackerman vehicle, or automobile. The total number of control degrees of freedom for such a vehicle is $\delta_M = 2$, one for steering and the second for actuation of the drive wheels. But what is the total degrees of freedom of the vehicle in its environment? In fact it is three: the car can position itself on the plane at any x, y point and with any angle θ.

Thus identifying a robot's space of possible configurations is important because surprisingly it can exceed δ_M. In addition to *workspace*, we care about how the robot is able to move between various configurations: what are the types of paths that it can follow and, furthermore, what are its possible trajectories through this configuration space? In the remainder of this discussion, we move away from inner kinematic details such as wheels and focus instead on the robot chassis pose and the chassis degrees of freedom. With this in mind, let us place the robot in the context of its workspace now.

3.4.1   Degrees of freedom

In defining the workspace of a robot, it is useful to first examine its *admissible velocity space*. Given the kinematic constraints of the robot, its velocity space describes the independent components of robot motion that the robot can control. For example, the velocity space of a unicycle can be represented with two axes, one representing the instantaneous forward speed of the unicycle and the second representing the instantaneous change in orientation, $\dot{\theta}$, of the unicycle.

The number of dimensions in the velocity space of a robot is the number of independently achievable velocities. This is also called the *differentiable degrees of freedom (DDOF)*. A robot's *DDOF* is *always* equal to its degree of mobility δ_m. For example, a bicycle has the following degree of maneuverability: $\delta_M = \delta_m + \delta_s = 1 + 1 = 2$. The *DDOF* of a bicycle is indeed 1.

In contrast to a bicycle, consider an *omnibot*, a robot with three Swedish wheels. We know that in this case there are zero standard wheels and therefore $\delta_M = \delta_m + \delta_s = 3 + 0 = 3$. So, the omnibot has three differential degrees of freedom. This is appropriate, given that because such a robot has no kinematic motion constraints, it is able to independently set all three pose variables: $\dot{x}, \dot{y}, \dot{\theta}$.

Given the difference in *DDOF* between a bicycle and an omnibot, consider the overall degrees of freedom in the workspace of each configuration. The omnibot can achieve any pose (x, y, θ) in its environment and can do so by directly achieving the goal positions of all three axes simultaneously because $DDOF = 3$. Clearly, it has a workspace with $DOF = 3$.

Can a bicycle achieve any pose (x, y, θ) in its environment? It can do so, but achieving some goal points may require more time and energy than an equivalent omnibot. For example, if a bicycle configuration must move laterally 1 m, the simplest successful maneuver would involve either a spiral or a back-and-forth motion similar to *parallel parking* of automobiles. Nevertheless, a bicycle can achieve any (x, y, θ) and therefore the workspace of a bicycle has *DOF* =3 as well.

Clearly, there is an inequality relation at work: $DDOF \leq \delta_M \leq DOF$. Although the dimensionality of a robot's workspace is an important attribute, it is clear from the example above that the particular paths available to a robot matter as well. Just as workspace *DOF* governs the robot's ability to achieve various poses, so the robot's *DDOF* governs its ability to achieve various paths.

3.4.2 Holonomic robots

In the robotics community, when describing the path space of a mobile robot, often the concept of holonomy is used. The term *holonomic* has broad applicability to several mathematical areas, including differential equations, functions and constraint expressions. In mobile robotics, the term refers specifically to the kinematic constraints of the robot chassis. A *holonomic robot* is a robot that has zero nonholonomic kinematic constraints. Conversely, a *nonholonomic robot* is a robot with one or more nonholonomic kinematic constraints.

A *holonomic kinematic constraint* can be expressed as an explicit function of position variables only. For example, in the case of a mobile robot with a single fixed standard wheel, a holonomic kinematic constraint would be expressible using $\alpha_1, \beta_1, l_1, r_1, \varphi_1, x, y, \theta$ only. Such a constraint may not use derivatives of these values, such as $\dot{\varphi}$ or $\dot{\xi}$. A *nonholonomic kinematic constraint* requires a differential relationship, such as the derivative of a position variable. Furthermore, it cannot be integrated to provide a constraint in terms of the position variables only. Because of this latter point of view, nonholonomic systems are often called *nonintegrable* systems.

Consider the fixed standard wheel sliding constraint:

$$\left[\cos(\alpha + \beta) \ \sin(\alpha + \beta) \ l\sin\beta\right] R(\theta)\dot{\xi}_I = 0 \tag{3.43}$$

This constraint must use robot motion $\dot{\xi}$ rather than pose ξ because the point is to constrain robot motion perpendicular to the wheel plane to be zero. The constraint is noninte-grable, depending explicitly on robot motion. Therefore, the sliding constraint is a nonholonomic constraint. Consider a bicycle configuration, with one fixed standard wheel and one steerable standard wheel. Because the fixed wheel sliding constraint will be in force for such a robot, we can conclude that the bicycle is a nonholonomic robot.

But suppose that one locks the bicycle steering system, so that it becomes two fixed standard wheels with separate but parallel axes. We know that $\delta_M = 1$ for such a configuration. Is it nonholonomic? Although it may not appear so because of the sliding and rolling constraints, the locked bicycle is actually holonomic. Consider the workspace of this locked bicycle. It consists of a single infinite line along which the bicycle can move (assuming the steering was frozen straight ahead). For formulaic simplicity, assume that this infinite line is aligned with X_I in the global reference frame and that $\{\beta_{1,2} = \pi/2, \alpha_1 = 0, \alpha_2 = \pi\}$. In this case the sliding constraints of both wheels can be replaced with an equally complete set of constraints on the robot pose: $\{y = 0, \theta = 0\}$. This eliminates two nonholonomic constraints, corresponding to the sliding constraints of the two wheels.

The only remaining nonholonomic kinematic constraints are the rolling constraints for each wheel:

$$\left[-\sin(\alpha + \beta) \ \cos(\alpha + \beta) \ l\cos\beta\right] R(\theta)\dot{\xi}_I + r\dot{\varphi} = 0 \tag{3.44}$$

This constraint is required for each wheel to relate the speed of wheel spin to the speed of motion projected along the wheel plane. But in the case of our locked bicycle, given the initial rotational position of a wheel at the origin, φ_o, we can replace this constraint with one that directly relates position on the line, x, with wheel rotation angle, φ: $\varphi = (x/r) + \varphi_o$.

The locked bicycle is an example of the first type of holonomic robot – where constraints do exist but are all holonomic kinematic constraints. This is the case for all holonomic robots with $\delta_M < 3$. The second type of holonomic robot exists when there are no kinematic constraints, that is, $N_f = 0$ and $N_s = 0$. Since there are no kinematic constraints, there are also no nonholonomic kinematic constraints and so such a robot is always holonomic. This is the case for all holonomic robots with $\delta_M = 3$.

An alternative way to describe a holonomic robot is based on the relationship between the differential degrees of freedom of a robot and the degrees of freedom of its workspace: *a robot is holonomic if and only if $DDOF = DOF$*. Intuitively, this is because it is only through nonholonomic constraints (imposed by steerable or fixed standard wheels) that a robot can achieve a workspace with degrees of freedom exceeding its differential degrees of freedom, $DOF > DDOF$. Examples include differential drive and bicycle/tricycle configurations.

In mobile robotics, useful chassis generally must achieve poses in a workspace with dimensionality 3, so in general we require $DOF = 3$ for the chassis. But the "holonomic" abilities to maneuver around obstacles without affecting orientation and to track at a target while following an arbitrary path are important additional considerations. For these reasons, the particular form of holonomy most relevant to mobile robotics is that of $DDOF = DOF = 3$. We define this class of robot configurations as omnidirectional: an *omnidirectional robot* is a holonomic robot with $DDOF = 3$.

3.4.3   Path and trajectory considerations

In mobile robotics, we care not only about the robot's ability to reach the required final configurations but also about *how* it gets there. Consider the issue of a robot's ability to follow paths: in the best case, a robot should be able to trace any path through its workspace of poses. Clearly, any omnidirectional robot can do this because it is holonomic in a three-dimensional workspace. Unfortunately, omnidirectional robots must use unconstrained wheels, limiting the choice of wheels to Swedish wheels, castor wheels, and spherical wheels. These wheels have not yet been incorporated into designs allowing far larger amounts of ground clearance and suspensions. Although powerful from a path space point of view, they are thus much less common than fixed and steerable standard wheels, mainly because their design and fabrication are somewhat complex and expensive.

Additionally, nonholonomic constraints might drastically improve stability of movements. Consider an omnidirectional vehicle driving at high speed on a curve with constant diameter. During such a movement the vehicle will be exposed to a non-negligible centripetal force. This lateral force pushing the vehicle out of the curve has to be counteracted by the motor torque of the omnidirectional wheels. In case of motor or control failure, the vehicle will be thrown out of the curve. However, for a car-like robot with kinematic constraints, the lateral forces are passively counteracted through the sliding constraints, mitigating the demands on motor torque.

But recall an earlier example of high maneuverability using standard wheels: the bicycle on which both wheels are steerable, often called the *two-steer*. This vehicle achieves a degree of steerability of 2, resulting in a high degree of maneuverability: $\delta_M = \delta_m + \delta_s = 1 + 2 = 3$. Interestingly, this configuration is not holonomic, yet has a high degree of maneuverability in a workspace with $DOF = 3$.

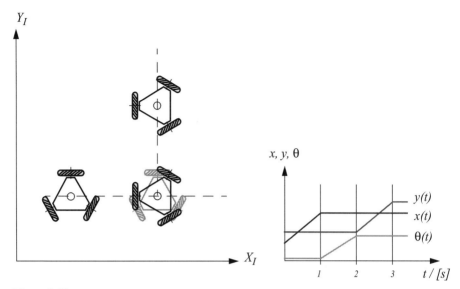

Figure 3.15
Example of robot trajectory with omnidirectional robot: move for 1 second with constant speed of 1 m/s along axis X_I; change orientation counterclockwise 90 degree, in 1 second; move for 1 second with constant speed of 1 m/s along axis Y_I.

The maneuverability result, $\delta_M = 3$, means that the two-steer can select any ICR by appropriately steering its two wheels. So, how does this compare to an omnidirectional robot? The ability to manipulate its ICR in the plane means that the two-steer can follow *any* path in its workspace. More generally, any robot with $\delta_M = 3$ can follow any path in its workspace from its initial pose to its final pose. An omnidirectional robot can also follow any path in its workspace and, not surprisingly, since $\delta_m = 3$ in an omnidirectional robot, then it must follow that $\delta_M = 3$.

But there is still a difference between a degree of freedom granted by steering versus by direct control of wheel velocity. This difference is clear in the context of *trajectories* rather than paths. A trajectory is like a path, except that it occupies an additional dimension: time. Therefore, for an omnidirectional robot on the ground plane a path generally denotes a trace through a 3D space of pose; for the same robot a trajectory denotes a trace through the 4D space of pose plus time.

For example, consider a goal trajectory in which the robot moves along axis X_I at a constant speed of 1 m/s for 1 second, then changes orientation counterclockwise 90 degrees also in 1 second, then moves parallel to axis Y_I for 1 final second. The desired 3-second trajectory is shown in figure 3.15, using plots of x, y and θ in relation to time.

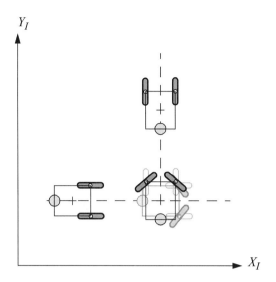

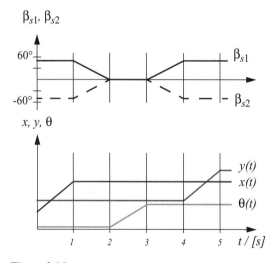

Figure 3.16
Example of robot trajectory similar to figure 3.15 with two steered wheels: move for 1 second with constant speed of 1 m/s along axis X_I; rotate steered wheels -50 / 50 degree respectively; change orientation counterclockwise 90 degree in 1 second; rotate steered wheels 50 / -50 degree respectively; move for 1 second with constant speed of 1 m/s along axis Y_I.

Can the omnidirectional robot accomplish this trajectory? We assume that the robot can achieve some arbitrary, finite velocity at each wheel. For simplicity, we further assume that acceleration is infinite; that is, it takes zero time to reach any desired velocity. Under these assumptions, the omnidirectional robot can indeed follow the trajectory of figure 3.15. The transition between the motion of second 1 and second 2, for example, involves only changes to the wheel velocities.

Because the two-steer has $\delta_M = 3$, it must be able to follow the path that would result from projecting this trajectory into timeless workspace. However, it cannot follow this 4D trajectory. Even if steering velocity is finite and arbitrary, although the two-steer would be able to change steering speed instantly, it would have to wait for the angle of the steerable wheels to change to the desired position before initiating a change in the robot chassis orientation. In short, the two-steer requires changes to internal degrees of freedom and because these changes take time, arbitrary trajectories are not attainable. Figure 3.16 depicts the most similar trajectory that a two-steer can achieve. In contrast to the desired three phases of motion, this trajectory has five phases.

3.5   Beyond Basic Kinematics

The above discussion of mobile robot kinematics is only an introduction to a far richer topic. When speed and force are also considered, as is particularly necessary in the case of high-speed mobile robots, dynamic constraints must be expressed in addition to kinematic constraints. Furthermore, many mobile robots such as tank-type chassis and four-wheel slip/skid systems violate the kinematic models above. When analyzing such systems, it is often necessary to explicitly model the dynamics of viscous friction between the robot and the ground plane.

More significantly, the kinematic analysis of a mobile robot system provides results concerning the theoretical workspace of that mobile robot. However to effectively move in this workspace a mobile robot must have appropriate actuation of its degrees of freedom. This problem, called motorization, requires further analysis of the forces that must be actively supplied to realize the kinematic range of motion available to the robot.

In addition to motorization, there is the question of controllability: under what conditions can a mobile robot travel from the initial pose to the goal pose in bounded time? Answering this question requires knowledge – both knowledge of the robot kinematics and knowledge of the control systems that can be used to actuate the mobile robot. Mobile robot control is therefore a return to the practical question of designing a real-world control algorithm that can drive the robot from pose to pose using the trajectories demanded for the application.

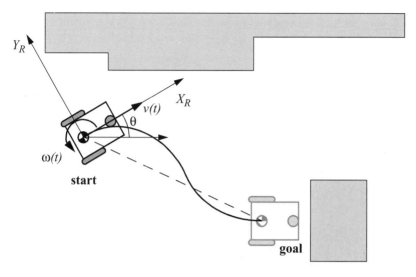

Figure 3.17
Typical situation for feedback control of a mobile robot

3.6   Motion Control (Kinematic Control)

As seen above, motion control might not be an easy task for nonholonomic systems. However, it has been studied by various research groups, for example, [8, 39, 52, 53, 137] and
some adequate solutions for motion control of a mobile robot system are available.

3.6.1   Open loop control (trajectory-following)

The objective of a kinematic controller is to follow a trajectory described by its position or
velocity profile as a function of time. This is often done by dividing the trajectory (path) in
motion segments of clearly defined shape, for example, straight *lines* and segments of a *circle*. The control problem is thus to precompute a smooth trajectory based on line and circle
segments which drives the robot from the initial position to the final position (figure 3.18).
This approach can be regarded as open-loop motion control, because the measured robot
position is not fed back for velocity or position control. It has several disadvantages:

- It is not at all an easy task to precompute a feasible trajectory if all limitations and constraints of the robot's velocities and accelerations have to be considered.

- The robot will not automatically adapt or correct the trajectory if dynamic changes of
  the environment occur.

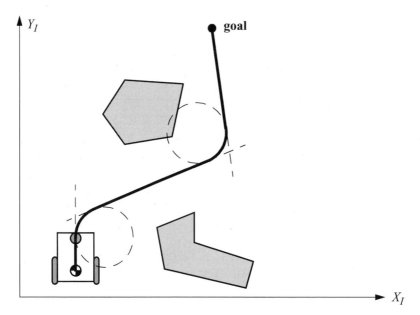

Figure 3.18
Open-loop control of a mobile robot based on straight lines and circular trajectory segments.

The resulting trajectories are usually not smooth, because the transitions from one trajectory segment to another are, for most of the commonly used segments (e.g., lines and
part of circles), not smooth. This means there is a discontinuity in the robot's acceleration.

3.6.2 Feedback control
A more appropriate approach in motion control of a mobile robot is to use a real-state feedback controller. With such a controller the robot's path-planning task is reduced to setting
intermediate positions (subgoals) lying on the requested path. One useful solution for a sta-
bilizing feedback control of differential-drive mobile robots is presented in section 3.6.2.1.
It is very similar to the controllers presented in [39, 100]. Others can be found in [8, 52, 53,
137].

3.6.2.1 Problem statement
Consider the situation shown in figure 3.17, with an arbitrary position and orientation of
the robot and a predefined goal position and orientation. The actual pose error vector given
in the robot reference frame $\{X_R, Y_R, \theta\}$ is $e = {}^R[x, y, \theta]^T$ with x, y, and θ being the goal
coordinates of the robot.

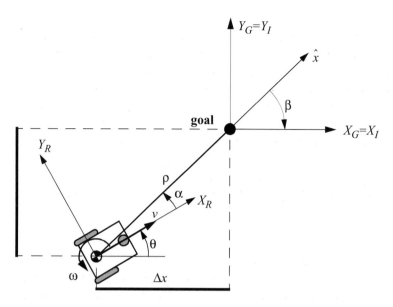

Figure 3.19
Robot kinematics and its frames of interests.

The task of the controller layout is to find a control matrix K, if it exists

$$K = \begin{bmatrix} k_{11} & k_{12} & k_{13} \\ k_{21} & k_{22} & k_{23} \end{bmatrix} \quad \text{with } k_{ij} = k(t, e) \tag{3.45}$$

such that the control of $v(t)$ and $\omega(t)$

$$\begin{bmatrix} v(t) \\ \omega(t) \end{bmatrix} = K \cdot e = K \,{}^{R}\!\begin{bmatrix} x \\ y \\ \theta \end{bmatrix} \tag{3.46}$$

drives the error e toward zero.[2]

$$\lim_{t \to \infty} e(t) = 0 \tag{3.47}$$

2. Remember that $v(t)$ is always heading in the X_R direction of the robot's reference frame due to the nonholonomic constraint.

3.6.2.2 Kinematic model

We assume, without loss of generality, that the goal is at the origin of the inertial frame (figure 3.19). In the following the position vector $[x, y, \theta]^T$ is always represented in the inertial frame.

The kinematics of a differential-drive mobile robot described in the inertial frame $\{X_I, Y_I, \theta\}$ is given by

$$
{}^I\begin{bmatrix} \dot{x} \\ \dot{y} \\ \dot{\theta} \end{bmatrix} = \begin{bmatrix} \cos\theta & 0 \\ \sin\theta & 0 \\ 0 & 1 \end{bmatrix} \begin{bmatrix} v \\ \omega \end{bmatrix}
\tag{3.48}
$$

where $\dot{x}$ and $\dot{y}$ are the linear velocities in the direction of the X_I and Y_I of the inertial frame.

Let α denote the angle between the x_R axis of the robot's reference frame and the vector $\hat{x}$ connecting the center of the axle of the wheels with the final position. If $\alpha \in I_1$, where

$$
I_1 = \left(-\frac{\pi}{2}, \frac{\pi}{2} \right]
\tag{3.49}
$$

then consider the coordinate transformation into polar coordinates with its origin at the goal position.

$$
\rho = \sqrt{\Delta x^2 + \Delta y^2}
\tag{3.50}
$$

$$
\alpha = -\theta + \mathrm{atan2}(\Delta y, \Delta x)
\tag{3.51}
$$

$$
\beta = -\theta - \alpha
\tag{3.52}
$$

This yields a system description, in the new polar coordinates, using a matrix equation

$$
\begin{bmatrix} \dot{\rho} \\ \dot{\alpha} \\ \dot{\beta} \end{bmatrix} = \begin{bmatrix} -\cos\alpha & 0 \\ \dfrac{\sin\alpha}{\rho} & -1 \\ -\dfrac{\sin\alpha}{\rho} & 0 \end{bmatrix} \begin{bmatrix} v \\ \omega \end{bmatrix}
\tag{3.53}
$$

where ρ is the distance between the center of the robot's wheel axle and the goal position,

θ denotes the angle between the X_R axis of the robot reference frame, and the X_I axis associated with the final position v and ω are the tangent and the angular velocity respectively.

On the other hand, if $\alpha \in I_2$, where

$$I_2 = (-\pi, -\pi/2] \cup (\pi/2, \pi]$$ (3.54)

redefining the forward direction of the robot by setting $v = -v$, we obtain a system described by a matrix equation of the form

$$\begin{bmatrix} \dot{\rho} \\ \dot{\alpha} \\ \dot{\beta} \end{bmatrix} = \begin{bmatrix} \cos\alpha & 0 \\ -\dfrac{\sin\alpha}{\rho} & 1 \\ \dfrac{\sin\alpha}{\rho} & 0 \end{bmatrix} \begin{bmatrix} v \\ \omega \end{bmatrix}$$ (3.55)

3.6.2.3 Remarks on the kinematic model in polar coordinates [eq. (3.53) and (3.55)]

- The coordinate transformation is not defined at $x = y = 0$; as in such a point the determinant of the Jacobian matrix of the transformation is not defined, that is unbounded.

- For $\alpha \in I_1$ the forward direction of the robot points toward the goal, for $\alpha \in I_2$ it is the reverse direction.

- By properly defining the forward direction of the robot at its initial configuration, it is always possible to have $\alpha \in I_1$ at $t = 0$. However, this does not mean that α remains in I_I for all time t. Hence, to avoid that the robot changes direction during approaching the goal, it is necessary to determine, if possible, the controller in such a way that $\alpha \in I_1$ for all t, whenever $\alpha(0) \in I_1$. The same applies for the reverse direction (see stability issues below).

3.6.2.4 The control law

The control signals v and ω must now be designed to drive the robot from its actual configuration, say $(\rho_0, \alpha_0, \beta_0)$, to the goal position. It is obvious that equation (3.53) presents a discontinuity at $\rho = 0$; thus the theorem of Brockett does not obstruct smooth stabilizability.

If we consider now the linear control law

$$v = k_\rho \rho$$ (3.56)

$$\omega = k_\alpha \alpha + k_\beta \beta$$ (3.57)

we get with equation (3.53) a closed-loop system described by

$$
\begin{bmatrix} \dot{\rho} \\ \dot{\alpha} \\ \dot{\beta} \end{bmatrix} = \begin{bmatrix} -k_\rho \rho \cos\alpha \\ k_\rho \sin\alpha - k_\alpha \alpha - k_\beta \beta \\ -k_\rho \sin\alpha \end{bmatrix} \tag{3.58}
$$

The system does not have any singularity at $\rho = 0$ and has a unique equilibrium point at $(\rho, \alpha, \beta) = (0, 0, 0)$. Thus it will drive the robot to this point, which is the goal position.

- In the Cartesian coordinate system the control law [equation (3.57)] leads to equations which are not defined at $x = y = 0$.

- Be aware of the fact that the angles α and β have always to be expressed in the range $(-\pi, \pi)$.

- Observe that the control signal v has always a constant sign, that is, it is positive whenever $\alpha(0) \in I_1$ and it is always negative otherwise. This implies that the robot performs its parking maneuver always in a single direction and without reversing its motion.

In figure 3.20 you find the resulting paths when the robot is initially on a circle in the xy plane. All movements have smooth trajectories toward the goal in the center. The control parameters for this simulation were set to

$$
k = (k_\rho, k_\alpha, k_\beta) = (3, 8, -1.5). \tag{3.59}
$$

3.6.2.5 Local stability issue

It can further be shown, that the closed-loop control system [equation (3.58)] is locally exponentially stable if

$$
k_\rho > 0 ; \quad k_\beta < 0 ; \quad k_\alpha - k_\rho > 0 \tag{3.60}
$$

Proof:
Linearized around the equilibrium ($\cos x = 1$, $\sin x = x$) position, equation (3.58) can be written as

$$
\begin{bmatrix} \dot{\rho} \\ \dot{\alpha} \\ \dot{\beta} \end{bmatrix} = \begin{bmatrix} -k_\rho & 0 & 0 \\ 0 & -(k_\alpha - k_\rho) & -k_\beta \\ 0 & -k_\rho & 0 \end{bmatrix} \begin{bmatrix} \rho \\ \alpha \\ \beta \end{bmatrix}, \tag{3.61}
$$

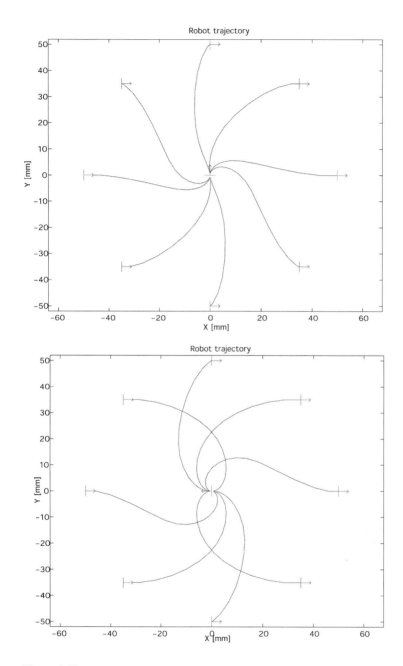

Figure 3.20
Resulting paths when the robot is initially on the unit circle in the *x,y* plane.

hence it is locally exponentially stable if the eigenvalues of the matrix

$$
A = \begin{bmatrix} -k_\rho & 0 & 0 \\ 0 & -(k_\alpha - k_\rho) & -k_\beta \\ 0 & -k_\rho & 0 \end{bmatrix}
\tag{3.62}
$$

all have a negative real part. The characteristic polynomial of the matrix A is

$$
(\lambda + k_\rho)(\lambda^2 + \lambda(k_\alpha - k_\rho) - k_\rho k_\beta)
\tag{3.63}
$$

and all roots have negative real part if

$$
k_\rho > 0 \ ; \quad -k_\beta > 0 \ ; \quad k_\alpha - k_\rho > 0
\tag{3.64}
$$

which proves the claim.

For robust position control, it might be advisable to apply the strong stability condition, which ensures that the robot does not change direction during its approach to the goal:

$$
k_\rho > 0 \ ; \quad k_\beta < 0 \ ; \quad k_\alpha + \frac{5}{3} k_\beta - \frac{2}{\pi} k_\rho > 0
\tag{3.65}
$$

This implies that $\alpha \in I_1$ for all t, whenever $\alpha(0) \in I_1$ and $\alpha \in I_2$ for all t, whenever $\alpha(0) \in I_2$ respectively. This strong stability condition has also been verified in applications.

4 Perception

One of the most important tasks of an autonomous system of any kind is to acquire knowledge about its environment. This is done by taking measurements using various sensors and then extracting meaningful information from those measurements.

In this chapter we present the most common sensors used in mobile robots and then discuss strategies for extracting information from the sensors. For more detailed information about many of the sensors used on mobile robots, refer to the comprehensive book *Sensors for Mobile Robots* by H.R. Everett [15].

4.1 Sensors for Mobile Robots

There are a wide variety of sensors used in mobile robots (figure 4.1). Some sensors are used to measure simple values like the internal temperature of a robot's electronics or the rotational speed of the motors. Other, more sophisticated sensors can be used to acquire information about the robot's environment or even to directly measure a robot's global position. In this chapter we focus primarily on sensors used to extract information about the robot's environment. Because a mobile robot moves around, it will frequently encounter unforeseen environmental characteristics, and therefore such sensing is particularly critical. We begin with a functional classification of sensors. Then, after presenting basic tools for describing a sensor's performance, we proceed to describe selected sensors in detail.

4.1.1 Sensor classification

We classify sensors using two important functional axes: *proprioceptive/exteroceptive* and *passive/active*.

Proprioceptive sensors measure values internal to the system (robot); for example, motor speed, wheel load, robot arm joint angles, battery voltage.

Exteroceptive sensors acquire information from the robot's environment; for example, distance measurements, light intensity, sound amplitude. Hence exteroceptive sensor measurements are interpreted by the robot in order to extract meaningful environmental features.

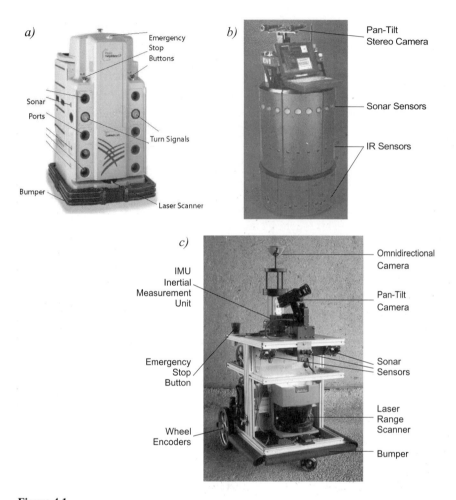

Figure 4.1
Examples of robots with multi-sensor systems: (a) HelpMate from Transition Research Corporation;
(b) B21 from Real World Interface; (c) BIBA Robot, BlueBotics SA.

Passive sensors measure ambient environmental energy entering the sensor. Examples
of passive sensors include temperature probes, microphones, and CCD or CMOS cameras.

Active sensors emit energy into the environment, then measure the environmental reaction. Because active sensors can manage more controlled interactions with the environment, they often achieve superior performance. However, active sensing introduces several
risks: the outbound energy may affect the very characteristics that the sensor is attempting
to measure. Furthermore, an active sensor may suffer from interference between its signal

and those beyond its control. For example, signals emitted by other nearby robots, or similar sensors on the same robot, may influence the resulting measurements. Examples of active sensors include wheel quadrature encoders, ultrasonic sensors, and laser rangefinders.

Table 4.1 provides a classification of the most useful sensors for mobile robot applications. The most interesting sensors are discussed in this chapter.

Table 4.1
Classification of sensors used in mobile robotics applications

General classification (typical use)	Sensor Sensor System	PC or EC	A or P
Tactile sensors (detection of physical contact or closeness; security switches)	Contact switches, bumpers	EC	P
	Optical barriers	EC	A
	Noncontact proximity sensors	EC	A
Wheel/motor sensors (wheel/motor speed and position)	Brush encoders	PC	P
	Potentiometers	PC	P
	Synchros, resolvers	PC	A
	Optical encoders	PC	A
	Magnetic encoders	PC	A
	Inductive encoders	PC	A
	Capacitive encoders	PC	A
Heading sensors (orientation of the robot in relation to a fixed reference frame)	Compass	EC	P
	Gyroscopes	PC	P
	Inclinometers	EC	A/P
Ground-based beacons (localization in a fixed reference frame)	GPS	EC	A
	Active optical or RF beacons	EC	A
	Active ultrasonic beacons	EC	A
	Reflective beacons	EC	A
Active ranging (reflectivity, time-of-flight, and geometric triangulation)	Reflectivity sensors	EC	A
	Ultrasonic sensor	EC	A
	Laser rangefinder	EC	A
	Optical triangulation (1D)	EC	A
	Structured light (2D)	EC	A
Motion/speed sensors (speed relative to fixed or moving objects)	Doppler radar	EC	A
	Doppler sound	EC	A
Vision-based sensors (visual ranging, whole-image analysis, segmentation, object recognition)	CCD/CMOS camera(s)	EC	P
	Visual ranging packages		
	Object tracking packages		

A, active; P, passive; P/A, passive/active; PC, proprioceptive; EC, exteroceptive.

The sensor classes in table 4.1 are arranged in ascending order of complexity and descending order of technological maturity. Tactile sensors and proprioceptive sensors are critical to virtually all mobile robots, and are well understood and easily implemented. Commercial quadrature encoders, for example, may be purchased as part of a gear-motor assembly used in a mobile robot. At the other extreme, visual interpretation by means of one or more CCD/CMOS cameras provides a broad array of potential functionalities, from obstacle avoidance and localization to human face recognition. However, commercially available sensor units that provide visual functionalities are only now beginning to emerge [90, 160].

4.1.2 Characterizing sensor performance

The sensors we describe in this chapter vary greatly in their performance characteristics. Some sensors provide extreme accuracy in well-controlled laboratory settings, but are overcome with error when subjected to real-world environmental variations. Other sensors provide narrow, high-precision data in a wide variety of settings. In order to quantify such performance characteristics, first we formally define the sensor performance terminology that will be valuable throughout the rest of this chapter.

4.1.2.1 Basic sensor response ratings

A number of sensor characteristics can be rated quantitatively in a laboratory setting. Such performance ratings will necessarily be best-case scenarios when the sensor is placed on a real-world robot, but are nevertheless useful.

Dynamic range is used to measure the spread between the lower and upper limits of input values to the sensor while maintaining normal sensor operation. Formally, the dynamic range is the ratio of the maximum input value to the minimum measurable input value. Because this raw ratio can be unwieldy, it is usually measured in *decibels,* which are computed as ten times the common logarithm of the dynamic range. However, there is potential confusion in the calculation of decibels, which are meant to measure the ratio between *powers*, such as watts or horsepower. Suppose your sensor measures motor current and can register values from a minimum of 1 mA to 20 Amps. The dynamic range of this current sensor is defined as

$$10 \cdot \log\left[\frac{20}{0.001}\right] = 43 \text{ dB} \qquad (4.1)$$

Now suppose you have a voltage sensor that measures the voltage of your robot's battery, measuring any value from 1 mV to 20 V. Voltage is not a unit of power, but the square of voltage is proportional to power. Therefore, we use 20 instead of 10:

$$20 \cdot \log \left[\frac{20}{0.001} \right] = 86 \text{ dB} \tag{4.2}$$

Range is also an important rating in mobile robot applications because often robot sensors operate in environments where they are frequently exposed to input values beyond their working range. In such cases, it is critical to understand how the sensor will respond. For example, an optical rangefinder will have a minimum operating range and can thus provide spurious data when measurements are taken with the object closer than that minimum.

Resolution is the minimum difference between two values that can be detected by a sensor. Usually, the lower limit of the dynamic range of a sensor is equal to its resolution. However, in the case of digital sensors, this is not necessarily so. For example, suppose that you have a sensor that measures voltage, performs an analog-to-digital (A/D) conversion, and outputs the converted value as an 8-bit number linearly corresponding to between 0 and 5 V. If this sensor is truly linear, then it has $2^8 - 1$ total output values, or a resolution of $5 \text{ V}(255) = 20 \text{ mV}$.

Linearity is an important measure governing the behavior of the sensor's output signal as the input signal varies. A linear response indicates that if two inputs x and y result in the two outputs $f(x)$ and $f(y)$, then for any values a and b, $f(ax + by) = af(x) + bf(y)$. This means that a plot of the sensor's input/output response is simply a straight line.

Bandwidth or *frequency* is used to measure the speed with which a sensor can provide a stream of readings. Formally, the number of measurements per second is defined as the sensor's frequency in *hertz*. Because of the dynamics of moving through their environment, mobile robots often are limited in maximum speed by the bandwidth of their obstacle detection sensors. Thus, increasing the bandwidth of ranging and vision-based sensors has been a high-priority goal in the robotics community.

4.1.2.2 In situ sensor performance

The above sensor characteristics can be reasonably measured in a laboratory environment with confident extrapolation to performance in real-world deployment. However, a number of important measures cannot be reliably acquired without deep understanding of the complex interaction between all environmental characteristics and the sensors in question. This is most relevant to the most sophisticated sensors, including active ranging sensors and visual interpretation sensors.

Sensitivity itself is a desirable trait. This is a measure of the degree to which an incremental change in the target input signal changes the output signal. Formally, sensitivity is the ratio of output change to input change. Unfortunately, however, the sensitivity of exteroceptive sensors is often confounded by undesirable sensitivity and performance coupling to other environmental parameters.

Cross-sensitivity is the technical term for sensitivity to environmental parameters that are orthogonal to the target parameters for the sensor. For example, a flux-gate compass can demonstrate high sensitivity to magnetic north and is therefore of use for mobile robot navigation. However, the compass will also demonstrate high sensitivity to ferrous building materials, so much so that its cross-sensitivity often makes the sensor useless in some indoor environments. High cross-sensitivity of a sensor is generally undesirable, especially when it cannot be modeled.

Error of a sensor is defined as the difference between the sensor's output measurements and the true values being measured, within some specific operating context. Given a true value v and a measured value m, we can define *error* as $error = m - v$.

Accuracy is defined as the degree of conformity between the sensor's measurement and the true value, and is often expressed as a proportion of the true value (e.g., 97.5% accuracy). Thus small error corresponds to high accuracy and vice versa:

$$\left(accuracy = 1 - \frac{|error|}{v} \right) \tag{4.3}$$

Of course, obtaining the ground truth, v, can be difficult or impossible, and so establishing a confident characterization of sensor accuracy can be problematic. Further, it is important to distinguish between two different sources of error:

Systematic errors are caused by factors or processes that can in theory be modeled. These errors are, therefore, deterministic (i.e., predictable). Poor calibration of a laser rangefinder, an unmodeled slope of a hallway floor, and a bent stereo camera head due to an earlier collision are all possible causes of systematic sensor errors.

Random errors cannot be predicted using a sophisticated model nor can they be mitigated by more precise sensor machinery. These errors can only be described in probabilistic terms (i.e., stochastically). Hue instability in a color camera, spurious rangefinding errors, and black level noise in a camera are all examples of random errors.

Precision is often confused with accuracy, and now we have the tools to clearly distinguish these two terms. Intuitively, high precision relates to reproducibility of the sensor results. For example, one sensor taking multiple readings of the same environmental state has high precision if it produces the same output. In another example, multiple copies of this sensor taking readings of the same environmental state have high precision if their outputs agree. Precision does not, however, have any bearing on the accuracy of the sensor's output with respect to the true value being measured. Suppose that the *random error* of a sensor is characterized by some mean value μ and a standard deviation σ. The formal definition of precision is the ratio of the sensor's output range to the standard deviation:

$$precision = \frac{range}{\sigma} \qquad (4.4)$$

Note that only σ and not μ has impact on precision. In contrast, mean error μ is directly proportional to overall sensor error and inversely proportional to sensor accuracy.

4.1.2.3 Characterizing error: the challenges in mobile robotics

Mobile robots depend heavily on exteroceptive sensors. Many of these sensors concentrate on a central task for the robot: acquiring information on objects in the robot's immediate vicinity so that it may interpret the state of its surroundings. Of course, these "objects" surrounding the robot are all detected from the viewpoint of its local reference frame. Since the systems we study are mobile, their ever-changing position and their motion have a significant impact on overall sensor behavior. In this section, empowered with the terminology of the earlier discussions, we describe how dramatically the sensor error of a mobile robot disagrees with the ideal picture drawn in the previous section.

Blurring of systematic and random errors. Active ranging sensors tend to have failure modes that are triggered largely by specific relative positions of the sensor and environment targets. For example, a sonar sensor will produce specular reflections, producing grossly inaccurate measurements of range, at specific angles to a smooth sheetrock wall. During motion of the robot, such relative angles occur at stochastic intervals. This is especially true in a mobile robot outfitted with a ring of multiple sonars. The chances of one sonar entering this error mode during robot motion is high. From the perspective of the moving robot, the sonar measurement error is a random error in this case. Yet, if the robot were to stop, becoming motionless, then a very different error modality is possible. If the robot's static position causes a particular sonar to fail in this manner, the sonar will fail consistently and will tend to return precisely the same (and incorrect!) reading time after time. Once the robot is motionless, the error appears to be systematic and of high precision.

The fundamental mechanism at work here is the cross-sensitivity of mobile robot sensors to robot pose and robot-environment dynamics. The models for such cross-sensitivity are not, in an underlying sense, truly random. However, these physical interrelationships are rarely modeled and therefore, from the point of view of an incomplete model, the errors appear random during motion and systematic when the robot is at rest.

Sonar is not the only sensor subject to this blurring of systematic and random error modality. Visual interpretation through the use of a CCD camera is also highly susceptible to robot motion and position because of camera dependence on lighting changes, lighting specularity (e.g., glare), and reflections. The important point is to realize that, while systematic error and random error are well-defined in a controlled setting, the mobile robot can exhibit error characteristics that bridge the gap between deterministic and stochastic error mechanisms.

Multimodal error distributions. It is common to characterize the behavior of a sensor's random error in terms of a probability distribution over various output values. In general, one knows very little about the causes of random error and therefore several simplifying assumptions are commonly used. For example, we can assume that the error is *zero-mean*, in that it symmetrically generates both positive and negative measurement error. We can go even further and assume that the probability density curve is Gaussian. Although we discuss the mathematics of this in detail in section 4.2, it is important for now to recognize the fact that one frequently assumes *symmetry* as well as *unimodal distribution*. This means that measuring the correct value is most probable, and any measurement that is further away from the correct value is less likely than any measurement that is closer to the correct value. These are strong assumptions that enable powerful mathematical principles to be applied to mobile robot problems, but it is important to realize how wrong these assumptions usually are.

Consider, for example, the sonar sensor once again. When ranging an object that reflects the sound signal well, the sonar will exhibit high accuracy, and will induce random error based on noise, for example, in the timing circuitry. This portion of its sensor behavior will exhibit error characteristics that are fairly symmetric and unimodal. However, when the sonar sensor is moving through an environment and is sometimes faced with materials that cause coherent reflection rather than returning the sound signal to the sonar sensor, then the sonar will grossly overestimate the distance to the object. In such cases, the error will be biased toward positive measurement error and will be far from the correct value. The error is not strictly systematic, and so we are left modeling it as a probability distribution of random error. So the sonar sensor has two separate types of operational modes, one in which the signal does return and some random error is possible, and the second in which the signal returns after a multipath reflection, and gross overestimation error occurs. The probability distribution could easily be at least bimodal in this case, and since overestimation is more common than underestimation it will also be asymmetric.

As a second example, consider ranging via stereo vision. Once again, we can identify two modes of operation. If the stereo vision system correctly correlates two images, then the resulting random error will be caused by camera noise and will limit the measurement accuracy. But the stereo vision system can also correlate two images *incorrectly*, matching two fence posts, for example, that are not the same post in the real world. In such a case stereo vision will exhibit gross measurement error, and one can easily imagine such behavior violating both the unimodal and the symmetric assumptions.

The thesis of this section is that sensors in a mobile robot *may* be subject to multiple modes of operation and, when the sensor error is characterized, unimodality and symmetry may be grossly violated. Nonetheless, as we shall see, many successful mobile robot systems make use of these simplifying assumptions and the resulting mathematical techniques with great empirical success.

The above sections have presented a terminology with which we can characterize the advantages and disadvantages of various mobile robot sensors. In the following sections, we do the same for a sampling of the most commonly used mobile robot sensors today.

4.1.3   Wheel/motor sensors

Wheel/motor sensors are devices used to measure the internal state and dynamics of a mobile robot. These sensors have vast applications outside of mobile robotics and, as a result, mobile robotics has enjoyed the benefits of high-quality, low-cost wheel and motor sensors that offer excellent resolution. In the next section, we sample just one such sensor, the optical incremental encoder.

4.1.3.1   Optical encoders

Optical incremental encoders have become the most popular device for measuring angular speed and position within a motor drive or at the shaft of a wheel or steering mechanism. In mobile robotics, encoders are used to control the position or speed of wheels and other motor-driven joints. Because these sensors are *proprioceptive*, their estimate of position is best in the reference frame of the robot and, when applied to the problem of robot *localization*, significant corrections are required as, discussed in chapter 5.

An optical encoder is basically a mechanical light chopper that produces a certain number of sine or square wave pulses for each shaft revolution. It consists of an illumination source, a fixed grating that masks the light, a rotor disc with a fine optical grid that rotates with the shaft, and fixed optical detectors. As the rotor moves, the amount of light striking the optical detectors varies based on the alignment of the fixed and moving gratings. In robotics, the resulting sine wave is transformed into a discrete square wave using a threshold to choose between *light* and *dark* states. Resolution is measured in *cycles per revolution* (CPR). The minimum angular resolution can be readily computed from an encoder's CPR rating. A typical encoder in mobile robotics may have 2000 CPR, while the optical encoder industry can readily manufacture encoders with 10000 CPR. In terms of required bandwidth, it is of course critical that the encoder be sufficiently fast to count at the shaft spin speeds that are expected. Industrial optical encoders present no bandwidth limitation to mobile robot applications.

Usually in mobile robotics the *quadrature encoder* is used. In this case, a second illumination and detector pair is placed 90 degrees shifted with respect to the original in terms of the rotor disc. The resulting twin square waves, shown in figure 4.2, provide significantly more information. The ordering of which square wave produces a rising edge first identifies the direction of rotation. Furthermore, the four detectably different states improve the resolution by a factor of four with no change to the rotor disc. Thus, a 2000 CPR encoder in quadrature yields 8000 counts. Further improvement is possible by retaining the sinusoidal

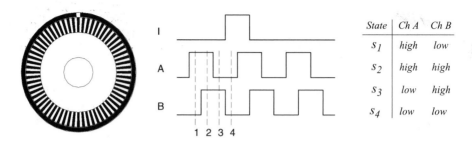

State	Ch A	Ch B
s_1	high	low
s_2	high	high
s_3	low	high
s_4	low	low

Figure 4.2
Quadrature optical wheel encoder: The observed phase relationship between channel A and B pulse trains are used to determine the direction of the rotation. A single slot in the outer track generates a reference (index) pulse per revolution.

wave measured by the optical detectors and performing sophisticated interpolation. Such methods, although rare in mobile robotics, can yield 1000-fold improvements in resolution.

As with most proprioceptive sensors, encoders are generally in the controlled environment of a mobile robot's internal structure, and so systematic error and cross-sensitivity can be engineered away. The accuracy of optical encoders is often assumed to be 100% and, although this may not be entirely correct, any errors at the level of an optical encoder are dwarfed by errors downstream of the motor shaft.

4.1.4 Heading sensors

Heading sensors can be *proprioceptive* (gyroscope, inclinometer) or *exteroceptive* (compass). They are used to determine the robot's orientation and inclination. They allow us, together with appropriate velocity information, to integrate the movement to a position estimate. This procedure, which has its roots in vessel and ship navigation, is called *dead reckoning*.

4.1.4.1 Compasses

The two most common modern sensors for measuring the direction of a magnetic field are the Hall effect and flux gate compasses. Each has advantages and disadvantages, as described below.

The Hall effect describes the behavior of electric potential in a semiconductor when in the presence of a magnetic field. When a constant current is applied across the length of a semiconductor, there will be a voltage difference in the perpendicular direction, across the semiconductor's width, based on the relative orientation of the semiconductor to magnetic flux lines. In addition, the sign of the voltage potential identifies the direction of the magnetic field. Thus, a single semiconductor provides a measurement of flux and direction along one dimension. Hall effect digital compasses are popular in mobile robotics, and con-

Figure 4.3
Digital compass: Sensors such as the digital/analog Hall effect sensor shown, available from Dins-
more (http://dinsmoregroup.com/dico), enable inexpensive (< $ 15) sensing of magnetic fields.

tain two such semiconductors at right angles, providing two axes of magnetic field (thresh-
olded) direction, thereby yielding one of eight possible compass directions. The
instruments are inexpensive but also suffer from a range of disadvantages. Resolution of a
digital Hall effect compass is poor. Internal sources of error include the nonlinearity of the
basic sensor and systematic bias errors at the semiconductor level. The resulting circuitry
must perform significant filtering, and this lowers the bandwidth of Hall effect compasses
to values that are slow in mobile robot terms. For example, the Hall effect compass pictured
in figure 4.3 needs 2.5 seconds to settle after a 90 degree spin.

The flux gate compass operates on a different principle. Two small coils are wound on
ferrite cores and are fixed perpendicular to one another. When alternating current is acti-
vated in both coils, the magnetic field causes shifts in the phase depending on its relative
alignment with each coil. By measuring both phase shifts, the direction of the magnetic
field in two dimensions can be computed. The flux gate compass can accurately measure
the strength of a magnetic field and has improved resolution and accuracy; however, it is
both larger and more expensive than a Hall effect compass.

Regardless of the type of compass used, a major drawback concerning the use of the
Earth's magnetic field for mobile robot applications involves disturbance of that magnetic
field by other magnetic objects and man-made structures, as well as the bandwidth limitations of electronic compasses and their susceptibility to vibration. Particularly in indoor
environments, mobile robotics applications have often avoided the use of compasses,
although a compass can conceivably provide useful *local* orientation information indoors,
even in the presence of steel structures.

4.1.4.2 Gyroscopes
Gyroscopes are heading sensors which preserve their orientation in relation to a fixed reference frame. Thus they provide an absolute measure for the heading of a mobile system.

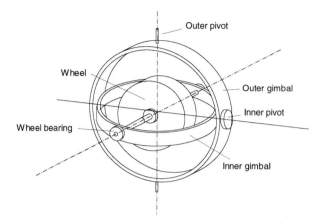

Figure 4.4
Two-axis mechanical gyroscope.

Gyroscopes can be classified in two categories, mechanical gyroscopes and optical gyro-scopes.

Mechanical gyroscopes. The concept of a mechanical gyroscope relies on the inertial properties of a fast-spinning rotor. The property of interest is known as the gyroscopic pre-cession. If you try to rotate a fast-spinning wheel around its vertical axis, you will feel a harsh reaction in the horizontal axis. This is due to the angular momentum associated with a spinning wheel and will keep the axis of the gyroscope inertially stable. The reactive torque τ and thus the tracking stability with the inertial frame are proportional to the spin-ning speed ω, the precession speed Ω, and the wheel's inertia I.

$$\tau = I\omega\Omega \tag{4.5}$$

By arranging a spinning wheel, as seen in figure 4.4, no torque can be transmitted from the outer pivot to the wheel axis. The spinning axis will therefore be space-stable (i.e., fixed in an inertial reference frame). Nevertheless, the remaining friction in the bearings of the gyro axis introduce small torques, thus limiting the long-term space stability and introduc-ing small errors over time. A high quality mechanical gyroscope can cost up to $100,000 and has an angular drift of about 0.1 degrees in 6 hours.

For navigation, the spinning axis has to be initially selected. If the spinning axis is aligned with the north-south meridian, the earth's rotation has no effect on the gyro's hor-izontal axis. If it points east-west, the horizontal axis reads the earth rotation.

Rate gyros have the same basic arrangement as shown in figure 4.4 but with a slight modification. The gimbals are restrained by a torsional spring with additional viscous damping. This enables the sensor to measure angular speeds instead of absolute orientation.

Optical gyroscopes. Optical gyroscopes are a relatively new innovation. Commercial use began in the early 1980s when they were first installed in aircraft. Optical gyroscopes are angular speed sensors that use two monochromatic light beams, or lasers, emitted from the same source, instead of moving, mechanical parts. They work on the principle that the speed of light remains unchanged and, therefore, geometric change can cause light to take a varying amount of time to reach its destination. One laser beam is sent traveling clockwise through a fiber while the other travels counterclockwise. Because the laser traveling in the direction of rotation has a slightly shorter path, it will have a higher frequency. The difference in frequency Δf of the two beams is a proportional to the angular velocity Ω of the cylinder. New solid-state optical gyroscopes based on the same principle are build using microfabrication technology, thereby providing heading information with resolution and bandwidth far beyond the needs of mobile robotic applications. Bandwidth, for instance, can easily exceed 100 kHz while resolution can be smaller than 0.0001 degrees/hr.

4.1.5 Ground-based beacons

One elegant approach to solving the localization problem in mobile robotics is to use active or passive beacons. Using the interaction of on-board sensors and the environmental beacons, the robot can identify its position precisely. Although the general intuition is identical to that of early human navigation beacons, such as stars, mountains, and lighthouses, modern technology has enabled sensors to localize an outdoor robot with accuracies of better than 5 cm within areas that are kilometers in size.

In the following section, we describe one such beacon system, the global positioning system (GPS), which is extremely effective for outdoor ground-based and flying robots. Indoor beacon systems have been generally less successful for a number of reasons. The expense of environmental modification in an indoor setting is not amortized over an extremely large useful area, as it is, for example, in the case of the GPS. Furthermore, indoor environments offer significant challenges not seen outdoors, including multipath and environmental dynamics. A laser-based indoor beacon system, for example, must disambiguate the one true laser signal from possibly tens of other powerful signals that have reflected off of walls, smooth floors, and doors. Confounding this, humans and other obstacles may be constantly changing the environment, for example, occluding the one true path from the beacon to the robot. In commercial applications, such as manufacturing plants, the environment can be carefully controlled to ensure success. In less structured indoor settings, beacons have nonetheless been used, and the problems are mitigated by careful beacon placement and the use of passive sensing modalities.

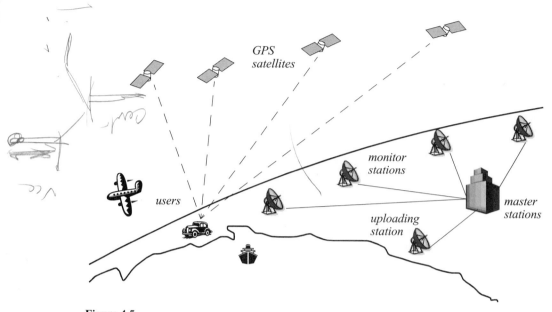

Figure 4.5
Calculation of position and heading based on GPS.

4.1.5.1 The global positioning system

The *global positioning system* (GPS) was initially developed for military use but is now freely available for civilian navigation. There are at least twenty-four operational GPS satellites at all times. The satellites orbit every 12 hours at a height of 20.190 km. Four satellites are located in each of six planes inclined 55 degrees with respect to the plane of the earth's equator (figure 4.5).

Each satellite continuously transmits data that indicate its location and the current time. Therefore, GPS receivers are completely passive but exteroceptive sensors. The GPS satellites synchronize their transmissions so that their signals are sent at the same time. When a GPS receiver reads the transmission of two or more satellites, the arrival time differences inform the receiver as to its relative distance to each satellite. By combining information regarding the arrival time and instantaneous location of four satellites, the receiver can infer its own position. In theory, such triangulation requires only three data points. However, timing is extremely critical in the GPS application because the time intervals being measured are in nanoseconds. It is, of course, mandatory that the satellites be well synchronized. To this end, they are updated by ground stations regularly and each satellite carries on-board atomic clocks for timing.

The GPS receiver clock is also important so that the travel time of each satellite's transmission can be accurately measured. But GPS receivers have a simple quartz clock. So, although three satellites would ideally provide position in three axes, the GPS receiver requires four satellites, using the additional information to solve for four variables: three position axes plus a time correction.

The fact that the GPS receiver must read the transmission of four satellites simultaneously is a significant limitation. GPS satellite transmissions are extremely low-power, and reading them successfully requires direct line-of-sight communication with the satellite. Thus, in confined spaces such as city blocks with tall buildings or in dense forests, one is unlikely to receive four satellites reliably. Of course, most indoor spaces will also fail to provide sufficient visibility of the sky for a GPS receiver to function. For these reasons, the GPS has been a popular sensor in mobile robotics, but has been relegated to projects involving mobile robot traversal of wide-open spaces and autonomous flying machines.

A number of factors affect the performance of a localization sensor that makes use of the GPS. First, it is important to understand that, because of the specific orbital paths of the GPS satellites, coverage is not geometrically identical in different portions of the Earth and therefore resolution is not uniform. Specifically, at the North and South Poles, the satellites are very close to the horizon and, thus, while resolution in the latitude and longitude directions is good, resolution of altitude is relatively poor as compared to more equatorial locations.

The second point is that GPS satellites are merely an information source. They can be employed with various strategies in order to achieve dramatically different levels of localization resolution. The basic strategy for GPS use, called *pseudorange* and described above, generally performs at a resolution of 15 m. An extension of this method is *differential GPS (DGPS)*, which makes use of a second receiver that is static and at a known exact position. A number of errors can be corrected using this reference, and so resolution improves to the order of 1 m or less. A disadvantage of this technique is that the stationary receiver must be installed, its location must be measured very carefully, and of course the moving robot must be within kilometers of this static unit in order to benefit from the DGPS technique.

A further improved strategy is to take into account the phase of the carrier signals of each received satellite transmission. There are two carriers, at 19 cm and 24 cm, and therefore significant improvements in precision are possible when the phase difference between multiple satellites is measured successfully. Such receivers can achieve 1 cm resolution for point positions and, with the use of multiple receivers, as in DGPS, sub-1 cm resolution.

A final consideration for mobile robot applications is bandwidth. The GPS will generally offer no better than 200 to 300 ms latency, and so one can expect no better than 5 Hz GPS updates. On a fast-moving mobile robot or flying robot, this can mean that local motion integration will be required for proper control due to GPS latency limitations.

4.1.6 Active ranging

Active ranging sensors continue to be the most popular sensors in mobile robotics. Many ranging sensors have a low price point, and, most importantly, all ranging sensors provide easily interpreted outputs: direct measurements of distance from the robot to objects in its vicinity. For obstacle detection and avoidance, most mobile robots rely heavily on active ranging sensors. But the local freespace information provided by ranging sensors can also be accumulated into representations beyond the robot's current local reference frame. Thus active ranging sensors are also commonly found as part of the localization and environmental modeling processes of mobile robots. It is only with the slow advent of successful visual interpretation competence that we can expect the class of active ranging sensors to gradually lose their primacy as the sensor class of choice among mobile roboticists.

Below, we present two *time-of-flight* active ranging sensors: the ultrasonic sensor and the laser rangefinder. Then, we present two geometric active ranging sensors: the optical triangulation sensor and the structured light sensor.

4.1.6.1 Time-of-flight active ranging

Time-of-flight ranging makes use of the propagation speed of sound or an electromagnetic wave. In general, the travel distance of a sound of electromagnetic wave is given by

$$d = c \cdot t \tag{4.6}$$

where

d = distance traveled (usually round-trip);

c = speed of wave propagation;

t = time of flight.

It is important to point out that the propagation speed v of sound is approximately 0.3 m/ms whereas the speed of electromagnetic signals is 0.3 m/ns, which is 1 million times faster. The time of flight for a typical distance, say 3 m, is 10 ms for an ultrasonic system but only 10 ns for a laser rangefinder. It is thus evident that measuring the time of flight t with electromagnetic signals is more technologically challenging. This explains why laser range sensors have only recently become affordable and robust for use on mobile robots.

The quality of time-of-flight range sensors depends mainly on

• uncertainties in determining the exact time of arrival of the reflected signal;

• inaccuracies in the time-of-flight measurement (particularly with laser range sensors);

• the dispersal cone of the transmitted beam (mainly with ultrasonic range sensors);

- interaction with the target (e.g., surface absorption, specular reflections);
- variation of propagation speed;
- the speed of the mobile robot and target (in the case of a dynamic target);

As discussed below, each type of time-of-flight sensor is sensitive to a particular subset of the above list of factors.

The ultrasonic sensor (time-of-flight, sound). The basic principle of an ultrasonic sensor is to transmit a packet of (ultrasonic) pressure waves and to measure the time it takes for this wave packet to reflect and return to the receiver. The distance d of the object causing the reflection can be calculated based on the propagation speed of sound c and the time of flight t.

$$d = \frac{c \cdot t}{2} \tag{4.7}$$

The speed of sound c in air is given by

$$c = \sqrt{\gamma R T} \tag{4.8}$$

where

γ = ratio of specific heats;

R = gas constant;

T = temperature in degrees Kelvin.

In air at standard pressure and 20° C the speed of sound is approximately $c = 343$ m/s.

Figure 4.6 shows the different signal output and input of an ultrasonic sensor. First, a series of sound pulses are emitted, comprising the *wave packet*. An integrator also begins to linearly climb in value, measuring the time from the transmission of these sound waves to detection of an echo. A threshold value is set for triggering an incoming sound wave as a valid echo. This threshold is often decreasing in time, because the amplitude of the expected echo decreases over time based on dispersal as it travels longer. But during transmission of the initial sound pulses and just afterward, the threshold is set very high to suppress triggering the echo detector with the outgoing sound pulses. A transducer will continue to ring for up to several milliseconds after the initial transmission, and this governs the *blanking time* of the sensor. Note that if, during the blanking time, the transmitted sound were to reflect off of an extremely close object and return to the ultrasonic sensor, it may fail to be detected.

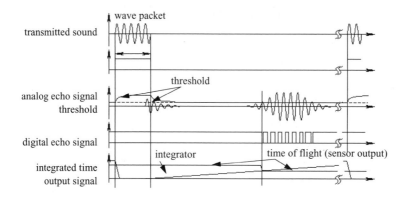

Figure 4.6
Signals of an ultrasonic sensor.

However, once the blanking interval has passed, the system will detect any above-threshold reflected sound, triggering a digital signal and producing the distance measurement using the integrator value.

The ultrasonic wave typically has a frequency between 40 and 180 kHz and is usually generated by a piezo or electrostatic transducer. Often the same unit is used to measure the reflected signal, although the required blanking interval can be reduced through the use of separate output and input devices. Frequency can be used to select a useful range when choosing the appropriate ultrasonic sensor for a mobile robot. Lower frequencies correspond to a longer range, but with the disadvantage of longer post-transmission ringing and, therefore, the need for longer blanking intervals. Most ultrasonic sensors used by mobile robots have an effective range of roughly 12 cm to 5 m. The published accuracy of commercial ultrasonic sensors varies between 98% and 99.1%. In mobile robot applications, specific implementations generally achieve a resolution of approximately 2 cm.

In most cases one may want a narrow opening angle for the sound beam in order to also obtain precise directional information about objects that are encountered. This is a major limitation since sound propagates in a cone-like manner (figure 4.7) with opening angles around 20 to 40 degrees. Consequently, when using ultrasonic ranging one does not acquire depth data points but, rather, entire regions of constant depth. This means that the sensor tells us only that there is an object at a certain distance within the area of the measurement cone. The sensor readings must be plotted as segments of an arc (sphere for 3D) and not as point measurements (figure 4.8). However, recent research developments show significant improvement of the measurement quality in using sophisticated echo processing [76].

Ultrasonic sensors suffer from several additional drawbacks, namely in the areas of error, bandwidth, and cross-sensitivity. The published accuracy values for ultrasonics are

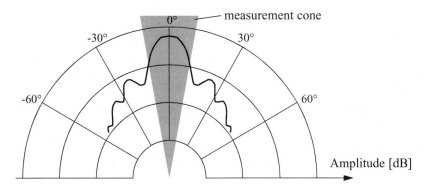

Figure 4.7
Typical intensity distribution of an ultrasonic sensor.

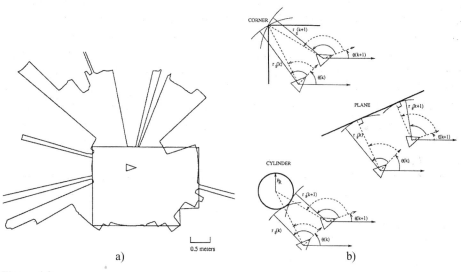

a)   b)

Figure 4.8
Typical readings of an ultrasonic system: (a) 360 degree scan; (b) results from different geometric primitives [23]. Courtesy of John Leonard, MIT.

nominal values based on successful, perpendicular reflections of the sound wave off of an acoustically reflective material. This does not capture the effective error modality seen on a mobile robot moving through its environment. As the ultrasonic transducer's angle to the object being ranged varies away from perpendicular, the chances become good that the sound waves will coherently reflect away from the sensor, just as light at a shallow angle reflects off of a smooth surface. Therefore, the true error behavior of ultrasonic sensors is compound, with a well-understood error distribution near the true value in the case of a successful retroreflection, and a more poorly understood set of range values that are grossly larger than the true value in the case of coherent reflection. Of course, the acoustic properties of the material being ranged have direct impact on the sensor's performance. Again, the impact is discrete, with one material possibly failing to produce a reflection that is sufficiently strong to be sensed by the unit. For example, foam, fur, and cloth can, in various circumstances, acoustically absorb the sound waves.

A final limitation of ultrasonic ranging relates to bandwidth. Particularly in moderately open spaces, a single ultrasonic sensor has a relatively slow cycle time. For example, measuring the distance to an object that is 3 m away will take such a sensor 20 ms, limiting its operating speed to 50 Hz. But if the robot has a ring of twenty ultrasonic sensors, each firing sequentially and measuring to minimize interference between the sensors, then the ring's cycle time becomes 0.4 seconds and the overall update frequency of any one sensor is just 2.5 Hz. For a robot conducting moderate speed motion while avoiding obstacles using ultrasonics, this update rate can have a measurable impact on the maximum speed possible while still sensing and avoiding obstacles safely.

Laser rangefinder (time-of-flight, electromagnetic). The laser rangefinder is a time-of-flight sensor that achieves significant improvements over the ultrasonic range sensor owing to the use of laser light instead of sound. This type of sensor consists of a transmitter which illuminates a target with a collimated beam (e.g., laser), and a receiver capable of detecting the component of light which is essentially coaxial with the transmitted beam. Often referred to as optical radar or *lidar* (light detection and ranging), these devices produce a range estimate based on the time needed for the light to reach the target and return. A mechanical mechanism with a mirror sweeps the light beam to cover the required scene in a plane or even in three dimensions, using a rotating, nodding mirror.

One way to measure the time of flight for the light beam is to use a pulsed laser and then measure the elapsed time directly, just as in the ultrasonic solution described earlier. Electronics capable of resolving picoseconds are required in such devices and they are therefore very expensive. A second method is to measure the beat frequency between a frequency-modulated continuous wave (FMCW) and its received reflection. Another, even easier method is to measure the phase shift of the reflected light. We describe this third approach in detail.

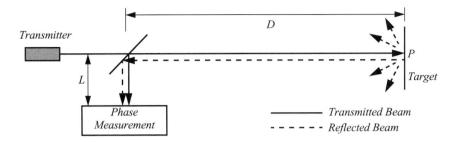

Figure 4.9
Schematic of laser rangefinding by phase-shift measurement.

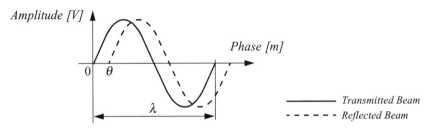

Figure 4.10
Range estimation by measuring the phase shift between transmitted and received signals.

Phase-shift measurement. Near-infrared light (from a light-emitting diode [LED] or laser) is collimated and transmitted from the transmitter in figure 4.9 and hits a point P in the environment. For surfaces having a roughness greater than the wavelength of the incident light, diffuse reflection will occur, meaning that the light is reflected almost isotropically. The wavelength of the infrared light emitted is 824 nm and so most surfaces, with the exception of only highly polished reflecting objects, will be diffuse reflectors. The component of the infrared light which falls within the receiving aperture of the sensor will return almost parallel to the transmitted beam for distant objects.

The sensor transmits 100% amplitude modulated light at a known frequency and measures the phase shift between the transmitted and reflected signals. Figure 4.10 shows how this technique can be used to measure range. The wavelength of the modulating signal obeys the equation $c = f \cdot \lambda$ where c is the speed of light and f the modulating frequency. For $f = 5$ MHz (as in the AT&T sensor), $\lambda = 60$ m. The total distance D' covered by the emitted light is

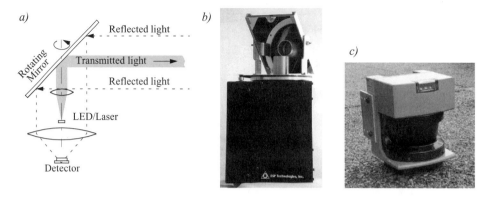

Figure 4.11
(a) Schematic drawing of laser range sensor with rotating mirror; (b) Scanning range sensor from EPS
Technologies Inc.; (c) Industrial 180 degree laser range sensor from Sick Inc., Germany

$$D' = L + 2D = L + \frac{\theta}{2\pi}\lambda \tag{4.9}$$

where D and L are the distances defined in figure 4.9. The required distance D, between
the beam splitter and the target, is therefore given by

$$D = \frac{\lambda}{4\pi}\theta \tag{4.10}$$

where θ is the electronically measured phase difference between the transmitted and
reflected light beams, and λ the known modulating wavelength. It can be seen that the
transmission of a single frequency modulated wave can theoretically result in ambiguous
range estimates since, for example, if $\lambda = 60$ m, a target at a range of 5 m would give an
indistinguishable phase measurement from a target at 65 m, since each phase angle would
be 360 degrees apart. We therefore define an "ambiguity interval" of λ, but in practice we
note that the range of the sensor is much lower than λ due to the attenuation of the signal
in air.

It can be shown that the confidence in the range (phase estimate) is inversely proportional to the square of the received signal amplitude, directly affecting the sensor's accuracy. Hence dark, distant objects will not produce as good range estimates as close, bright
objects.

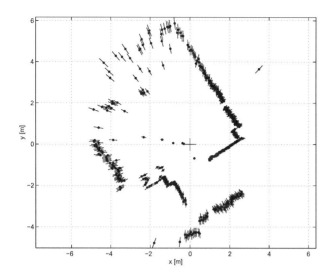

Figure 4.12
Typical range image of a 2D laser range sensor with a rotating mirror. The length of the lines through the measurement points indicate the uncertainties.

In figure 4.11 the schematic of a typical 360 degrees laser range sensor and two examples are shown. figure 4.12 shows a typical range image of a 360 degrees scan taken with a laser range sensor.

As expected, the angular resolution of laser rangefinders far exceeds that of ultrasonic sensors. The Sick laser scanner shown in Figure 4.11 achieves an angular resolution of 0.5 degree. Depth resolution is approximately 5 cm, over a range from 5 cm up to 20 m or more, depending upon the brightness of the object being ranged. This device performs twenty five 180 degrees scans per second but has no mirror nodding capability for the vertical dimension.

As with ultrasonic ranging sensors, an important error mode involves coherent reflection of the energy. With light, this will only occur when striking a highly polished surface. Practically, a mobile robot may encounter such surfaces in the form of a polished desktop, file cabinet or, of course, a mirror. Unlike ultrasonic sensors, laser rangefinders cannot detect the presence of optically transparent materials such as glass, and this can be a significant obstacle in environments, for example, museums, where glass is commonly used.

4.1.6.2 Triangulation-based active ranging
Triangulation-based ranging sensors use geometric properties manifest in their measuring strategy to establish distance readings to objects. The simplest class of triangulation-based

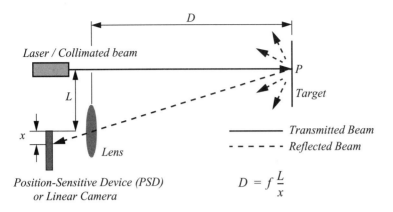

Figure 4.13
Principle of 1D laser triangulation.

rangers are *active* because they project a known light pattern (e.g., a point, a line, or a texture) onto the environment. The reflection of the known pattern is captured by a receiver and, together with known geometric values, the system can use simple triangulation to establish range measurements. If the receiver measures the position of the reflection along a single axis, we call the sensor an optical triangulation sensor in 1D. If the receiver measures the position of the reflection along two orthogonal axes, we call the sensor a structured light sensor. These two sensor types are described in the two sections below.

Optical triangulation (1D sensor). The principle of optical triangulation in 1D is straightforward, as depicted in figure 4.13. A collimated beam (e.g., focused infrared LED, laser beam) is transmitted toward the target. The reflected light is collected by a lens and projected onto a position-sensitive device (PSD) or linear camera. Given the geometry of figure 4.13, the distance D is given by

$$D = f \frac{L}{x} \tag{4.11}$$

The distance is proportional to $1/x$; therefore the sensor resolution is best for close objects and becomes poor at a distance. Sensors based on this principle are used in range sensing up to 1 or 2 m, but also in high-precision industrial measurements with resolutions far below 1 μm.

Optical triangulation devices can provide relatively high accuracy with very good resolution (for close objects). However, the operating range of such a device is normally fairly limited by geometry. For example, the optical triangulation sensor pictured in figure 4.14

Figure 4.14
A commercially available, low-cost optical triangulation sensor: the Sharp GP series infrared rangefinders provide either analog or digital distance measures and cost only about $ 15.

operates over a distance range of between 8 and 80 cm. It is inexpensive compared to ultrasonic and laser rangefinder sensors. Although more limited in range than sonar, the optical triangulation sensor has high bandwidth and does not suffer from cross-sensitivities that are more common in the sound domain.

Structured light (2D sensor). If one replaces the linear camera or PSD of an optical triangulation sensor with a 2D receiver such as a CCD or CMOS camera, then one can recover distance to a large set of points instead of to only one point. The emitter must project a known pattern, or *structured light*, onto the environment. Many systems exist which either project light textures (figure 4.15b) or emit collimated light (possibly laser) by means of a rotating mirror. Yet another popular alternative is to project a laser stripe (figure 4.15a) by turning a laser beam into a plane using a prism. Regardless of how it is created, the projected light has a known structure, and therefore the image taken by the CCD or CMOS receiver can be filtered to identify the pattern's reflection.

Note that the problem of recovering depth is in this case far simpler than the problem of passive image analysis. In passive image analysis, as we discuss later, existing features in the environment must be used to perform *correlation*, while the present method projects a known pattern upon the environment and thereby avoids the standard correlation problem altogether. Furthermore, the structured light sensor is an active device so it will continue to work in dark environments as well as environments in which the objects are featureless (e.g., uniformly colored and edgeless). In contrast, stereo vision would fail in such texture-free circumstances.

Figure 4.15c shows a 1D active triangulation geometry. We can examine the trade-off in the design of triangulation systems by examining the geometry in figure 4.15c. The mea-

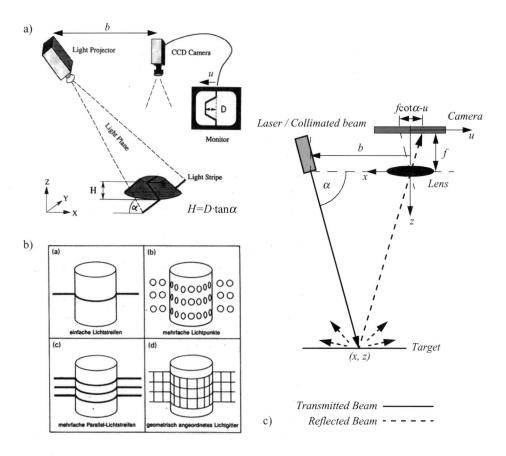

Figure 4.15
(a) Principle of active two dimensional triangulation. (b) Other possible light structures. (c) 1D schematic of the principle. Image (a) and (b) courtesy of Albert-Jan Baerveldt, Halmstad University.

sured values in the system are α and u, the distance of the illuminated point from the origin in the imaging sensor. (Note the imaging sensor here can be a camera or an array of photo diodes of a position-sensitive device (e.g., a 2D PSD).

From figure 4.15c, simple geometry shows that

$$x = \frac{b \cdot u}{f \cot \alpha - u} \; ; \quad z = \frac{b \cdot f}{f \cot \alpha - u} \tag{4.12}$$

where f is the distance of the lens to the imaging plane. In the limit, the ratio of image resolution to range resolution is defined as the triangulation gain G_p and from equation (4.12) is given by

$$\frac{\partial u}{\partial z} = G_p = \frac{b \cdot f}{z^2} \tag{4.13}$$

This shows that the ranging accuracy, for a given image resolution, is proportional to source/detector separation b and focal length f, and decreases with the square of the range z. In a scanning ranging system, there is an additional effect on the ranging accuracy, caused by the measurement of the projection angle α. From equation 4.12 we see that

$$\frac{\partial \alpha}{\partial z} = G_\alpha = \frac{b \sin \alpha^2}{z^2} \tag{4.14}$$

We can summarize the effects of the parameters on the sensor accuracy as follows:

- *Baseline length (b)*: the smaller b is, the more compact the sensor can be. The larger b is, the better the range resolution will be. Note also that although these sensors do not suffer from the correspondence problem, the disparity problem still occurs. As the baseline length b is increased, one introduces the chance that, for close objects, the illuminated point(s) may not be in the receiver's field of view.

- *Detector length and focal length (f)*: A larger detector length can provide either a larger field of view or an improved range resolution or partial benefits for both. Increasing the detector length, however, means a larger sensor head and worse electrical characteristics (increase in random error and reduction of bandwidth). Also, a short focal length gives a large field of view at the expense of accuracy, and vice versa.

At one time, laser stripe-based structured light sensors were common on several mobile robot bases as an inexpensive alternative to laser rangefinding devices. However, with the increasing quality of laser rangefinding sensors in the 1990s, the structured light system has become relegated largely to vision research rather than applied mobile robotics.

4.1.7 Motion/speed sensors

Some sensors measure directly the relative motion between the robot and its environment. Since such motion sensors detect relative motion, so long as an object is moving relative to the robot's reference frame, it will be detected and its speed can be estimated. There are a number of sensors that inherently measure some aspect of motion or change. For example, a pyroelectric sensor detects change in heat. When a human walks across the sensor's field

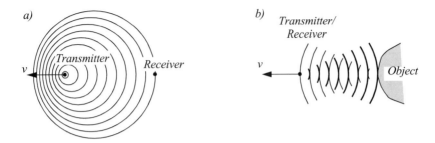

Figure 4.16
Doppler effect between two moving objects (a) or a moving and a stationary object (b).

of view, his or her motion triggers a change in heat in the sensor's reference frame. In the next section, we describe an important type of motion detector based on the Doppler effect. These sensors represent a well-known technology with decades of general applications behind them. For fast-moving mobile robots such as autonomous highway vehicles and unmanned flying vehicles, Doppler-based motion detectors are the obstacle detection sensor of choice.

4.1.7.1 Doppler effect-based sensing (radar or sound)

Anyone who has noticed the change in siren pitch that occurs when an approaching fire engine passes by and recedes is familiar with the Doppler effect.

A transmitter emits an electromagnetic or sound wave with a frequency f_t. It is either received by a receiver (figure 4.16a) or reflected from an object (figure 4.16b). The measured frequency f_r at the receiver is a function of the relative speed v between transmitter and receiver according to

$$f_r = f_t \frac{1}{1 + v/c} \qquad (4.15)$$

if the transmitter is moving and

$$f_r = f_t (1 + v/c) \qquad (4.16)$$

if the receiver is moving.

In the case of a reflected wave (figure 4.16b) there is a factor of 2 introduced, since any change x in relative separation affects the round-trip path length by $2x$. Furthermore, in such situations it is generally more convenient to consider the change in frequency Δf, known as the *Doppler shift*, as opposed to the *Doppler frequency* notation above.

$$\Delta f = f_t - f_r = \frac{2f_t v \cos\theta}{c} \tag{4.17}$$

$$v = \frac{\Delta f \cdot c}{2f_t \cos\theta} \tag{4.18}$$

where

Δf = Doppler frequency shift;

θ = relative angle between direction of motion and beam axis.

The Doppler effect applies to sound and electromagnetic waves. It has a wide spectrum of applications:

- *Sound waves*: for example, industrial process control, security, fish finding, measure of ground speed.

- *Electromagnetic waves*: for example, vibration measurement, radar systems, object tracking.

A current application area is both autonomous and manned highway vehicles. Both microwave and laser radar systems have been designed for this environment. Both systems have equivalent range, but laser can suffer when visual signals are deteriorated by environmental conditions such as rain, fog, and so on. Commercial microwave radar systems are already available for installation on highway trucks. These systems are called VORAD (vehicle on-board radar) and have a total range of approximately 150 m. With an accuracy of approximately 97%, these systems report range rates from 0 to 160 km/hr with a resolution of 1 km/hr. The beam is approximately 4 degrees wide and 5 degrees in elevation. One of the key limitations of radar technology is its bandwidth. Existing systems can provide information on multiple targets at approximately 2 Hz.

4.1.8 Vision-based sensors

Vision is our most powerful sense. It provides us with an enormous amount of information about the environment and enables rich, intelligent interaction in dynamic environments. It is therefore not surprising that a great deal of effort has been devoted to providing machines with sensors that mimic the capabilities of the human vision system. The first step in this process is the creation of sensing devices that capture the same raw information light that the human vision system uses. The next section describes the two current technologies for creating vision sensors: CCD and CMOS. These sensors have specific limitations in performance when compared to the human eye, and it is important that the reader understand these limitations. Afterward, the second and third sections describe vision-based sensors

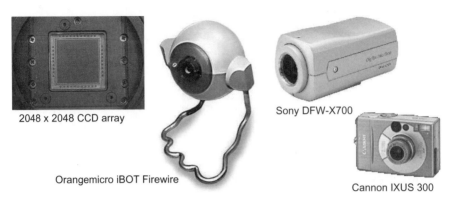

Figure 4.17
Commercially available CCD chips and CCD cameras. Because this technology is relatively mature, cameras are available in widely varying forms and costs (http://www.howstuffworks.com/digital-camera2.htm).

that are commercially available, like the sensors discussed previously in this chapter, along with their disadvantages and most popular applications.

4.1.8.1 CCD and CMOS sensors

CCD technology. The charged coupled device is the most popular basic ingredient of robotic vision systems today. The CCD chip (see figure 4.17) is an array of light-sensitive picture elements, or pixels, usually with between 20,000 and several million pixels total. Each pixel can be thought of as a light-sensitive, discharging capacitor that is 5 to 25 μm in size. First, the capacitors of all pixels are charged fully, then the integration period begins. As photons of light strike each pixel, they liberate electrons, which are captured by electric fields and retained at the pixel. Over time, each pixel accumulates a varying level of charge based on the total number of photons that have struck it. After the integration period is complete, the relative charges of all pixels need to be frozen and read. In a CCD, the reading process is performed at one corner of the CCD chip. The bottom row of pixel charges is transported to this corner and read, then the rows above shift down and the process is repeated. This means that each charge must be transported across the chip, and it is critical that the value be preserved. This requires specialized control circuitry and custom fabrication techniques to ensure the stability of transported charges.

The photodiodes used in CCD chips (and CMOS chips as well) are not equally sensitive to all frequencies of light. They are sensitive to light between 400 and 1000 nm wavelength. It is important to remember that photodiodes are less sensitive to the ultraviolet end of the spectrum (e.g., blue) and are overly sensitive to the infrared portion (e.g., heat).

You can see that the basic light-measuring process is colorless: it is just measuring the total number of photons that strike each pixel in the integration period. There are two common approaches for creating *color* images. If the pixels on the CCD chip are grouped into 2 x 2 sets of four, then red, green, and blue dyes can be applied to a color filter so that each individual pixel receives only light of one color. Normally, two pixels measure green while one pixel each measures red and blue light intensity. Of course, this one-chip color CCD has a geometric resolution disadvantage. The number of pixels in the system has been effectively cut by a factor of four, and therefore the image resolution output by the CCD camera will be sacrificed.

The three-chip color camera avoids these problems by splitting the incoming light into three complete (lower intensity) copies. Three separate CCD chips receive the light, with one red, green, or blue filter over each entire chip. Thus, in parallel, each chip measures light intensity for one color, and the camera must combine the CCD chips' outputs to create a joint color image. Resolution is preserved in this solution, although the three-chip color cameras are, as one would expect, significantly more expensive and therefore more rarely used in mobile robotics.

Both three-chip and single-chip color CCD cameras suffer from the fact that photo-diodes are much more sensitive to the near-infrared end of the spectrum. This means that the overall system detects blue light much more poorly than red and green. To compensate, the gain must be increased on the blue channel, and this introduces greater absolute noise on blue than on red and green. It is not uncommon to assume at least one to two bits of additional noise on the blue channel. Although there is no satisfactory solution to this problem today, over time the processes for blue detection have been improved and we expect this positive trend to continue.

The CCD camera has several camera parameters that affect its behavior. In some cameras, these values are fixed. In others, the values are constantly changing based on built-in feedback loops. In higher-end cameras, the user can modify the values of these parameters via software. The *iris position* and *shutter speed* regulate the amount of light being measured by the camera. The iris is simply a mechanical aperture that constricts incoming light, just as in standard 35 mm cameras. Shutter speed regulates the integration period of the chip. In higher-end cameras, the effective shutter speed can be as brief at 1/30,000 seconds and as long as 2 seconds. *Camera gain* controls the overall amplification of the analog signal, prior to A/D conversion. However, it is very important to understand that, even though the image may appear brighter after setting high gain, the shutter speed and iris may not have changed at all. Thus gain merely amplifies the signal, and amplifies along with the signal all of the associated noise and error. Although useful in applications where imaging is done for human consumption (e.g., photography, television), gain is of little value to a mobile roboticist.

In color cameras, an additional control exists for *white balance*. Depending on the source of illumination in a scene (e.g., fluorescent lamps, incandescent lamps, sunlight, underwater filtered light, etc.), the relative measurements of red, green, and blue light that define pure white light will change dramatically. The human eye compensates for all such effects in ways that are not fully understood, but, the camera can demonstrate glaring inconsistencies in which the same table looks blue in one image, taken during the night, and yellow in another image, taken during the day. White balance controls enable the user to change the relative gains for red, green, and blue in order to maintain more consistent color definitions in varying contexts.

The key disadvantages of CCD cameras are primarily in the areas of inconstancy and dynamic range. As mentioned above, a number of parameters can change the brightness and colors with which a camera creates its image. Manipulating these parameters in a way to provide consistency over time and over environments, for example, ensuring that a green shirt always looks green, and something dark gray is always dark gray, remains an open problem in the vision community. For more details on the fields of color constancy and luminosity constancy, consult [40].

The second class of disadvantages relates to the behavior of a CCD chip in environments with extreme illumination. In cases of very low illumination, each pixel will receive only a small number of photons. The longest possible integration period (i.e., shutter speed) and camera optics (i.e., pixel size, chip size, lens focal length and diameter) will determine the minimum level of light for which the signal is stronger than random error noise. In cases of very high illumination, a pixel fills its well with free electrons and, as the well reaches its limit, the probability of trapping additional electrons falls and therefore the linearity between incoming light and electrons in the well degrades. This is termed *saturation* and can indicate the existence of a further problem related to cross-sensitivity. When a well has reached its limit, then additional light within the remainder of the integration period may cause further charge to leak into neighboring pixels, causing them to report incorrect values or even reach secondary saturation. This effect, called *blooming*, means that individual pixel values are not truly independent.

The camera parameters may be adjusted for an environment with a particular light level, but the problem remains that the dynamic range of a camera is limited by the well capacity of the individual pixels. For example, a high-quality CCD may have pixels that can hold 40,000 electrons. The noise level for reading the well may be 11 electrons, and therefore the dynamic range will be 40,000:11, or 3600:1, which is 35 dB.

CMOS technology. The complementary metal oxide semiconductor chip is a significant departure from the CCD. It too has an array of pixels, but located alongside each pixel are several transistors specific to that pixel. Just as in CCD chips, all of the pixels accumulate charge during the integration period. During the data collection step, the CMOS takes a new

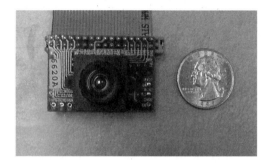

Figure 4.18
A commercially available, low-cost CMOS camera with lens attached.

approach: the pixel-specific circuitry next to every pixel measures and amplifies the pixel's signal, all in parallel for every pixel in the array. Using more traditional traces from general semiconductor chips, the resulting pixel values are all carried to their destinations.

CMOS has a number of advantages over CCD technologies. First and foremost, there is no need for the specialized clock drivers and circuitry required in the CCD to transfer each pixel's charge down all of the array columns and across all of its rows. This also means that specialized semiconductor manufacturing processes are not required to create CMOS chips. Therefore, the same production lines that create microchips can create inexpensive CMOS chips as well (see figure 4.18). The CMOS chip is so much simpler that it consumes significantly less power; incredibly, it operates with a power consumption that is one-hundredth the power consumption of a CCD chip. In a mobile robot, power is a scarce resource and therefore this is an important advantage.

On the other hand, the CMOS chip also faces several disadvantages. Most importantly, the circuitry next to each pixel consumes valuable real estate on the face of the light-detecting array. Many photons hit the transistors rather than the photodiode, making the CMOS chip significantly less sensitive than an equivalent CCD chip. Second, the CMOS technology is younger and, as a result, the best resolution that one can purchase in CMOS format continues to be far inferior to the best CCD chips available. Time will doubtless bring the high-end CMOS imagers closer to CCD imaging performance.

Given this summary of the mechanism behind CCD and CMOS chips, one can appreciate the sensitivity of any vision-based robot sensor to its environment. As compared to the human eye, these chips all have far poorer adaptation, cross-sensitivity, and dynamic range. As a result, vision sensors today continue to be fragile. Only over time, as the underlying performance of imaging chips improves, will significantly more robust vision-based sensors for mobile robots be available.

Camera output considerations. Although digital cameras have inherently digital output, throughout the 1980s and early 1990s, most affordable vision modules provided analog output signals, such as NTSC (National Television Standards Committee) and PAL (Phase Alternating Line). These camera systems included a D/A converter which, ironically, would be counteracted on the computer using a *framegrabber*, effectively an A/D converter board situated, for example, on a computer's bus. The D/A and A/D steps are far from noisefree, and furthermore the color depth of the analog signal in such cameras was optimized for human vision, not computer vision.

More recently, both CCD and CMOS technology vision systems provide digital signals that can be directly utilized by the roboticist. At the most basic level, an imaging chip provides parallel digital I/O (input/output) pins that communicate discrete pixel level values. Some vision modules make use of these direct digital signals, which must be handled subject to hard-time constraints governed by the imaging chip. To relieve the real-time demands, researchers often place an *image buffer chip* between the imager's digital output and the computer's digital inputs. Such chips, commonly used in webcams, capture a complete image snapshot and enable non real time access to the pixels, usually in a single, ordered pass.

At the highest level, a roboticist may choose instead to utilize a higher-level digital transport protocol to communicate with an imager. Most common are the IEEE 1394 (*Firewire*) standard and the USB (and USB 2.0) standards, although some older imaging modules also support serial (RS-232). To use any such high-level protocol, one must locate or create driver code both for that communication layer and for the particular implementation details of the imaging chip. Take note, however, of the distinction between lossless digital video and the standard digital video stream designed for human visual consumption. Most digital video cameras provide digital output, but often only in compressed form. For vision researchers, such compression must be avoided as it not only discards information but even introduces image detail that does not actually exist, such as MPEG (Moving Picture Experts Group) discretization boundaries.

4.1.8.2 Visual ranging sensors

Range sensing is extremely important in mobile robotics as it is a basic input for successful obstacle avoidance. As we have seen earlier in this chapter, a number of sensors are popular in robotics explicitly for their ability to recover depth estimates: ultrasonic, laser rangefinder, optical rangefinder, and so on. It is natural to attempt to implement ranging functionality using vision chips as well.

However, a fundamental problem with visual images makes rangefinding relatively difficult. Any vision chip collapses the 3D world into a 2D image plane, thereby losing depth information. If one can make strong assumptions regarding the size of objects in the world, or their particular color and reflectance, then one can directly interpret the appearance of the 2D image to recover depth. But such assumptions are rarely possible in real-world

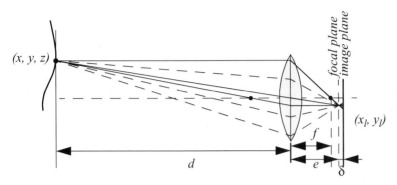

Figure 4.19
Depiction of the camera optics and its impact on the image. In order to get a sharp image, the image plane must coincide with the focal plane. Otherwise the image of the point (x,y,z) will be blurred in the image, as can be seen in the drawing above.

mobile robot applications. Without such assumptions, a single picture does not provide enough information to recover spatial information.

The general solution is to recover depth by looking at *several* images of the scene to gain more information, hopefully enough to at least partially recover depth. The images used must be different, so that taken together they provide additional information. They could differ in viewpoint, yielding *stereo* or *motion* algorithms. An alternative is to create different images, not by changing the viewpoint, but by changing the camera geometry, such as the focus position or lens iris. This is the fundamental idea behind depth from focus and depth from defocus techniques.

In the next section, we outline the general approach to the depth from focus techniques because it presents a straightforward and efficient way to create a vision-based range sensor. Subsequently, we present details for the correspondence-based techniques of depth from stereo and motion.

Depth from focus. The depth from focus class of techniques relies on the fact that image properties not only change as a function of the scene but also as a function of the camera parameters. The relationship between camera parameters and image properties is depicted in figure 4.19.

The basic formula governing image formation relates the distance of the object from the lens, d in the above figure, to the distance e from the lens to the focal point, based on the focal length f of the lens:

$$\frac{1}{f} = \frac{1}{d} + \frac{1}{e} \tag{4.19}$$

If the image plane is located at distance e from the lens, then for the specific object voxel depicted, all light will be focused at a single point on the image plane and the object voxel will be *focused*. However, when the image plane is not at e, as is depicted in figure 4.19, then the light from the object voxel will be cast on the image plane as a *blur circle*. To a first approximation, the light is homogeneously distributed throughout this blur circle, and the radius R of the circle can be characterized according to the equation

$$R = \frac{L\delta}{2e} \tag{4.20}$$

L is the diameter of the lens or aperture and δ is the displacement of the image plan from the focal point.

Given these formulas, several basic optical effects are clear. For example, if the aperture or lens is reduced to a point, as in a pinhole camera, then the radius of the blur circle approaches zero. This is consistent with the fact that decreasing the iris aperture opening causes the *depth of field* to increase until all objects are in focus. Of course, the disadvantage of doing so is that we are allowing less light to form the image on the image plane and so this is practical only in bright circumstances.

The second property that can be deduced from these optics equations relates to the sensitivity of blurring as a function of the distance from the lens to the object. Suppose the image plane is at a fixed distance 1.2 from a lens with diameter $L = 0.2$ and focal length $f = 0.5$. We can see from equation (4.20) that the size of the blur circle R changes proportionally with the image plane displacement δ. If the object is at distance $d = 1$, then from equation (4.19) we can compute $e = 1$ and therefore $\delta = 0.2$. Increase the object distance to $d = 2$ and as a result $\delta = 0.533$. Using equation (4.20) in each case we can compute $R = 0.02$ and $R = 0.08$ respectively. This demonstrates high sensitivity for defocusing when the object is close to the lens.

In contrast, suppose the object is at $d = 10$. In this case we compute $e = 0.526$. But if the object is again moved one unit, to $d = 11$, then we compute $e = 0.524$. The resulting blur circles are $R = 0.117$ and $R = 0.129$, far less than the quadrupling in R when the obstacle is one-tenth the distance from the lens. This analysis demonstrates the fundamental limitation of depth from focus techniques: they lose sensitivity as objects move farther away (given a fixed focal length). Interestingly, this limitation will turn out to apply to virtually all visual ranging techniques, including depth from stereo and depth from motion.

Nevertheless, camera optics can be customized for the depth range of the intended application. For example, a zoom lens with a very large focal length f will enable range resolu-

Figure 4.20
Two images of the same scene taken with a camera at two different focusing positions. Note the significant change in texture sharpness between the near surface and far surface. The scene is an outdoor concrete step.

tion at significant distances, of course at the expense of field of view. Similarly, a large lens diameter, coupled with a very fast shutter speed, will lead to larger, more detectable blur circles.

Given the physical effects summarized by the above equations, one can imagine a visual ranging sensor that makes use of multiple images in which camera optics are varied (e.g., image plane displacement δ) and the same scene is captured (see figure 4.20). In fact, this approach is not a new invention. The human visual system uses an abundance of cues and techniques, and one system demonstrated in humans is depth from focus. Humans vary the focal length of their lens continuously at a rate of about 2 Hz. Such approaches, in which the lens optics are actively searched in order to maximize focus, are technically called *depth from focus*. In contrast, *depth from defocus* means that depth is recovered using a series of images that have been taken with different camera geometries.

The depth from focus method is one of the simplest visual ranging techniques. To determine the range to an object, the sensor simply moves the image plane (via focusing) until maximizing the sharpness of the object. When the sharpness is maximized, the corresponding position of the image plane directly reports range. Some autofocus cameras and virtually all autofocus video cameras use this technique. Of course, a method is required for measuring the sharpness of an image or an object within the image. The most common techniques are approximate measurements of the subimage *intensity* (I) *gradient*:

$$sharpness_1 = \sum_{x,y} |I(x, y) - I(x - 1, y)| \qquad (4.21)$$

$$sharpness_2 = \sum_{x,y} (I(x, y) - I(x - 2, y - 2))^2 \qquad (4.22)$$

Figure 4.21
The Cheshm robot uses three monochrome cameras as its only ranging sensor for obstacle avoidance in the context of humans, static obstacles such as bushes, and convex obstacles such as ledges and steps.

A significant advantage of the horizontal sum of differences technique [equation (4.21)] is that the calculation can be implemented in analog circuitry using just a rectifier, a low-pass filter, and a high-pass filter. This is a common approach in commercial cameras and video recorders. Such systems will be sensitive to contrast along one particular axis, although in practical terms this is rarely an issue.

However depth from focus is an active search method and will be slow because it takes time to change the focusing parameters of the camera, using, for example, a servo-controlled focusing ring. For this reason this method has not been applied to mobile robots.

A variation of the depth from focus technique has been applied to a mobile robot, demonstrating obstacle avoidance in a variety of environments, as well as avoidance of concave obstacles such as steps and ledges [117]. This robot uses three monochrome cameras placed as close together as possible with different, fixed lens focus positions (figure 4.21).

Several times each second, all three frame-synchronized cameras simultaneously capture three images of the same scene. The images are each divided into five columns and three rows, or fifteen subregions. The approximate sharpness of each region is computed using a variation of equation (4.22), leading to a total of forty-five sharpness values. Note that equation (4.22) calculates sharpness along diagonals but skips one row. This is due to a subtle but important issue. Many cameras produce images in *interlaced* mode. This means that the odd rows are captured first, then afterward the even rows are captured. When such a camera is used in dynamic environments, for example, on a moving robot, then adjacent rows show the dynamic scene at two different time points, differing by up to one-thirtieth of a second. The result is an artificial blurring due to motion and not optical defocus. By comparing only even-numbered rows we avoid this interlacing side effect.

Recall that the three images are each taken with a camera using a different focus position. Based on the focusing position, we call each image *close, medium* or *far*. A 5 x 3 coarse depth map of the scene is constructed quickly by simply comparing the sharpness values of each of the three corresponding regions. Thus, the depth map assigns only two bits of depth information to each region using the values *close, medium,* and *far*. The critical step is to adjust the focus positions of all three cameras so that flat ground in front of the obstacle results in *medium* readings in one row of the depth map. Then, unexpected readings of either *close* or *far* will indicate convex and concave obstacles respectively, enabling basic obstacle avoidance in the vicinity of objects on the ground as well as drop-offs into the ground.

Although sufficient for obstacle avoidance, the above depth from focus algorithm presents unsatisfyingly coarse range information. The alternative is *depth from defocus*, the most desirable of the focus-based vision techniques.

Depth from defocus methods take as input two or more images of the same scene, taken with different, known camera geometry. Given the images and the camera geometry settings, the goal is to recover the depth information of the 3D scene represented by the images. We begin by deriving the relationship between the actual scene properties (irradiance and depth), camera geometry settings, and the image g that is formed at the image plane.

The *focused image* $f(x, y)$ of a scene is defined as follows. Consider a pinhole aperture ($L = 0$) in lieu of the lens. For every point p at position (x, y) on the image plane, draw a line through the pinhole aperture to the corresponding, visible point P in the actual scene. We define $f(x, y)$ as the irradiance (or light intensity) at p due to the light from P. Intuitively, $f(x, y)$ represents the intensity image of the scene perfectly in focus.

The *point spread function* $h(x_g, y_g, x_f, y_f, R_{x, y})$ is defined as the amount of irradiance from point P in the scene (corresponding to (x_f, y_f) in the focused image f that contributes to point (x_g, y_g) in the observed, defocused image g. Note that the point spread function depends not only upon the source, (x_f, y_f), and the target, (x_g, y_g), but also on R, the blur circle radius. R, in turn, depends upon the distance from point P to the lens, as can be seen by studying equations (4.19) and (4.20).

Given the assumption that the blur circle is homogeneous in intensity, we can define h as follows:

$$h(x_g, y_g, x_f, y_f, R_{x,y}) = \begin{bmatrix} \dfrac{1}{\pi R^2} & \text{if } ((x_g - x_f)^2 + (y_g - y_f)^2) \leq R^2 \\ 0 & \text{if } ((x_g - x_f)^2 + (y_g - y_f)^2) > R^2 \end{bmatrix} \tag{4.23}$$

Intuitively, point P contributes to the image pixel (x_g, y_g) only when the blur circle of point P contains the point (x_g, y_g). Now we can write the general formula that computes the value of each pixel in the image, $f(x, y)$, as a function of the point spread function and the focused image:

$$g(x_g, y_g) = \sum_{x,y} h(x_g, y_g, x, y, R_{x,y}) f(x, y) \tag{4.24}$$

This equation relates the depth of scene points via R to the observed image g. Solving for R would provide us with the depth map. However, this function has another unknown, and that is f, the focused image. Therefore, one image alone is insufficient to solve the depth recovery problem, assuming we do *not* know how the fully focused image would look.

Given two images of the same scene, taken with varying camera geometry, in theory it will be possible to solve for g as well as R because f stays constant. There are a number of algorithms for implementing such a solution accurately and quickly. The classic approach is known as *inverse filtering* because it attempts to directly solve for R, then extract depth information from this solution. One special case of the inverse filtering solution has been demonstrated with a real sensor. Suppose that the incoming light is split and sent to two cameras, one with a large aperture and the other with a pinhole aperture [121]. The pinhole aperture results in a fully focused image, directly providing the value of f. With this approach, there remains a single equation with a single unknown, and so the solution is straightforward. Pentland [121] has demonstrated such a sensor, with several meters of range and better than 97% accuracy. Note, however, that the pinhole aperture necessitates a large amount of incoming light, and that furthermore the actual image intensities must be normalized so that the pinhole and large-diameter images have equivalent total radiosity. More recent depth from defocus methods use statistical techniques and characterization of the problem as a set of linear equations [64]. These matrix-based methods have recently achieved significant improvements in accuracy over all previous work.

In summary, the basic advantage of the depth from defocus method is its extremely fast speed. The equations above do not require search algorithms to find the solution, as would the correlation problem faced by depth from stereo methods. Perhaps more importantly, the depth from defocus methods also need not capture the scene at different perspectives, and are therefore unaffected by occlusions and the disappearance of objects in a second view.

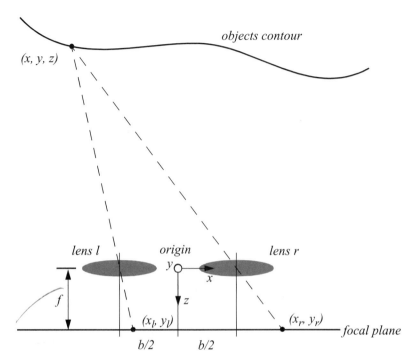

Figure 4.22
Idealized camera geometry for stereo vision.

As with all visual methods for ranging, accuracy decreases with distance. Indeed, the accuracy can be extreme; these methods have been used in microscopy to demonstrate ranging at the micrometer level.

Stereo vision. Stereo vision is one of several techniques in which we recover depth information from two images that depict the scene from different perspectives. The theory of depth from stereo has been well understood for years, while the engineering challenge of creating a practical stereo sensor has been formidable [16, 29, 30]. Recent times have seen the first successes on this front, and so after presenting a basic formalism of stereo ranging, we describe the state-of-the-art algorithmic approach and one of the recent, commercially available stereo sensors.

First, we consider a simplified case in which two cameras are placed with their optical axes parallel, at a separation (called the *baseline*) of b, shown in figure 4.22.

In this figure, a point on the object is described as being at coordinate (x, y, z) with respect to a central origin located between the two camera lenses. The position of this point's light rays on each camera's image is depicted in camera-specific local coordinates. Thus, the origin for the coordinate frame referenced by points of the form (x_l,y_l) is located at the center of lens l.

From the figure 4.22, it can be seen that

$$\frac{x_l}{f} = \frac{x + b/2}{z} \quad \text{and} \quad \frac{x_r}{f} = \frac{x - b/2}{z} \tag{4.25}$$

and (out of the plane of the page)

$$\frac{y_l}{f} = \frac{y_r}{f} = \frac{y}{z} \tag{4.26}$$

where f is the distance of both lenses to the image plane. Note from equation (4.25) that

$$\frac{x_l - x_r}{f} = \frac{b}{z} \tag{4.27}$$

where the *difference* in the image coordinates, $x_l - x_r$ is called the *disparity*. This is an important term in stereo vision, because it is only by measuring disparity that we can recover depth information. Using the disparity and solving all three above equations provides formulas for the three dimensions of the scene point being imaged:

$$x = b\frac{(x_l + x_r)/2}{x_l - x_r} \; ; \; y = b\frac{(y_l + y_r)/2}{x_l - x_r} \; ; \; z = b\frac{f}{x_l - x_r} \tag{4.28}$$

Observations from these equations are as follows:

- Distance is inversely proportional to disparity. The distance to near objects can therefore be measured more accurately than that to distant objects, just as with depth from focus techniques. In general, this is acceptable for mobile robotics, because for navigation and obstacle avoidance closer objects are of greater importance.

- Disparity is proportional to b. For a given disparity error, the accuracy of the depth estimate increases with increasing baseline b.

- As b is increased, because the physical separation between the cameras is increased, some objects may appear in one camera but not in the other. Such objects by definition will not have a disparity and therefore will not be ranged successfully.

• A point in the scene visible to both cameras produces a pair of image points (one via each lens) known as a *conjugate pair*. Given one member of the conjugate pair, we know that the other member of the pair lies somewhere along a line known as an *epipolar line*. In the case depicted by figure 4.22, because the cameras are perfectly aligned with one another, the epipolar lines are horizontal lines (i.e., along the x direction).

However, the assumption of perfectly aligned cameras is normally violated in practice. In order to optimize the range of distances that can be recovered, it is often useful to turn the cameras inward toward one another, for example. Figure 4.22 shows the *orientation* vectors that are necessary to solve this more general problem. We will express the position of a scene point P in terms of the reference frame of each camera separately. The reference frames of the cameras need not be aligned, and can indeed be at any arbitrary orientation relative to one another.

For example the position of point P will be described in terms of the left camera frame as $r'_l = (x'_l, y'_l, z'_l)$. Note that these are the coordinates of point P, not the position of its counterpart in the left camera image. P can also be described in terms of the right camera frame as $r'_r = (x'_r, y'_r, z'_r)$. If we have a rotation matrix R and translation matrix r_0 relating the relative positions of cameras l and r, then we can define r'_r in terms of r'_l:

$$r'_r = R \cdot r'_l + r_0 \qquad\qquad\qquad (4.29)$$

where R is a 3 x 3 rotation matrix and r_0 is an offset translation matrix between the two cameras.

Expanding equation (4.29) yields

$$\begin{bmatrix} x'_r \\ y'_r \\ z'_r \end{bmatrix} = \begin{bmatrix} r_{11} & r_{12} & r_{13} \\ r_{21} & r_{22} & r_{21} \\ r_{31} & r_{32} & r_{33} \end{bmatrix} \begin{bmatrix} x'_l \\ y'_l \\ z'_l \end{bmatrix} + \begin{bmatrix} r_{01} \\ r_{02} \\ r_{03} \end{bmatrix} \qquad\qquad (4.30)$$

The above equations have two uses:

1. We could find r'_r if we knew R, r'_l and r_0. Of course, if we knew r'_l then we would have complete information regarding the position of P relative to the left camera, and so the depth recovery problem would be solved. Note that, for perfectly aligned cameras as in figure 4.22, $R = I$ (the identify matrix).

2. We could calibrate the system and find r_{11}, r_{12} ... given a set of conjugate pairs $\{(x'_l, y'_l, z'_l), (x'_r, y'_r, z'_r)\}$.

In order to carry out the calibration step of step 2 above, we must find values for twelve unknowns, requiring twelve equations. This means that calibration requires, for a given scene, four conjugate points.

The above example supposes that regular translation and rotation are all that are required to effect sufficient calibration for stereo depth recovery using two cameras. In fact, single-camera calibration is itself an active area of research, particularly when the goal includes any 3D recovery aspect. When researchers intend to use even a single camera with high precision in 3D, internal errors relating to the exact placement of the imaging chip relative to the lens optical axis, as well as aberrations in the lens system itself, must be calibrated against. Such single-camera calibration involves finding solutions for the values for the exact offset of the imaging chip relative to the optical axis, both in translation and angle, and finding the relationship between distance along the imaging chip surface and external viewed surfaces. Furthermore, even without optical aberration in play, the lens is an inherently radial instrument, and so the image projected upon a flat imaging surface is radially distorted (i.e., parallel lines in the viewed world converge on the imaging chip).

A commonly practiced technique for such single-camera calibration is based upon acquiring multiple views of an easily analyzed planar pattern, such as a grid of black squares on a white background. The corners of such squares can easily be extracted, and using an interactive refinement algorithm the intrinsic calibration parameters of a camera can be extracted. Because modern imaging systems are capable of spatial accuracy greatly exceeding the pixel size, the payoff of such refined calibration can be significant. For further discussion of calibration and to download and use a standard calibration program, see [158].

Assuming that the calibration step is complete, we can now formalize the range recovery problem. To begin with, we do not have the position of P available, and therefore (x'_l, y'_l, z'_l) and (x'_r, y'_r, z'_r) are unknowns. Instead, by virtue of the two cameras we have pixels on the image planes of each camera, (x_l, y_l, z_l) and (x_r, y_r, z_r). Given the focal length f of the cameras we can relate the position of P to the left camera image as follows:

$$\frac{x_l}{f} = \frac{x'_l}{z'_l} \text{ and } \frac{y_l}{f} = \frac{y'_l}{z'_l} \tag{4.31}$$

Let us concentrate first on recovery of the values z'_l and z'_r. From equations (4.30) and (4.31) we can compute these values from any two of the following equations:

$$\left(r_{11}\frac{x_l}{f} + r_{12}\frac{y_l}{f} + r_{13} \right)z'_l + r_{01} = \frac{x_r}{f}z'_r \tag{4.32}$$

$$\left(r_{21}\frac{x_l}{f} + r_{22}\frac{y_l}{f} + r_{23} \right) z'_l + r_{02} = \frac{y_r}{f}z'_r \tag{4.33}$$

$$\left(r_{31}\frac{x_l}{f} + r_{32}\frac{y_l}{f} + r_{33} \right) z'_l + r_{03} = z'_r \tag{4.34}$$

The same process can be used to identify values for x' and y', yielding complete information about the position of point P. However, using the above equations requires us to have identified conjugate pairs in the left and right camera images: image points that originate at the same object point P in the scene. This fundamental challenge, identifying the conjugate pairs and thereby recovering disparity, is the *correspondence problem*. Intuitively, the problem is, given two images of the same scene from different perspectives, how can we identify the same object points in both images? For every such identified object point, we will be able to recover its 3D position in the scene.

The correspondence problem, or the problem of matching the same object in two different inputs, has been one of the most challenging problems in the computer vision field and the artificial intelligence fields. The basic approach in nearly all proposed solutions involves converting each image in order to create more stable and more information-rich data. With more reliable data in hand, stereo algorithms *search* for the best conjugate pairs representing as many of the images' pixels as possible.

The search process is well understood, but the quality of the resulting depth maps depends heavily upon the way in which images are treated to reduce noise and improve stability. This has been the chief technology driver in stereo vision algorithms, and one particular method has become widely used in commercially available systems.

The zero crossings of Laplacian of Gaussian (ZLoG). ZLoG is a strategy for identifying features in the left and right camera images that are stable and will match well, yielding high-quality stereo depth recovery. This approach has seen tremendous success in the field of stereo vision, having been implemented commercially in both software and hardware with good results. It has led to several commercial stereo vision systems and yet it is extremely simple. Here we summarize the approach and explain some of its advantages.

The core of ZLoG is the Laplacian transformation of an image. Intuitively, this is nothing more than the second derivative. Formally, the Laplacian $L(x, y)$ of an image with intensities $I(x, y)$ is defined as

$$L(x, y) = \frac{\partial^2 I}{\partial x^2} + \frac{\partial^2 I}{\partial y^2} \tag{4.35}$$

So the Laplacian represents the second derivative of the image, and is computed along both axes. Such a transformation, called a *convolution*, must be computed over the discrete space of image pixel values, and therefore an approximation of equation (4.35) is required for application:

$$L = P \otimes I \qquad (4.36)$$

We depict a discrete operator P, called a *kernel*, that approximates the second derivative operation along both axes as a 3 x 3 table:

$$\begin{bmatrix} 0 & 1 & 0 \\ 1 & -4 & 1 \\ 0 & 1 & 0 \end{bmatrix} \qquad (4.37)$$

Application of the kernel P to convolve an image is straightforward. The kernel defines the contribution of each pixel in the image to the corresponding pixel in the target as well as its neighbors. For example, if a pixel (5,5) in the image I has value $I(5, 5) = 10$, then application of the kernel depicted by equation (4.37) causes pixel $I(5, 5)$ to make the following contributions to the target image L:

$L(5, 5)$ += -40;

$L(4, 5)$ += 10;

$L(6, 5)$ += 10;

$L(5, 4)$ += 10;

$L(5, 6)$ += 10.

Now consider the graphic example of a step function, representing a pixel row in which the intensities are dark, then suddenly there is a jump to very bright intensities. The second derivative will have a sharp positive peak followed by a sharp negative peak, as depicted in figure 4.23. The Laplacian is used because of this extreme sensitivity to changes in the image. But the second derivative is in fact oversensitive. We would like the Laplacian to trigger large peaks due to real changes in the scene's intensities, but we would like to keep signal noise from triggering false peaks.

For the purpose of removing noise due to sensor error, the ZLoG algorithm applies Gaussian smoothing first, then executes the Laplacian convolution. Such smoothing can be effected via convolution with a 3×3 table that approximates Gaussian smoothing:

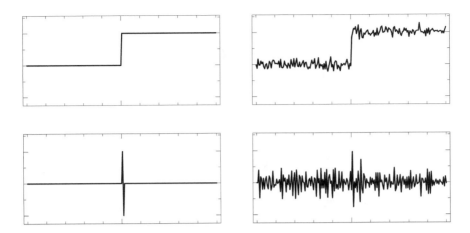

Figure 4.23
Step function example of second derivative shape and the impact of noise.

$$
\begin{bmatrix}
\dfrac{1}{16} & \dfrac{2}{16} & \dfrac{1}{16} \\[2mm]
\dfrac{2}{16} & \dfrac{4}{16} & \dfrac{2}{16} \\[2mm]
\dfrac{1}{16} & \dfrac{2}{16} & \dfrac{1}{16}
\end{bmatrix}
\tag{4.38}
$$

Gaussian smoothing does not really remove error; it merely distributes image variations over larger areas. This should seem familiar. In fact, Gaussian smoothing is almost identical to the blurring caused by defocused optics. It is, nonetheless, very effective at removing high-frequency noise, just as blurring removes fine-grained detail. Note that, like defocusing, this kernel does not change the total illumination but merely redistributes it (by virtue of the divisor 16).

The result of Laplacian of Gaussian (LoG) image filtering is a target array with sharp positive and negative spikes identifying boundaries of change in the original image. For example, a sharp edge in the image will result in both a positive spike and a negative spike, located on either side of the edge.

To solve the correspondence problem, we would like to identify specific *features* in LoG that are amenable to matching between the left camera and right camera filtered images. A very effective feature has been to identify each *zero crossing* of the LoG as such a feature.

Figure 4.25
The SVM module mounted on EPFL's Shrimp robot.

Many zero crossings do lie at edges in images, but their occurrence is somewhat broader than that. An interesting characteristic of zero crossings is that they are very sharply defined, covering just one "pixel" width in the filtered image. The accuracy can even be further enhanced by using interpolation to establish the position of the zero crossing with subpixel accuracy. All told, the accuracy of the zero crossing features in ZLoG have made them the preferred features in state-of-the-art stereo depth recovery algorithms.

Figure 4.24 shows on an example the various steps required to extract depth information from a stereo image.

Several commercial stereo vision depth recovery sensors have been available for researchers over the past 10 years. A popular unit in mobile robotics today is the digital stereo head (or SVM) from Videre Design shown in figure 4.25.

The SVM uses the LoG operator, following it by tessellating the resulting array into subregions within which the sum of absolute values is computed. The correspondence problem is solved at the level of these subregions, a process called *area correlation,* and after correspondence is solved the results are interpolated to one-fourth pixel precision. An important feature of the SVM is that it produces not just a depth map but distinct measures of

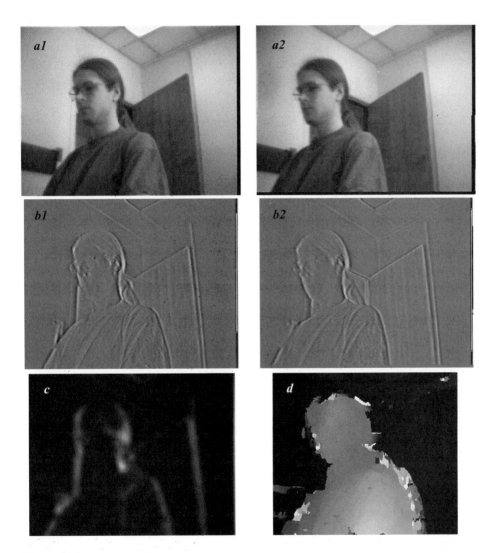

Figure 4.24
Extracting depth information from a stereo image. (a1 and a2) Left and right image. (b1 and b2) Vertical edge filtered left and right image: filter = [1 2 4 -2 -10 -2 4 2 1]. (c) Confidence image: bright = high confidence (good texture); dark = low confidence (no texture). (d) Depth image (disparity): bright = close; dark = far.

match quality for each pixel. This is valuable because such additional information can be used over time to eliminate spurious, incorrect stereo matches that have poor match quality.

The performance of SVM provides a good representative of the state of the art in stereo ranging today. The SVM consists of sensor hardware, including two CMOS cameras and DSP (Digital Signal Processor) hardware. In addition, the SVM includes stereo vision software that makes use of a standard computer (e.g., a Pentium processor). On a 320 x 240 pixel image pair, the SVM assigns one of thirty-two discrete levels of disparity (i.e., depth) to every pixel at a rate of twelve frames per second (based on the speed of a 233 MHz Pentium II). This compares favorably to both laser rangefinding and ultrasonics, particularly when one appreciates that ranging information with stereo is being computed for not just one target point, but all target points in the image.

It is important to note that the SVM uses CMOS chips rather than CCD chips, demonstrating that resolution sufficient for stereo vision algorithms is readily available using the less expensive, power efficient CMOS technology.

The resolution of a vision-based ranging system will depend upon the range to the object, as we have stated before. It is instructive to observe the published resolution values for the SVM sensor. Although highly dependent on the camera optics, using a standard 6 mm focal length lens pair, the SVM claims a resolution of 10 mm at 3 m range, and a resolution of 60 mm at 10 m range. These values are based on ideal circumstances, but nevertheless exemplify the rapid loss in resolution that will accompany vision-based ranging.

4.1.8.3 Motion and optical flow

A great deal of information can be recovered by recording time-varying images from a fixed (or moving) camera. First, we distinguish between the motion field and optical flow:

- Motion field: this assigns a velocity vector to every point in an image. If a point in the environment moves with velocity v_0, then this induces a velocity v_i in the image plane. It is possible to determine mathematically the relationship between v_i and v_0.

- Optical flow: it can also be true that brightness patterns in the image move as the object that causes them moves (light source). Optical flow is the apparent motion of these brightness patterns.

In our analysis here we assume that the optical flow pattern will correspond to the motion field, although this is not always true in practice. This is illustrated in figure 4.26a where a sphere exhibits spatial variation of brightness, or shading, in the image of the sphere since its surface is curved. If the surface moves, however, this shading pattern will not move hence the optical flow is zero everywhere even though the motion field is not zero. In figure 4.26b, the opposite occurs. Here we have a fixed sphere with a moving light source. The shading in the image will change as the source moves. In this case the optical

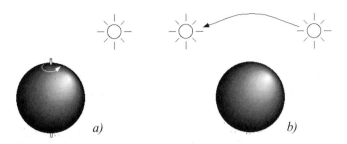

Figure 4.26
Motion of the sphere or the light source here demonstrates that optical flow is not always the same as the motion field.

flow is nonzero but the motion field is zero. If the only information accessible to us is the optical flow and we depend on this, we will obtain incorrect results in both cases.

Optical Flow. There are a number of techniques for attempting to measure optical flow and thereby obtain the scene's motion field. Most algorithms use local information, attempting to find the motion of a local patch in two consecutive images. In some cases, global information regarding smoothness and consistency can help to further disambiguate such *matching* processes. Below we present details for the optical flow constraint equation method. For more details on this and other methods refer to [41, 77, 146].

Suppose first that the time interval between successive snapshots is so fast that we can assume that the measured intensity of a portion of the same object is effectively constant. Mathematically, let $E(x, y, t)$ be the image irradiance at time t at the image point (x, y). If $u(x, y)$ and $v(x, y)$ are the x and y components of the optical flow vector at that point, we need to search a new image for a point where the irradiance will be the same at time $t + \delta t$, that is, at point $(x + \delta t, y + \delta t)$, where $\delta x = u\delta t$ and $\delta y = v\delta t$. That is,

$$E(x + u\delta t, y + v\delta t, t + \delta t) = E(x, y, t) \tag{4.39}$$

for a small time interval, δt. This will capture the motion of a constant-intensity *patch* through time. If we further assume that the brightness of the image varies smoothly, then we can expand the left hand side of equation (4.39) as a Taylor series to obtain

$$E(x, y, t) + \delta x \frac{\partial E}{\partial x} + \delta y \frac{\partial E}{\partial y} + \delta t \frac{\partial E}{\partial t} + e = E(x, y, t) \tag{4.40}$$

where e contains second- and higher-order terms in δx, and so on. In the limit as δt tends to zero we obtain

$$\frac{\partial E}{\partial x}\frac{dx}{dt} + \frac{\partial E}{\partial y}\frac{dy}{dt} + \frac{\partial E}{\partial t} = 0 \qquad\qquad (4.41)$$

from which we can abbreviate

$$u = \frac{dx}{dt} \; ; \; v = \frac{dy}{dt} \qquad\qquad (4.42)$$

and

$$E_x = \frac{\partial E}{\partial x} \; ; \; E_y = \frac{\partial E}{\partial y} \; ; \; E_t = \frac{\partial E}{\partial t} = 0 \qquad\qquad (4.43)$$

so that we obtain

$$E_x u + E_y v + E_t = 0 \qquad\qquad (4.44)$$

The derivative E_t represents how quickly the intensity changes with time while the derivatives E_x and E_y represent the spatial rates of intensity change (how quickly intensity changes across the image). Altogether, equation (4.44) is known as the *optical flow constraint equation* and the three derivatives can be estimated for each pixel given successive images.

We need to calculate both u and v for each pixel, but the optical flow constraint equation only provides one equation per pixel, and so this is insufficient. The ambiguity is intuitively clear when one considers that a number of equal-intensity pixels can be inherently ambiguous – it may be unclear which pixel is the resulting location for an equal-intensity originating pixel in the prior image.

The solution to this ambiguity requires an additional constraint. We assume that in general the motion of adjacent pixels will be similar, and that therefore the overall optical flow of all pixels will be smooth. This constraint is interesting in that we know it will be violated to *some* degree, but we enforce the constraint nonetheless in order to make the optical flow computation tractable. Specifically, this constraint will be violated precisely when different objects in the scene are moving in different directions with respect to the vision system. Of course, such situations will tend to include edges, and so this may introduce a useful visual cue.

Because we know that this smoothness constraint will be somewhat incorrect, we can mathematically define the degree to which we violate this constraint by evaluating the formula

$$e_s = \iint (u^2 + v^2) dx dy \tag{4.45}$$

which is the integral of the square of the magnitude of the gradient of the optical flow. We also determine the error in the optical flow constraint equation (which in practice will not quite be zero).

$$e_c = \iint (E_x u + E_y v + E_t)^2 dx dy \tag{4.46}$$

Both of these equations should be as small as possible so we want to minimize $e_s + \lambda e_c$, where λ is a parameter that weights the error in the image motion equation relative to the departure from smoothness. A large parameter should be used if the brightness measurements are accurate and small if they are noisy. In practice the parameter λ is adjusted manually and interactively to achieve the best performance.

The resulting problem then amounts to the calculus of variations, and the Euler equations yield

$$\nabla^2 u = \lambda (E_x u + E_y v + E_t) E_x \tag{4.47}$$

$$\nabla^2 v = \lambda (E_x u + E_y v + E_t) E_y \tag{4.48}$$

where

$$\nabla^2 = \frac{\partial^2}{\delta x^2} + \frac{\partial^2}{\delta y^2} \tag{4.49}$$

which is the Laplacian operator.

Equations (4.47) and (4.48) form a pair of elliptical second-order partial differential equations which can be solved iteratively.

Where silhouettes (one object occluding another) occur, discontinuities in the optical flow will occur. This of course violates the smoothness constraint. One possibility is to try and find edges that are indicative of such occlusions, excluding the pixels near such edges from the optical flow computation so that smoothness is a more realistic assumption. Another possibility is to opportunistically make use of these distinctive edges. In fact, corners can be especially easy to *pattern-match* across subsequent images and thus can serve as fiducial markers for optical flow computation in their own right.

Optical flow promises to be an important ingredient in future vision algorithms that combine cues across multiple algorithms. However, obstacle avoidance and navigation

Figure 4.27
Color markers on the top of EPFL's STeam Engine soccer robots enable a color-tracking sensor to locate the robots and the ball in the soccer field.

control systems for mobile robots exclusively using optical flow have not yet proved to be broadly effective.

4.1.8.4   Color-tracking sensors
Although depth from stereo will doubtless prove to be a popular application of vision-based methods to mobile robotics, it mimics the functionality of existing sensors, including ultrasonic, laser, and optical rangefinders. An important aspect of vision-based sensing is that the vision chip can provide sensing modalities and cues that no other mobile robot sensor provides. One such novel sensing modality is detecting and tracking color in the environment.

Color represents an environmental characteristic that is orthogonal to range, and it represents both a natural cue and an artificial cue that can provide new information to a mobile robot. For example, the annual robot soccer events make extensive use of color both for environmental marking and for robot localization (see figure 4.27).

Color sensing has two important advantages. First, detection of color is a straightforward function of a single image, therefore no correspondence problem need be solved in such algorithms. Second, because color sensing provides a new, independent environmental cue, if it is combined (i.e., *sensor fusion*) with existing cues, such as data from stereo vision or laser rangefinding, we can expect significant information gains.

Efficient color-tracking sensors are now available commercially. Below, we briefly describe two commercial, hardware-based color-tracking sensors, as well as a publicly available software-based solution.

Cognachrome color-tracking system. The Cognachrome Vision System form Newton Research Labs is a color-tracking hardware-based sensor capable of extremely fast color tracking on a dedicated processor [162]. The system will detect color blobs based on three user-defined colors at a rate of 60 Hz. The Cognachrome system can detect and report on a maximum of twenty-five objects per frame, providing centroid, bounding box, area, aspect ratio, and principal axis orientation information for each object independently.

This sensor uses a technique called *constant thresholding* to identify each color. In RGB (red, green and blue) space, the user defines for each of R, G, and B a minimum and maximum value. The 3D box defined by these six constraints forms a color bounding box, and any pixel with RGB values that are all within this bounding box is identified as a target. Target pixels are merged into larger objects that are then reported to the user.

The Cognachrome sensor achieves a position resolution of one pixel for the centroid of each object in a field that is 200 x 250 pixels in size. The key advantage of this sensor, just as with laser rangefinding and ultrasonics, is that there is no load on the mobile robot's main processor due to the sensing modality. All processing is performed on sensor-specific hardware (i.e., a Motorola 68332 processor and a mated framegrabber). The Cognachrome system costs several thousand dollars, but is being superseded by higher-performance hardware vision processors at Newton Labs, Inc.

CMUcam robotic vision sensor. Recent advances in chip manufacturing, both in terms of CMOS imaging sensors and high-speed, readily available microprocessors at the 50+ MHz range, have made it possible to manufacture low-overhead intelligent vision sensors with functionality similar to Cognachrome for a fraction of the cost. The CMUcam sensor is a recent system that mates a low-cost microprocessor with a consumer CMOS imaging chip to yield an intelligent, self-contained vision sensor for $100, as shown in figure 4.29.

This sensor is designed to provide high-level information extracted from the camera image to an external processor that may, for example, control a mobile robot. An external processor configures the sensor's streaming data mode, for instance, specifying tracking mode for a bounded RGB or YUV value set. Then, the vision sensor processes the data in real time and outputs high-level information to the external consumer. At less than 150 mA of current draw, this sensor provides image color statistics and color-tracking services at approximately twenty frames per second at a resolution of 80 x 143 [126].

Figure 4.29 demonstrates the color-based object tracking service as provided by CMUcam once the sensor is trained on a human hand. The approximate shape of the object is extracted as well as its bounding box and approximate center of mass.

CMVision color tracking software library. Because of the rapid speedup of processors in recent times, there has been a trend toward executing basic vision processing on a main

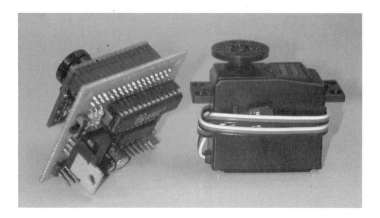

Figure 4.28
The CMUcam sensor consists of three chips: a CMOS imaging chip, a SX28 microprocessor, and a
Maxim RS232 level shifter [126].

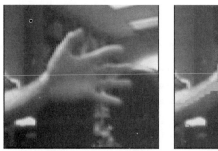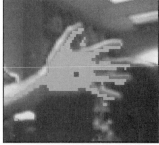

Figure 4.29
Color-based object extraction as applied to a human hand.

processor within the mobile robot. Intel Corporation's computer vision library is an optimized library for just such processing [160]. In this spirit, the CMVision color-tracking
software represents a state-of-the-art software solution for color tracking in dynamic environments [47]. CMVision can track up to thirty-two colors at 30 Hz on a standard 200 MHz
Pentium computer.

The basic algorithm this sensor uses is constant thresholding, as with Cognachrome,
with the chief difference that the YUV color space is used instead of the RGB color space
when defining a six-constraint bounding box for each color. While R, G, and B values
encode the intensity of each color, YUV separates the color (or *chrominance*) measure
from the brightness (or *luminosity*) measure. Y represents the image's luminosity while U

and V together capture its chrominance. Thus, a bounding box expressed in YUV space can achieve greater stability with respect to changes in illumination than is possible in RGB space.

The CMVision color sensor achieves a resolution of 160 x 120 and returns, for each object detected, a bounding box and a centroid. The software for CMVision is available freely with a Gnu Public License at [161].

Key performance bottlenecks for both the CMVision software, the CMUcam hardware system, and the Cognachrome hardware system continue to be the quality of imaging chips and available computational speed. As significant advances are made on these frontiers one can expect packaged vision systems to witness tremendous performance improvements.

4.2   Representing Uncertainty

In section 4.1.2 we presented a terminology for describing the performance characteristics of a sensor. As mentioned there, sensors are imperfect devices with errors of both systematic and random nature. Random errors, in particular, cannot be corrected, and so they represent atomic levels of sensor uncertainty.

But when you build a mobile robot, you combine information from many sensors, even using the same sensors repeatedly, over time, to possibly build a model of the environment. How can we scale up, from characterizing the uncertainty of a single sensor to the uncertainty of the resulting robot system?

We begin by presenting a statistical representation for the random error associated with an individual sensor [12]. With a quantitative tool in hand, the standard Gaussian uncertainty model can be presented and evaluated. Finally, we present a framework for computing the uncertainty of conclusions drawn from a set of quantifiably uncertain measurements, known as the *error propagation law*.

4.2.1   Statistical representation

We have already defined *error* as the difference between a sensor measurement and the true value. From a statistical point of view, we wish to characterize the error of a sensor, not for one specific measurement but for any measurement. Let us formulate the problem of sensing as an estimation problem. The sensor has taken a set of n measurements with values ρ_i. The goal is to characterize the estimate of the true value $E[X]$ given these measurements:

$$E[X] = g(\rho_1, \rho_2, \ldots, \rho_n) \tag{4.50}$$

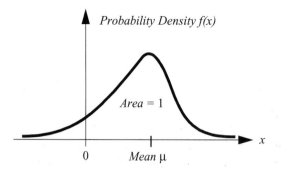

Probability Density f(x)

Area = 1

0   *Mean* μ

x

Figure 4.30
A sample probability density function, showing a single probability peak (i.e., unimodal) with asymptotic drops in both directions.

From this perspective, the true value is represented by a random (and therefore unknown) variable X. We use a *probability density function* to characterize the statistical properties of the value of X.

In figure 4.30, the density function identifies for each possible value x of X a probability density $f(x)$ along the y-axis. The area under the curve is 1, indicating the complete chance of X having *some* value:

$$\int_{-\infty}^{\infty} f(x)dx \; = \; 1 \tag{4.51}$$

The probability of the value of X falling between two limits a and b is computed as the bounded integral:

$$P[a < X \leq b] \; = \; \int_{a}^{b} f(x)dx \tag{4.52}$$

The probability density function is a useful way to characterize the possible values of X because it not only captures the range of X but also the comparative probability of different values for X. Using $f(x)$ we can quantitatively define the mean, variance, and standard deviation as follows.

The *mean value* μ is equivalent to the expected value $E[X]$ if we were to measure X an infinite number of times and average all of the resulting values. We can easily define $E[X]$:

$$\mu = E[X] = \int_{-\infty}^{\infty} xf(x)dx \qquad (4.53)$$

Note in the above equation that calculation of $E[X]$ is identical to the weighted average of all possible values of x. In contrast, the *mean square value* is simply the weighted average of the squares of all values of x:

$$E[X^2] = \int_{-\infty}^{\infty} x^2 f(x)dx \qquad (4.54)$$

Characterization of the "width" of the possible values of X is a key statistical measure, and this requires first defining the *variance* σ^2:

$$Var(X) = \sigma^2 = \int_{-\infty}^{\infty} (x - \mu)^2 f(x)dx \qquad (4.55)$$

Finally, the *standard deviation* σ is simply the square root of variance σ, and σ^2 will play important roles in our characterization of the error of a single sensor as well as the error of a model generated by combining multiple sensor readings.

4.2.1.1 Independence of random variables.

With the tools presented above, we often evaluate systems with multiple random variables. For instance, a mobile robot's laser rangefinder may be used to measure the position of a feature on the robot's right and, later, another feature on the robot's left. The position of each feature in the real world may be treated as random variables, X_1 and X_2.

Two random variables X_1 and X_2 are *independent* if the particular value of one has no bearing on the particular value of the other. In this case we can draw several important conclusions about the statistical behavior of X_1 and X_2. First, the expected value (or mean value) of the product of random variables is equal to the product of their mean values:

$$E[X_1 X_2] = E[X_1]E[X_2] \qquad (4.56)$$

Second, the variance of their sums is equal to the sum of their variances:

$$Var(X_1 + X_2) = Var(X_1) + Var(X_2) \qquad (4.57)$$

In mobile robotics, we often assume the independence of random variables even when this assumption is not strictly true. The simplification that results makes a number of the existing mobile robot-mapping and navigation algorithms tenable, as described in

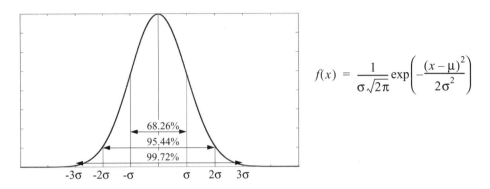

$$f(x) = \frac{1}{\sigma\sqrt{2\pi}} \exp\left(-\frac{(x-\mu)^2}{2\sigma^2}\right)$$

Figure 4.31
The Gaussian function with $\mu = 0$ and $\sigma = 1$. We shall refer to this as the reference Gaussian. The value 2σ is often refereed to as the signal quality; 95.44% of the values are falling within $\pm 2\sigma$.

chapter 5. A further simplification, described in section 4.2.1.2, revolves around one specific probability density function used more often than any other when modeling error: the Gaussian distribution.

4.2.1.2 Gaussian distribution

The Gaussian distribution, also called the *normal distribution,* is used across engineering disciplines when a well-behaved error model is required for a random variable for which no error model of greater felicity has been discovered. The Gaussian has many characteristics that make it mathematically advantageous to other ad hoc probability density functions. It is symmetric around the mean μ. There is no particular bias for being larger than or smaller than μ, and this makes sense when there is no information to the contrary. The Gaussian distribution is also unimodal, with a single peak that reaches a maximum at μ (necessary for any symmetric, unimodal distribution). This distribution also has tails (the value of $f(x)$ as x approaches $-\infty$ and ∞) that only approach zero asymptotically. This means that all amounts of error are possible, although very large errors may be highly improbable. In this sense, the Gaussian is conservative. Finally, as seen in the formula for the Gaussian probability density function, the distribution depends only on two parameters:

$$f(x) = \frac{1}{\sigma\sqrt{2\pi}} \exp\left(-\frac{(x-\mu)^2}{2\sigma^2}\right) \tag{4.58}$$

The Gaussian's basic shape is determined by the structure of this formula, and so the only two parameters required to fully specify a particular Gaussian are its mean, μ, and its

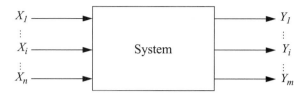

Figure 4.32
Error propagation in a multiple-input multi-output system with n inputs and m outputs.

standard deviation, σ. Figure 4.31 shows the Gaussian function with $\mu = 0$ and $\sigma = 1$.

Suppose that a random variable X is modeled as a Gaussian. How does one identify the chance that the value of X is within one standard deviation of μ? In practice, this requires integration of $f(x)$, the Gaussian function to compute the area under a portion of the curve:

$$Area = \int_{-\sigma}^{\sigma} f(x)dx \qquad (4.59)$$

Unfortunately, there is no closed-form solution for the integral in equation (4.59), and so the common technique is to use a Gaussian *cumulative probability table*. Using such a table, one can compute the probability for various value ranges of X:

$P[\mu - \sigma < X \leq \mu + \sigma] = 0.68$;

$P[\mu - 2\sigma < X \leq \mu + 2\sigma] = 0.95$;

$P[\mu - 3\sigma < X \leq \mu + 3\sigma] = 0.997$.

For example, 95% of the values for X fall within two standard deviations of its mean. This applies to *any* Gaussian distribution. As is clear from the above progression, under the Gaussian assumption, once bounds are relaxed to 3σ, the overwhelming proportion of values (and, therefore, probability) is subsumed.

4.2.2 Error propagation: combining uncertain measurements
The probability mechanisms above may be used to describe the errors associated with a single sensor's attempts to measure a real-world value. But in mobile robotics, one often uses a series of measurements, all of them uncertain, to extract a single environmental measure. For example, a series of uncertain measurements of single points can be fused to extract the position of a line (e.g., a hallway wall) in the environment (figure 4.36).

Consider the system in figure 4.32, where X_i are n input signals with a known probability distribution and Y_i are m outputs. The question of interest is: what can we say about

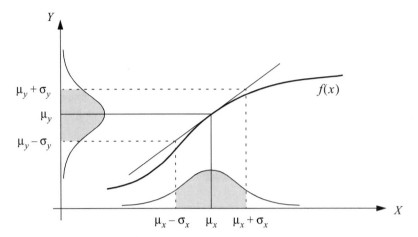

Figure 4.33
One-dimensional case of a nonlinear error propagation problem.

the probability distribution of the output signals Y_i if they depend with known functions f_i upon the input signals? Figure 4.33 depicts the 1D version of this error propagation problem as an example.

The general solution can be generated using the first order Taylor expansion of f_i. The output covariance matrix C_Y is given by the error propagation law:

$$C_Y = F_X C_X F_X^T \qquad (4.60)$$

where

C_X = covariance matrix representing the input uncertainties;

C_Y = covariance matrix representing the propagated uncertainties for the outputs;

F_x is the *Jacobian* matrix defined as

$$F_X = \nabla f = \left[\nabla_X \cdot f(X)^T \right]^T = \begin{bmatrix} f_1 \\ \vdots \\ f_m \end{bmatrix} \begin{bmatrix} \dfrac{\partial}{\partial X_1} & \cdots & \dfrac{\partial}{\partial X_n} \end{bmatrix} = \begin{bmatrix} \dfrac{\partial f_1}{\partial X_1} & \cdots & \dfrac{\partial f_1}{\partial X_n} \\ \vdots & \cdots & \vdots \\ \dfrac{\partial f_m}{\partial X_1} & \cdots & \dfrac{\partial f_m}{\partial X_n} \end{bmatrix}. \qquad (4.61)$$

This is also the transpose of the gradient of $f(X)$.

We will not present a detailed derivation here but will use equation (4.60) to solve an example problem in section 4.3.1.1.

4.3   Feature Extraction

An autonomous mobile robot must be able to determine its relationship to the environment by making measurements with its sensors and then using those measured signals. A wide variety of sensing technologies are available, as shown in the previous section. But every sensor we have presented is imperfect: measurements always have error and, therefore, uncertainty associated with them. Therefore, sensor inputs must be used in a way that enables the robot to interact with its environment successfully in spite of measurement uncertainty.

There are two strategies for using uncertain sensor input to guide the robot's behavior. One strategy is to use each sensor measurement as a raw and individual value. Such raw sensor values could, for example, be tied directly to robot behavior, whereby the robot's actions are a function of its sensor inputs. Alternatively, the raw sensor values could be used to update an intermediate model, with the robot's actions being triggered as a function of this model rather than the individual sensor measurements.

The second strategy is to extract information from one or more sensor readings first, generating a higher-level *percept* that can then be used to inform the robot's model and perhaps the robot's actions directly. We call this process *feature extraction, and* it is this next, optional step in the perceptual interpretation pipeline (figure 4.34) that we will now discuss.

In practical terms, mobile robots do not necessarily use feature extraction and scene interpretation for every activity. Instead, robots will interpret sensors to varying degrees depending on each specific functionality. For example, in order to guarantee emergency stops in the face of immediate obstacles, the robot may make direct use of raw forward-facing range readings to stop its drive motors. For local obstacle avoidance, raw ranging sensor strikes may be combined in an occupancy grid model, enabling smooth avoidance of obstacles meters away. For map-building and precise navigation, the range sensor values and even vision sensor measurements may pass through the complete perceptual pipeline, being subjected to feature extraction followed by scene interpretation to minimize the impact of individual sensor uncertainty on the robustness of the robot's mapmaking and navigation skills. The pattern that thus emerges is that, as one moves into more sophisticated, long-term perceptual tasks, the feature extraction and scene interpretation aspects of the perceptual pipeline become essential.

Feature definition. Features are recognizable structures of elements in the environment. They usually can be extracted from measurements and mathematically described. Good features are always perceivable and easily detectable from the environment. We distinguish

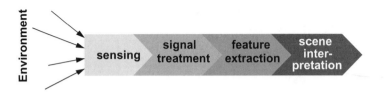

Figure 4.34
The perceptual pipeline: from sensor readings to knowledge models.

between *low-level features* (*geometric primitives*) like lines, circles, or polygons, and *high-level features* (*objects*) such as edges, doors, tables, or a trash can. At one extreme, raw sensor data provide a large volume of data, but with low distinctiveness of each individual quantum of data. Making use of raw data has the potential advantage that every bit of information is fully used, and thus there is a high conservation of information. Low-level features are abstractions of raw data, and as such provide a lower volume of data while increasing the distinctiveness of each feature. The hope, when one incorporates low-level features, is that the features are filtering out poor or useless data, but of course it is also likely that some valid information will be lost as a result of the feature extraction process. High-level features provide maximum abstraction from the raw data, thereby reducing the volume of data as much as possible while providing highly distinctive resulting features. Once again, the abstraction process has the risk of filtering away important information, potentially lowering data utilization.

Although features must have some spatial locality, their geometric extent can range widely. For example, a corner feature inhabits a specific coordinate location in the geometric world. In contrast, a visual "fingerprint" identifying a specific room in an office building applies to the entire room, but has a location that is spatially limited to the one particular room.

In mobile robotics, features play an especially important role in the creation of environmental models. They enable more compact and robust descriptions of the environment, helping a mobile robot during both map-building and localization. When designing a mobile robot, a critical decision revolves around choosing the appropriate features for the robot to use. A number of factors are essential to this decision:

Target environment. For geometric features to be useful, the target geometries must be readily detected in the actual environment. For example, line features are extremely useful in office building environments due to the abundance of straight wall segments, while the same features are virtually useless when navigating Mars.

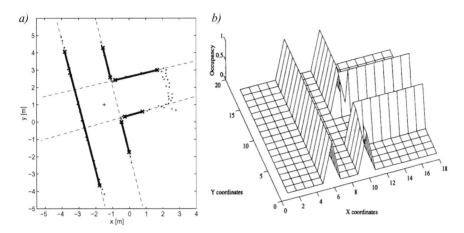

Figure 4.35
Environment representation and modeling: (a) feature based (continuous metric); (b) occupancy grid (discrete metric). Courtesy of Sjur Vestli.

Available sensors. Obviously, the specific sensors and sensor uncertainty of the robot impacts the appropriateness of various features. Armed with a laser rangefinder, a robot is well qualified to use geometrically detailed features such as corner features owing to the high-quality angular and depth resolution of the laser scanner. In contrast, a sonar-equipped robot may not have the appropriate tools for corner feature extraction.

Computational power. Vision-based feature extraction can effect a significant computational cost, particularly in robots where the vision sensor processing is performed by one of the robot's main processors.

Environment representation. Feature extraction is an important step toward scene interpretation, and by this token the features extracted must provide information that is consonant with the representation used for the environmental model. For example, nongeometric vision-based features are of little value in purely geometric environmental models but can be of great value in topological models of the environment. Figure 4.35 shows the application of two different representations to the task of modeling an office building hallway. Each approach has advantages and disadvantages, but extraction of line and corner features has much more relevance to the representation on the left. Refer to chapter 5, section 5.5 for a close look at map representations and their relative trade-offs.

In the following two sections, we present specific feature extraction techniques based on the two most popular sensing modalities of mobile robotics: range sensing and visual appearance-based sensing.

4.3.1 Feature extraction based on range data (laser, ultrasonic, vision-based ranging)

Most of today's features extracted from ranging sensors are geometric primitives such as line segments or circles. The main reason for this is that for most other geometric primitives the parametric description of the features becomes too complex and no closed-form solution exists. Here we describe line extraction in detail, demonstrating how the uncertainty models presented above can be applied to the problem of combining multiple sensor measurements. Afterward, we briefly present another very successful feature of indoor mobile robots, the corner feature, and demonstrate how these features can be combined in a single representation.

4.3.1.1 Line extraction

Geometric feature extraction is usually the process of comparing and matching measured sensor data against a predefined description, or template, of the expect feature. Usually, the system is overdetermined in that the number of sensor measurements exceeds the number of feature parameters to be estimated. Since the sensor measurements all have some error, there is no perfectly consistent solution and, instead, the problem is one of optimization. One can, for example, extract the feature that minimizes the discrepancy with all sensor measurements used (e.g,. least-squares estimation).

In this section we present an optimization-based solution to the problem of extracting a line feature from a set of uncertain sensor measurements. For greater detail than is presented below, refer to [14, pp. 15 and 221].

Probabilistic line extraction from uncertain range sensor data. Our goal is to extract a line feature based on a set of sensor measurements as shown in figure 4.36. There is uncertainty associated with each of the noisy range sensor measurements, and so there is no single line that passes through the set. Instead, we wish to select the best possible match, given some optimization criterion.

More formally, suppose n ranging measurement points in polar coordinates $x_i = (\rho_i, \theta_i)$ are produced by the robot's sensors. We know that there is uncertainty associated with each measurement, and so we can model each measurement using two random variables $X_i = (P_i, Q_i)$. In this analysis we assume that uncertainty with respect to the actual value of P and Q is independent. Based on equation (4.56) we can state this formally:

$$E[P_i \cdot P_j] = E[P_i]E[P_j] \qquad \forall\, i, j = 1, ..., n \qquad\qquad (4.62)$$

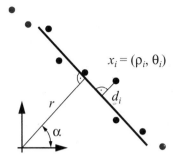

Figure 4.36
Estimating a line in the least-squares sense. The model parameters y (length of the perpendicular) and α (its angle to the abscissa) uniquely describe a line.

$$E[Q_i \cdot Q_j] = E[Q_i]E[Q_j] \qquad \forall \; i,j = 1, ..., n \tag{4.63}$$

$$E[P_i \cdot Q_j] = E[P_i]E[Q_j] \qquad \forall \; i,j = 1, ..., n \tag{4.64}$$

Furthermore, we assume that each random variable is subject to a Gaussian probability density curve, with a mean at the true value and with some specified variance:

$$P_i \sim N(\rho_i, \sigma_{\rho_i}^2) \tag{4.65}$$

$$Q_i \sim N(\theta_i, \sigma_{\theta_i}^2) \tag{4.66}$$

Given some measurement point (ρ, θ), we can calculate the corresponding Euclidean coordinates as $x = \rho \cos\theta$ and $y = \rho \sin\theta$. If there were no error, we would want to find a line for which all measurements lie on that line:

$$\rho \cos\theta \cos\alpha + \rho \sin\theta \sin\alpha - r = \rho \cos(\theta - \alpha) - r = 0 \tag{4.67}$$

Of course there is measurement error, and so this quantity will not be zero. When it is nonzero, this is a measure of the error between the measurement point (ρ, θ) and the line, specifically in terms of the minimum orthogonal distance between the point and the line. It is always important to understand how the error that shall be minimized is being measured. For example a number of line extraction techniques do not minimize this orthogonal point-line distance, but instead the distance parallel to the y-axis between the point and the line. A good illustration of the variety of optimization criteria is available in [17] where several algorithms for fitting circles and ellipses are presented which minimize algebraic and geometric distances.

For each specific (ρ_i, θ_i), we can write the orthogonal distance d_i between (ρ_i, θ_i) and the line as

$$\rho_i \cos(\theta_i - \alpha) - r = d_i .$$ (4.68)

If we consider each measurement to be equally uncertain, we can sum the square of all errors together, for all measurement points, to quantify an overall fit between the line and all of the measurements:

$$S = \sum_i d_i^2 = \sum_i (\rho_i \cos(\theta_i - \alpha) - r)^2$$ (4.69)

Our goal is to minimize S when selecting the line parameters (α, r). We can do so by solving the nonlinear equation system

$$\frac{\partial S}{\partial \alpha} = 0 \qquad \frac{\partial S}{\partial r} = 0 .$$ (4.70)

The above formalism is considered an *unweighted least-squares* solution because no distinction is made from among the measurements. In reality, each sensor measurement may have its own, unique uncertainty based on the geometry of the robot and environment when the measurement was recorded. For example, we know with regard to vision-based stereo ranging that uncertainty and, therefore, variance increases as a square of the distance between the robot and the object. To make use of the variance σ_i^2 that models the uncertainty regarding distance ρ_i of a particular sensor measurement, we compute an individual weight w_i for each measurement using the formula

$$w_i = 1/\sigma_i^2 .$$ (4.71)

Then, equation (4.69) becomes

---

2. The issue of determining an adequate weight when σ_i is given (and perhaps some additional information) is complex in general and beyond the scope of this text. See [9] for a careful treatment.

$$S = \sum w_i d_i^2 = \sum w_i (\rho_i \cos(\theta_i - \alpha) - r)^2. \tag{4.72}$$

It can be shown that the solution to equation (4.70) in the *weighted* least-squares sense[3] is

$$\alpha = \frac{1}{2} \text{atan} \left(\frac{\sum w_i \rho_i^2 \sin 2\theta_i - \frac{2}{\sum w_i} \sum \sum w_i w_j \rho_i \rho_j \cos \theta_i \sin \theta_j}{\sum w_i \rho_i^2 \cos 2\theta_i - \frac{1}{\sum w_i} \sum \sum w_i w_j \rho_i \rho_j \cos(\theta_i + \theta_j)} \right) \tag{4.73}$$

$$r = \frac{\sum w_i \rho_i \cos(\theta_i - \alpha)}{\sum w_i} \tag{4.74}$$

In practice, equation (4.73) uses the four-quadrant arc tangent (atan2)[4].

Let us demonstrate equations (4.73) and (4.74) with a concrete example. The seventeen measurements (ρ_i, θ_i) in table 4.2 have been taken with a laser range sensor installed on a mobile robot. We assume that the uncertainties of all measurements are equal, uncorrelated, and that the robot was static during the measurement process.

Direct application of the above solution equations yields the line defined by $\alpha = 37.36$ and $r = 0.4$. This line represents the best fit in a least-squares sense and is shown visually in figure 4.37.

Propagation of uncertainty during line extraction. Returning to the subject of section 4.2.3, we would like to understand how the uncertainties of specific range sensor measurements propagate to govern the uncertainty of the extracted line. In other words, how does uncertainty in ρ_i and θ_i propagate in equations (4.73) and (4.74) to affect the uncertainty of α and r?

---

3. We follow here the notation of [14] and distinguish a weighted least-squares problem if C_X is diagonal (input errors are mutually independent) and a generalized least-squares problem if C_X is nondiagonal.
4. Atan2 computes $\tan(x/y)^{-1}$ but uses the signs of both x and y to determine the quadrant in which the resulting angles lies. For example $\text{atan2}(-2, -2) = -135°$, whereas $\text{atan2}(2, 2) = -45°$, a distinction which would be lost with a single-argument arc tangent function.

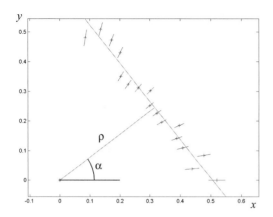

Figure 4.37
Extracted line from laser range measurements (+). The small lines at each measurement point represent the measurement uncertainty σ that is proportional to the square of the measurement distance.

Table 4.2
Measured values

pointing angle of sensor θ_i [deg]	range ρ_i [m]
0	0.5197
5	0.4404
10	0.4850
15	0.4222
20	0.4132
25	0.4371
30	0.3912
35	0.3949
40	0.3919
45	0.4276
50	0.4075
55	0.3956
60	0.4053
65	0.4752
70	0.5032
75	0.5273
80	0.4879

This requires direct application of equation (4.60) with A and R representing the random output variables of α and r respectively. The goal is to derive the 2×2 output covariance matrix

$$C_{AR} = \begin{bmatrix} \sigma_A^2 & \sigma_{AR} \\ \sigma_{AR} & \sigma_R^2 \end{bmatrix}, \tag{4.75}$$

given the $2n \times 2n$ input covariance matrix

$$C_X = \begin{bmatrix} C_P & 0 \\ 0 & C_Q \end{bmatrix} = \begin{bmatrix} diag(\sigma_{\rho_i}^2) & 0 \\ 0 & diag(\sigma_{\theta_i}^2) \end{bmatrix} \tag{4.76}$$

and the system relationships [equations (4.73) and (4.74)]. Then by calculating the Jacobian,

$$F_{PQ} = \begin{bmatrix} \dfrac{\partial \alpha}{\partial P_1} & \dfrac{\partial \alpha}{\partial P_2} & \cdots & \dfrac{\partial \alpha}{\partial P_n} & \dfrac{\partial \alpha}{\partial Q_1} & \dfrac{\partial \alpha}{\partial Q_2} & \cdots & \dfrac{\partial \alpha}{\partial Q_n} \\[2mm] \dfrac{\partial r}{\partial P_1} & \dfrac{\partial r}{\partial P_2} & \cdots & \dfrac{\partial r}{\partial P_n} & \dfrac{\partial r}{\partial Q_1} & \dfrac{\partial r}{\partial Q_2} & \cdots & \dfrac{\partial r}{\partial Q_n} \end{bmatrix} \tag{4.77}$$

we can instantiate the uncertainty propagation equation (4.63) to yield C_{AR}:

$$C_{AR} = F_{PQ} C_X F_{PQ}^T \tag{4.78}$$

Thus we have calculated the probability C_{AR} of the extracted line (α, r) based on the probabilities of the measurement points. For more details about this method refer to [6, 37]

4.3.1.2 Segmentation for line extraction
The previous section described how to extract a line feature given a set of range measurements. Unfortunately, the feature extraction process is significantly more complex than that. A mobile robot does indeed acquire a set of range measurements, but in general the range measurements are not all part of one line. Rather, only some of the range measurements should play a role in line extraction and, further, there may be more than one line

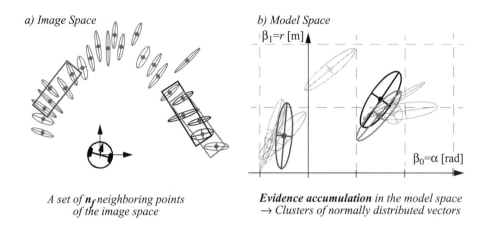

a) Image Space

b) Model Space

A set of n_f neighboring points
of the image space

Evidence accumulation in the model space
→ *Clusters of normally distributed vectors*

Figure 4.38
Clustering: finding neighboring segments of a common line [37].

feature represented in the measurement set. This more realistic scenario is shown in figure 4.38.

The process of dividing up a set of measurements into subsets that can be interpreted one by one is termed *segmentation* and is an important aspect of both range-based and vision-based perception. A diverse set of techniques exist for segmentation of sensor input in general. This general problem is beyond the scope of this text and for details concerning segmentation algorithms, refer to [91, 131].

For example, one segmentation technique is the merging, or *bottom-up* technique in which smaller features are identified and then merged together based on decision criteria to extract the goal features. Suppose that the problem of figure 4.38. is solved through merging. First, one may generate a large number of line segments based on adjacent groups of range measurements. The second step would be to identify line segments that have a high probability of belonging to the same extracted light feature. The simplest measure of the closeness of two line segments[5] $x_1 = [\alpha_1, r_1]$ and $x_2 = [\alpha_2, r_2]$ in the model space is given by Euclidean distance:

$$(x_1 - x_2)^T(x_1 - x_2) = (\alpha_1 - \alpha_2)^2 + (r_1 - r_2)^2 \qquad (4.79)$$

5. Note: The lines are represented in polar coordinates.

The selection of all line segments x_j that contribute to the same line can now be done in a threshold-based manner according to

$$(x_j - \bar{x})^T (x_j - \bar{x}) \leq d_m \tag{4.80}$$

where d_m is a threshold value and $\bar{x}$ is the representation of the reference line (from a model, average of a group of lines, etc.).

But the approach of equation (4.80) does not take into account the fact that for each measurement and therefore for each line segment we have a measure of uncertainty. One can improve upon this equation by selecting line segments that are weighted by their covariance matrix C_j:

$$(x_j - \bar{x})^T (C_j + \bar{C})^{-1} (x_j - \bar{x}) \leq d_m \tag{4.81}$$

The distance measure of equation (4.81) discriminates the distance of uncertain points in model space considerably more effectively by taking uncertainty into account explicitly.

4.3.1.3 Range histogram features
A histogram is a simple way to combine characteristic elements of an image. An angle histogram, as presented in figure 4.39, plots the statistics of lines extracted by two adjacent range measurements. First, a 360-degree scan of the room is taken with the range scanner, and the resulting "hits" are recorded in a map. Then the algorithm measures the relative angle between any two adjacent hits (see figure 4.39b). After compensating for noise in the readings (caused by the inaccuracies in position between adjacent hits), the angle histogram shown in figure 4.39c can be built. The uniform direction of the main walls are clearly visible as peaks in the angle histogram. Detection of peaks yields only two main peaks: one for each pair of parallel walls. This algorithm is very robust with regard to openings in the walls, such as doors and windows, or even cabinets lining the walls.

4.3.1.4 Extracting other geometric features
Line features are of particular value for mobile robots operating in man-made environments, where, for example, building walls and hallway walls are usually straight. In general, a mobile robot makes use of multiple features simultaneously, comprising a *feature set* that is most appropriate for its operating environment. For indoor mobile robots, the line feature is certainly a member of the optimal feature set.

In addition, other geometric kernels consistently appear throughout the indoor man-made environment. *Corner* features are defined as a point feature with an orientation. *Step discontinuities*, defined as a step change perpendicular to the direction of hallway travel,

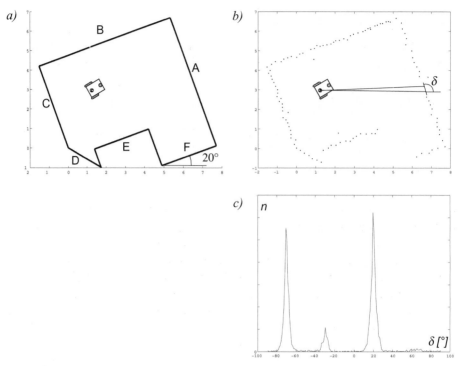

Figure 4.39
Angle histogram [155].

are characterized by their form (convex or concave) and step size. *Doorways*, defined as openings of the appropriate dimensions in walls, are characterized by their width.

Thus, the standard segmentation problem is not so simple as deciding on a mapping from sensor readings to line segments, but rather it is a process in which features of different types are extracted based on the available sensor measurements. Figure 4.40 shows a model of an indoor hallway environment along with both indentation features (i.e., step discontinuities) and doorways.

Note that different feature types can provide quantitatively different information for mobile robot localization. The line feature, for example, provides two degrees of information, angle and distance. But the step feature provides 2D relative position information as well as angle.

The set of useful geometric features is essentially unbounded, and as sensor performance improves we can only expect greater success at the feature extraction level. For example, an interesting improvement upon the line feature described above relates to the

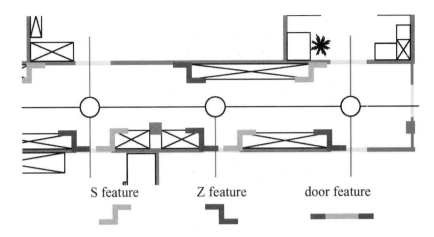

Figure 4.40
Multiple geometric features in a single hallway, including doorways and discontinuities in the width of the hallway.

advent of successful vision-based ranging systems. Because stereo vision provides a full 3D set of range measurements, one can extract plane features in addition to line features from the resulting data set. Plane features are valuable in man-made environments due to the flat walls, floors, and ceilings of our indoor environments. Thus they are promising as another highly informative feature for mobile robots to use for mapping and localization.

4.3.2 Visual appearance based feature extraction

Visual interpretation is, as we have mentioned before, an extremely challenging problem to fully solve. Significant research effort has been dedicated over the past several decades, to inventing algorithms for understanding a scene based on 2D images and the research efforts have slowly produced fruitful results. Covering the field of computer vision and image processing is, of course, beyond the scope of this book. To explore these disciplines, refer to [18, 29, 159]. An overview on some of the most popular approaches can be seen in figure 4.41.

In section 4.1.8 we have already seen vision-based ranging and color-tracking sensors that are commercially available for mobile robots. These specific vision applications have witnessed commercial solutions primarily because the challenges are in both cases relatively well focused and the resulting, problem-specific algorithms are straightforward. But images contain much more than implicit depth information and color blobs. We would like to solve the more general problem of extracting a large number of feature types from images.

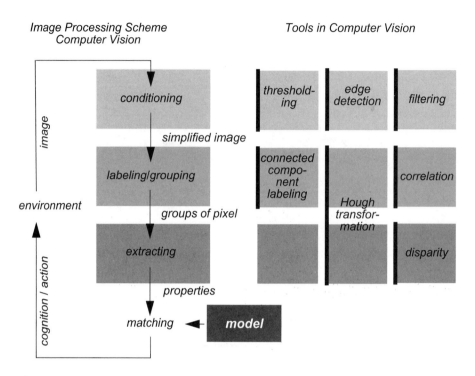

Figure 4.41
Scheme and tools in computer vision. See also [18].

This section presents some appearance-based feature extraction techniques that are relevant to mobile robotics along these lines. Two key requirements must be met for a vision-based feature extraction technique to have mobile robotic relevance. First, the method must operate in real time. Mobile robots move through their environment, and so the processing simply cannot be an off-line operation. Second, the method must be robust to the real-world conditions outside of a laboratory. This means that carefully controlled illumination assumptions and carefully painted objects are unacceptable requirements.

Throughout the following descriptions, keep in mind that vision-based interpretation is primarily about the challenge of *reducing information*. A sonar unit produces perhaps fifty bits of information per second. By contrast, a CCD camera can output 240 *million* bits per second! The sonar produces a tiny amount of information from which we hope to draw broader conclusions. But the CCD chip produces too much information, and this overabundance of information mixes together relevant and irrelevant information haphazardly. For example, we may intend to measure the color of a landmark. The CCD camera does not simply report its color, but also measures the general illumination of the environment, the direction of illumination, the defocusing caused by optics, the side effects imposed by nearby objects with different colors, and so on. Therefore the problem of visual feature extraction is largely one of removing the majority of irrelevant information in an image so that the remaining information unambiguously describes specific features in the environment.

We divide vision-based feature extraction methods into two classes based on their spatial extent. *Spatially localized features* are those features found in subregions of one or more images, corresponding to specific locations in the physical world. *Whole-image features* are those features that are functions of the entire image or set of images, corresponding to a large visually connected area in the physical world.

Before continuing it is important to note that all vision-based sensors supply images with such a significant amount of noise that a first step usually consists of "cleaning" the image before launching any feature extraction algorithm. Therefore, we first describe the process of initial image filtering, or preprocessing.

Image preprocessing. Many image-processing algorithms make use of the second derivative of the image intensity. Indeed, the Laplacian of Gaussian method we studied in section 4.1.8.2 for stereo ranging is such an example. Because of the susceptibility of such high-order derivative algorithms to changes in illumination in the basic signal, it is important to smooth the signal so that changes in intensity are due to real changes in the luminosity of objects in the scene rather than random variations due to imaging noise. A standard approach is convolution with a Gaussian distribution function, as we described earlier in section 4.1.8.2:

$$\hat{I} = G \otimes I \tag{4.82}$$

Of course, when approximated by a discrete kernel, such as a 3 x 3 table, the result is essentially local, weighted averaging:

$$G = \frac{1}{16} \begin{bmatrix} 1 & 2 & 1 \\ 2 & 4 & 2 \\ 1 & 2 & 1 \end{bmatrix} \tag{4.83}$$

Such a low-pass filter effectively removes high-frequency noise, and this in turn causes the first derivative and especially the second derivative of intensity to be far more stable. Because of the importance of gradients and derivatives to image processing, such Gaussian smoothing preprocessing is a popular first step of virtually all computer vision algorithms.

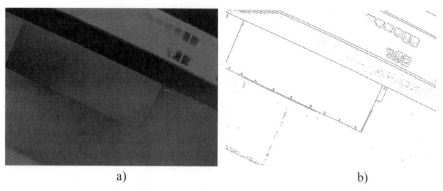

a)   b)

Figure 4.42
(a) Photo of a ceiling lamp. (b) Edges computed from (a).

4.3.2.1   Spatially localized features

In the computer vision community many algorithms assume that the object of interest occupies only a sub-region of the image, and therefore the features being sought are localized spatially within images of the scene. Local image-processing techniques find features that are local to a subset of pixels, and such local features map to specific locations in the physical world. This makes them particularly applicable to geometric models of the robot's environment.

The single most popular local feature extractor used by the mobile robotics community is the edge detector, and so we begin with a discussion of this classic topic in computer vision. However, mobile robots face the specific mobility challenges of obstacle avoidance and localization. In view of obstacle avoidance, we present vision-based extraction of the floor plane, enabling a robot to detect all areas that can be safely traversed. Finally, in view of the need for localization we discuss the role of vision-based feature extraction in the detection of robot navigation landmarks.

Edge detection. Figure 4.42 shows an image of a scene containing a part of a ceiling lamp as well as the edges extracted from this image. Edges define regions in the image plane where a *significant* change in the image brightness takes place. As shown in this example, edge detection significantly reduces the amount of information in an image, and is therefore a useful potential feature during image interpretation. The hypothesis is that edge contours in an image correspond to important scene contours. As figure 4.42b shows, this is not entirely true. There is a difference between the output of an edge detector and an ideal line drawing. Typically, there are missing contours, as well as noise contours, that do not correspond to anything of significance in the scene.

The basic challenge of edge detection is visualized in figure 4.23. Figure 4.23 (top left) shows the 1D section of an ideal edge. But the signal produced by a camera will look more like figure 4.23 (top right). The location of the edge is still at the same x value, but a significant level of high-frequency noise affects the signal quality.

A naive edge detector would simply differentiate, since an edge by definition is located where there are large transitions in intensity. As shown in figure 4.23 (bottom right), differentiation of the noisy camera signal results in subsidiary peaks that can make edge detection very challenging. A far more stable derivative signal can be generated simply by preprocessing the camera signal using the Gaussian smoothing function described above. Below, we present several popular edge detection algorithms, all of which operate on this same basic principle, that the derivative(s) of intensity, following some form of smoothing, comprises the basic signal from which to extract edge features.

Optimal edge detection Canny. The current reference edge detector throughout the vision community was invented by John Canny in 1983 [30]. This edge detector was born out of a formal approach in which Canny treated edge detection as a signal-processing problem in which there are three explicit goals:

- Maximizing the signal-to-noise ratio;

- Achieving the highest precision possible on the location of edges;

- Minimizing the number of edge responses associated with each edge.

The Canny edge extractor smooths the image I via Gaussian convolution and then looks for maxima in the (rectified) derivative. In practice the smoothing and differentiation are combined into one operation because

$$(G \otimes I)' = G' \otimes I \tag{4.84}$$

Thus, smoothing the image by convolving with a Gaussian G_σ and then differentiating is equivalent to convolving the image with G'_σ, the first derivative of a Gaussian (figure 4.43b).

We wish to detect edges in any direction. Since G' is directional, this requires application of two perpendicular filters, just as we did for the Laplacian in equation (4.35). We define the two filters as $f_V(x, y) = G'_\sigma(x)G_\sigma(y)$ and $f_H(x, y) = G'_\sigma(y)G_\sigma(x)$. The result is a basic algorithm for detecting edges at arbitrary orientations:

The algorithm for detecting edge pixels at an arbitrary orientation is as follows:

1. Convolve the image $I(x, y)$ with $f_V(x, y)$ and $f_H(x, y)$ to obtain the gradient components $R_V(x, y)$ and $R_H(x, y)$, respectively.

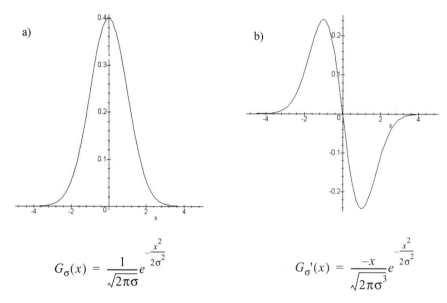

$$G_\sigma(x) = \frac{1}{\sqrt{2\pi}\sigma}e^{-\frac{x^2}{2\sigma^2}}$$

$$G_\sigma'(x) = \frac{-x}{\sqrt{2\pi}\sigma^3}e^{-\frac{x^2}{2\sigma^2}}$$

Figure 4.43
(a) A Gaussian function. (b) The first derivative of a Gaussian function.

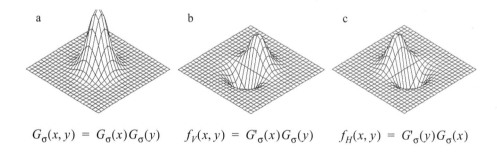

$$G_\sigma(x, y) = G_\sigma(x)G_\sigma(y) \qquad f_V(x, y) = G'_\sigma(x)G_\sigma(y) \qquad f_H(x, y) = G'_\sigma(y)G_\sigma(x)$$

Figure 4.44
(a) Two-dimensional Gaussian function. (b) Vertical filter. (c) Horizontal filter.

2. Define the square of the gradient magnitude $R(x, y) = R_V^2(x, y) + R_H^2(x, y)$.

3. Mark those peaks in $R(x, y)$ that are above some predefined threshold T.

Once edge pixels are extracted, the next step is to construct complete edges. A popular next step in this process is *nonmaxima suppression*. Using edge direction information, the process involves revisiting the gradient value and determining whether or not it is at a local

Figure 4.45
(a) Example of an edge image; (b) Nonmaxima suppression of (a).

maximum. If not, then the value is set to zero. This causes only the maxima to be preserved, and thus reduces the thickness of all edges to a single pixel (figure 4.45).

Finally, we are ready to go from edge pixels to complete edges. First, find adjacent (or connected) sets of edges and group them into ordered lists. Second, use thresholding to eliminate the weakest edges.

Gradient edge detectors. On a mobile robot, computation time must be minimized to retain the real-time behavior of the robot. Therefore simpler, discrete kernel operators are commonly used to approximate the behavior of the Canny edge detector. One such early operator was developed by Roberts in 1965 [29]. He used two 2 x 2 masks to calculate the gradient across the edge in two diagonal directions. Let r_1 be the value calculated from the first mask and r_2 from the second mask. Roberts obtained the gradient magnitude $|G|$ with the equation

$$|G| \cong \sqrt{r_1^2 + r_2^2} \; ; \quad r_1 = \begin{bmatrix} -1 & 0 \\ 0 & 1 \end{bmatrix} \; ; \quad r_2 = \begin{bmatrix} 0 & -1 \\ 1 & 0 \end{bmatrix} \qquad (4.85)$$

Prewitt (1970) [29] used two 3 x 3 masks oriented in the row and column directions. Let p_1 be the value calculated from the first mask and p_2 the value calculated from the second mask. Prewitt obtained the gradient magnitude $|G|$ and the gradient direction θ taken in a clockwise angle with respect to the column axis shown in the following equation.

$$|G| \cong \sqrt{p_1^2 + p_2^2} \; ;$$

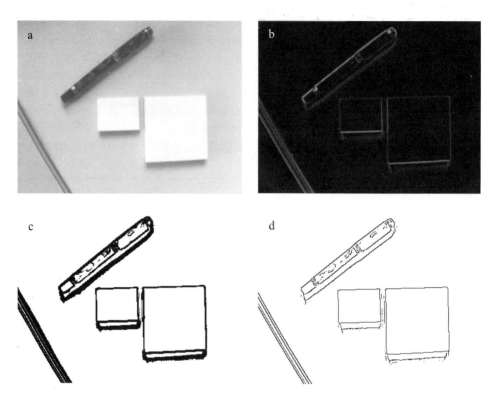

Figure 4.46
Example of vision-based feature extraction with the different processing steps: (a) raw image data; (b) filtered image using a Sobel filter; (c) thresholding, selection of edge pixels (d) nonmaxima suppression.

$$\theta \cong \mathrm{atan}\left(\frac{p_1}{p_2}\right) \; ; \quad p_1 = \begin{bmatrix} -1 & -1 & -1 \\ 0 & 0 & 0 \\ 1 & 1 & 1 \end{bmatrix} \; ; \; p_2 = \begin{bmatrix} -1 & 0 & 1 \\ -1 & 0 & 1 \\ -1 & 0 & 1 \end{bmatrix} \qquad (4.86)$$

In the same year Sobel [29] used, like Prewitt, two 3 x 3 masks oriented in the row and column direction. Let s_1 be the value calculated from the first mask and s_2 the value calculated from the second mask. Sobel obtained the same results as Prewitt for the gradient magnitude $|G|$ and the gradient direction θ taken in a clockwise angle with respect to the column axis. Figure 4.46 shows application of the Sobel filter to a visual scene.

$$|G| \cong \sqrt{s_1^2 + s_2^2} \; ;$$

$$\theta \cong \operatorname{atan}\!\left(\frac{s_1}{s_2}\right) ; \quad s_1 = \begin{bmatrix} -1 & -2 & -1 \\ 0 & 0 & 0 \\ 1 & 2 & 1 \end{bmatrix} ; \quad s_2 = \begin{bmatrix} -1 & 0 & 1 \\ -2 & 0 & 2 \\ -1 & 0 & 1 \end{bmatrix} \tag{4.87}$$

Dynamic thresholding. Many image-processing algorithms have generally been tested in laboratory conditions or by using static image databases. Mobile robots, however, operate in dynamic real-world settings where there is no guarantee regarding optimal or even stable illumination. A vision system for mobile robots has to adapt to the changing illumination. Therefore a constant threshold level for edge detection is not suitable. The same scene with different illumination results in edge images with considerable differences. To dynamically adapt the edge detector to the ambient light, a more adaptive threshold is required, and one approach involves calculating that threshold based on a statistical analysis of the image about to be processed.

To do this, a histogram of the gradient magnitudes of the processed image is calculated (figure 4.47). With this simple histogram it is easy to consider only the n pixels with the highest gradient magnitude for further calculation steps. The pixels are counted backward starting at the highest magnitude. The gradient magnitude of the point where n is reached will be used as the temporary threshold value.

The motivation for this technique is that the n pixels with the highest gradient are expected to be the most relevant ones for the processed image. Furthermore, for each image, the same number of relevant edge pixels is considered, independent of illumination. It is important to pay attention to the fact that the number of pixels in the edge image delivered by the edge detector is not n. Because most detectors use nonmaxima suppression, the number of edge pixels will be further reduced.

Straight edge extraction: Hough transforms. In mobile robotics the straight edge is often extracted as a specific feature. Straight vertical edges, for example, can be used as clues to the location of doorways and hallway intersections. The Hough transform is a simple tool for extracting edges of a particular shape[16, 18]. Here we explain its application to the problem of extracting straight edges.

Suppose a pixel (x_p, y_p) in the image I is part of an edge. Any straight-line edge including point (x_p, y_p) must satisfy the equation: $y_p = m_1 x_p + b_1$. This equation can only be satisfied with a constrained set of possible values for m_1 and b_1. In other words, this equation is satisfied only by lines through I that pass through (x_p, y_p).

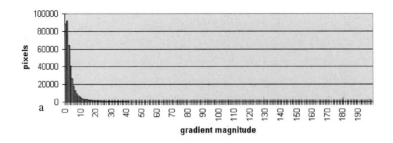

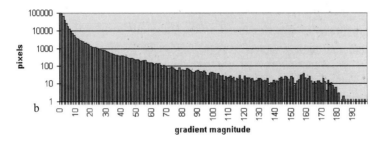

Figure 4.47
(a) Number of pixels with a specific gradient magnitude in the image of figure 4.46(b). (b) Same as (a), but with logarithmic scale

Now consider a second pixel, (x_q, y_q) in I. Any line passing through this second pixel must satisfy the equation: $y_q = m_2 x_q + b_2$. What if $m_1 = m_2$ and $b_1 = b_2$? Then the line defined by both equations is one and the same: it is the line that passes through both (x_p, y_p) and (x_q, y_q).

More generally, for all pixels that are part of a single straight line through I, they must all lie on a line defined by the *same* values for m and b. The general definition of this line is, of course, $y = mx + b$. The Hough transform uses this basic property, creating a mechanism so that each edge pixel can "vote" for various values of the (m, b) parameters. The lines with the most votes at the end are straight edge features:

• Create a 2D array A with axes that tessellate the values of m and b.

• Initialize the array to zero: $A[m, b] = 0$ for all values of m, b.

• For each edge pixel (x_p, y_p) in I, loop over all values of m and b:
  if $y_p = mx_p + b$ then $A[m, b]$+=1.

• Search the cells in A to identify those with the largest value. Each such cell's indices (m, b) correspond to an extracted straight-line edge in I.

Floor plane extraction. Obstacle avoidance is one of the basic tasks required of most mobile robots. Range-based sensors provide effective means for identifying most types of obstacles facing a mobile robot. In fact, because they directly measure range to objects in the world, range-based sensors such as ultrasonic and laser rangefinders are inherently well suited for the task of obstacle detection. However, each ranging sensor has limitations. Ultrasonics have poor angular resolution and suffer from coherent reflection at shallow angles. Most laser rangefinders are 2D, only detecting obstacles penetrating a specific sensed plane. Stereo vision and depth from focus require the obstacles and floor plane to have texture in order to enable correspondence and blurring respectively.

In addition to each individual shortcoming, range-based obstacle detection systems will have difficulty detecting small or flat objects that are on the ground. For example, a vacuum cleaner may need to avoid large, flat objects, such as paper or money left on the floor. In addition, different types of floor surfaces cannot easily be discriminated by ranging. For example, a sidewalk-following robot will have difficulty discriminating grass from pavement using range sensing alone.

Floor plane extraction is a vision-based approach for identifying the traversable portions of the ground. Because it makes use of edges and color in a variety of implementations, such obstacle detection systems can easily detect obstacles in cases that are difficult for traditional ranging devices.

As is the case with all vision-based algorithms, floor plane extraction succeeds only in environments that satisfy several important assumptions:

• Obstacles differ in appearance from the ground.

• The ground is flat and its angle to the camera is known.

• There are no overhanging obstacles.

The first assumption is a requirement in order to discriminate the ground from obstacles using its appearance. A stronger version of this assumption, sometimes invoked, states that the ground is uniform in appearance and different from all obstacles. The second and third assumptions allow floor plane extraction algorithms to estimate the robot's distance to obstacles detected.

Floor plane extraction in artificial environments. In a controlled environment, the floor, walls and obstacles can be designed so that the walls and obstacles appear significantly different from the floor in a camera image. Shakey, the first autonomous robot developed from 1966 through 1972 at SRI, used vision-based floor plane extraction in a manufactured environment for obstacle detection [115]. Shakey's artificial environment used textureless, homogeneously white floor tiles. Furthermore, the base of each wall was painted with a high-contrast strip of black paint and the edges of all simple polygonal obstacles were also painted black.

In Shakey's environment, edges corresponded to nonfloor objects, and so the floor plane extraction algorithm simply consisted of the application of an edge detector to the monochrome camera image. The lowest edges detected in an image corresponded to the closest obstacles, and the direction of straight-line edges extracted from the image provided clues regarding not only the position but also the orientation of walls and polygonal obstacles.

Although this very simple appearance-based obstacle detection system was successful, it should be noted that special care had to be taken at the time to create indirect lighting in the laboratory such that shadows were not cast, as the system would falsely interpret the edges of shadows as obstacles.

Adaptive floor plane extraction. Floor plane extraction has succeeded not only in artificial environments but in real-world mobile robot demonstrations in which a robot avoids both static obstacles such as walls and dynamic obstacles such as passersby, based on segmentation of the floor plane at a rate of several hertz. Such floor plane extraction algorithms tend to use edge detection and color detection jointly while making certain assumptions regarding the floor, for example, the floor's maximum texture or approximate color range [78].

Each system based on fixed assumptions regarding the floor's appearance is limited to only those environments satisfying its constraints. A more recent approach is that of adaptive floor plane extraction, whereby the parameters defining the expected appearance of the floor are allowed to vary over time. In the simplest instance, one can assume that the pixels at the bottom of the image (i.e., closest to the robot) are part of the floor and contain no obstacles. Then, statistics computed on these "floor sample" pixels can be used to classify the remaining image pixels.

The key challenge in adaptive systems is the choice of what statistics to compute using the "floor sample" pixels. The most popular solution is to construct one or more *histograms* based on the floor sample pixel values. Under "edge detection" above, we found histograms to be useful in determining the best cut point in edge detection thresholding algorithms. Histograms are also useful as discrete representations of distributions. Unlike the Gaussian representation, a histogram can capture multi-modal distributions. Histograms can also be updated very quickly and use very little processor memory. An intensity histogram of the "floor sample" subregion I_f of image I is constructed as follows:

- As preprocessing, smooth I_f, using a Gaussian smoothing operator.

- Initialize a histogram array H with n intensity values: $H[i] = 0$ for $i = 1, ..., n$.

- For every pixel (x, y) in I_f increment the histogram: $H[I_f(x, y)] += 1$.

The histogram array H serves as a characterization of the appearance of the floor plane. Often, several 1D histograms are constructed, corresponding to intensity, hue, and saturation, for example. Classification of each pixel in I as floor plane or obstacle is performed

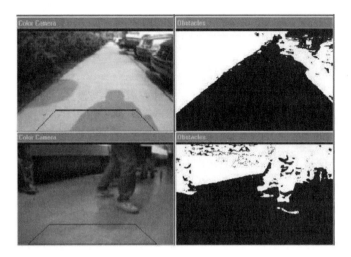

Figure 4.48
Examples of adaptive floor plane extraction. The trapezoidal polygon identifies the floor sampling region.

by looking at the appropriate histogram counts for the qualities of the target pixel. For example, if the target pixel has a hue that never occurred in the "floor sample," then the corresponding hue histogram will have a count of zero. When a pixel references a histogram value below a predefined threshold, that pixel is classified as an obstacle.

Figure 4.48 shows an appearance-based floor plane extraction algorithm operating on both indoor and outdoor images [151]. Note that, unlike the static floor extraction algorithm, the adaptive algorithm is able to successfully classify a human shadow due to the adaptive histogram representation. An interesting extension of the work has been to not use the static floor sample assumption, but rather to record visual history and to use, as the floor sample, only the portion of prior visual images that has successfully rolled under the robot during mobile robot motion.

Appearance-based extraction of the floor plane has been demonstrated on both indoor and outdoor robots for real-time obstacle avoidance with a bandwidth of up to 10 Hz. Applications include robotics lawn mowing, social indoor robots, and automated electric wheelchairs.

4.3.2.2 Whole-image features
A single visual image provides so much information regarding a robot's immediate surroundings that an alternative to searching the image for spatially localized features is to make use of the information captured by the entire image to extract a whole-image feature.

 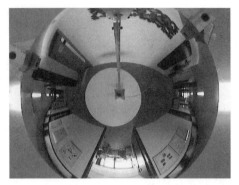

Figure 4.49
Two typical images acquired by the OmniCam catadioptric camera system.

Whole-image features are not designed to identify specific spatial structures such as obstacles or the position of specific landmarks. Rather, they serve as compact representations of the entire local region. From the perspective of robot localization, the goal is to extract one or more features from the image that are correlated well with the robot's position. In other words, small changes in robot position should cause only small changes to whole-image features, while large changes in robot position should cause correspondingly large changes to whole-image features.

We present two techniques for whole-image feature extraction below. The first technique is another popular application of the image histogramming approach. The resulting image histogram comprises a set of whole-image features derived directly from the pixel information of an image. The second technique, tiered extraction, covers approaches in which a whole-image feature is built by first extracting spatially localized features, then composing these features together to form a single metafeature.

Direct extraction: image histograms. Recall that we wish to design whole-image features that are insensitive to a small amount of robot motion while registering significant changes for large-scale robot motion. A logical first step in designing a vision-based sensor for this purpose is to maximize the field of view of the camera. As the field of view increases, a small-scale structure in the robot's environment occupies a smaller proportion of the image, thereby mitigating the impact of individual scene objects on image characteristics. The catadioptric camera system, now very popular in mobile robotics, offers an extremely wide field of view [114]. This imaging system consists of a high-quality CCD camera mounted, together with customized optics, toward a parabolic mirror. The image provides a 360-degree view of the robot's environment, as shown in figure 4.49.

The catadioptric image is a 360-degree image warped onto a 2D image surface. Because of this, it offers another critical advantage in terms of sensitivity to small-scale robot motion. If the camera is mounted vertically on the robot so that the image represents the environment surrounding the robot (i.e., its horizon), then rotation of the camera and robot simply results in image rotation. In short, the catadioptric camera can be rotationally invariant to field of view.

Of course, mobile robot rotation will still change the image; that is, pixel positions will change, although the new image will simply be a rotation of the original image. But we intend to extract image features via histogramming. Because histogramming is a function of the set of pixel values and not the position of each pixel, the process is pixel position invariant. When combined with the catadioptric camera's field of view invariance, we can create a system that is invariant to robot rotation and insensitive to small-scale robot translation.

A color camera's output image generally contains useful information along multiple *bands*: r, g, and b values as well as hue, saturation, and luminance values. The simplest histogram-based extraction strategy is to build separate 1D histograms characterizing each band. Given a color camera image, G, the first step is to create mappings from G to each of the n available bands. We use G_i to refer to an array storing the values in band i for all pixels in G. Each band-specific histogram H_i is calculated as before:

- As preprocessing, smooth G_i using a Gaussian smoothing operator.

- Initialize H_i with n levels: $H[j] = 0$ for $j = 1, ..., n$.

- For every pixel (x,y) in G_i, increment the histogram: $H_i[G_i[x, y]]+=1$.

Given the image shown in figure 4.49, the image histogram technique extracts six histograms (for each of r, g, b, hue, saturation, and luminance) as shown in figure 4.50. In order to make use of such histograms as whole-image features, we need ways to compare to histograms to quantify the likelihood that the histograms map to nearby robot positions. The problem of defining useful histogram distance metrics is itself an important subfield within the image retrieval field. For an overview refer to [127]. One of the most successful distance metrics encountered in mobile robot localization is the *Jeffrey divergence*. Given two histograms H and K, with h_i and k_i denoting the histogram entries, the Jeffrey divergence $d(H, K)$ is defined as

$$d(H, K) = \sum_i \left(h_i \log \frac{2h_i}{h_i + k_i} + k_i \log \frac{2k_i}{h_i + k_i} \right) \tag{4.88}$$

Using measures such as the Jeffrey divergence, mobile robots have used whole-image histogram features to identify their position in real time against a database of previously

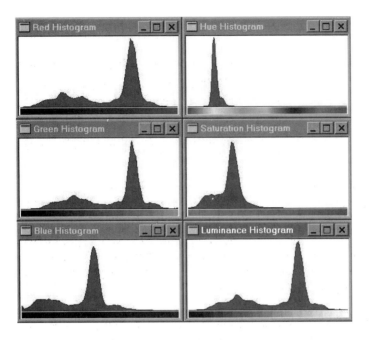

Figure 4.50
Six 1D histograms of the image above. A 5 x 5 smoothing filter was convolved with each band before histogramming.

recorded images of locations in their environment. Using this whole-image extraction approach, a robot can readily recover the particular hallway or particular room in which it is located [152].

Tiered extraction: image fingerprint extraction. An alternative to extracting a whole-image feature directly from pixel values is to use a tiered approach: first identify spatially localized features in the image, then translate from this set of local features to a single metafeature for the whole image. We describe one particular implementation of this approach, in which the resulting whole-image feature is called the image *fingerprint* [95]. As with other whole-image extraction techniques, because low sensitivity to small robot motions is desired, the system makes use of a 360-degree panoramic image, here constructed as a mosaic of images captured with a standard CMOS chip camera.

The first extraction tier searches the panoramic image for spatially localized features: vertical edges and sixteen discrete hues of color. The vertical edge detector is a straightforward gradient approach implementing a horizontal difference operator. Vertical edges are "voted upon" by each edge pixel just as in a vertical edge Hough transform. As described

VBvvvOvvvLvBEvvvvvvBvL (Pc)

KvLvvvJvvvvvvBvvvLvBEvOvN (Pw3)

Figure 4.51
Two panoramic images and their associated fingerprint sequences [95].

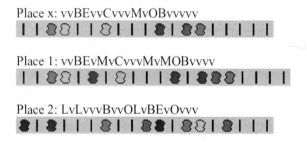

Place x: vvBEvvCvvvMvOBvvvvv

Place 1: vvBEvMvCvvvMvMOBvvvv

Place 2: LvLvvvBvvOLvBEvOvvv

Figure 4.52
Three actual string sequences. The top two are strings extracted by the robot at the same position [95].

in section 4.3.2.1, an adaptive threshold is used to reduce the number of edges. Suppose the Hough table's tallies for each candidate vertical line have a mean μ and a standard deviation σ. The chosen threshold is simply $\mu + \sigma$.

Vertical color bands are identified in largely the same way, identifying statistics over the occurrence of each color, then filtering out all candidate color patches except those with tallies greater than $\mu + \sigma$. Figure 4.51 shows two sample panoramic images and their associated fingerprints. Note that each fingerprint is converted to an ASCII string representation.

Just as with histogram distance metrics in the case of image histogramming, we need a quantifiable measure of the distance between two fingerprint strings. String-matching algorithms are yet another large field of study, with particularly interesting applications today in the areas of genetics [34]. Note that we may have strings that differ not just in a single element value, but even in their overall length. For example, figure 4.52 depicts three actual sequences generated using the above algorithm. The top string should match *Place 1*, but note that there are deletions and insertions between the two strings.

The technique used in the fingerprinting approach for string differencing is known as a *minimum energy algorithm*. Taken from the stereo vision community, this optimization-based algorithm will find the minimum energy required to "transform" one sequence into another sequence. The result is a distance metric that is relatively insensitive to the addition or subtraction of individual local features while still able to robustly identify the correct matching string in a variety of circumstances.

It should be clear from the previous two sections that whole-image feature extraction is straightforward with vision-based perception and can be applicable to mobile robot local-ization. But it is spatially localized features that continue to play a dominant role because of their immediate application to the more urgent need for real-time obstacle avoidance.

5 Mobile Robot Localization

5.1 Introduction

Navigation is one of the most challenging competences required of a mobile robot. Success in navigation requires success at the four building blocks of navigation: *perception,* the robot must interpret its sensors to extract meaningful data; *localization,* the robot must determine its position in the environment (figure 5.1); *cognition,* the robot must decide how to act to achieve its goals; and *motion control,* the robot must modulate its motor outputs to achieve the desired trajectory.

Of these four components (figure 5.2), localization has received the greatest research attention in the past decade and, as a result, significant advances have been made on this front. In this chapter, we explore the successful localization methodologies of recent years. First, section 5.2 describes how sensor and effector uncertainty is responsible for the difficulties of localization. Then, section 5.3 describes two extreme approaches to dealing with the challenge of robot localization: avoiding localization altogether, and performing explicit map-based localization. The remainder of the chapter discusses the question of rep-

Figure 5.1
Where am I?

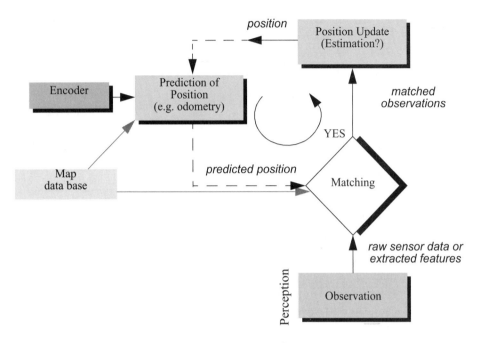

Figure 5.2
General schematic for mobile robot localization.

resentation, then presents case studies of successful localization systems using a variety of representations and techniques to achieve mobile robot localization competence.

5.2   The Challenge of Localization: Noise and Aliasing

If one could attach an accurate GPS (global positioning system) sensor to a mobile robot, much of the localization problem would be obviated. The GPS would inform the robot of its exact position, indoors and outdoors, so that the answer to the question, "Where am I?", would always be immediately available. Unfortunately, such a sensor is not currently practical. The existing GPS network provides accuracy to within several meters, which is unacceptable for localizing human-scale mobile robots as well as miniature mobile robots such as desk robots and the body-navigating nanorobots of the future. Furthermore, GPS technologies cannot function indoors or in obstructed areas and are thus limited in their workspace.

But, looking beyond the limitations of GPS, localization implies more than knowing one's absolute position in the Earth's reference frame. Consider a robot that is interacting with humans. This robot may need to identify its absolute position, but its relative position with respect to target humans is equally important. Its localization task can include identifying humans using its sensor array, then computing its relative position to the humans. Furthermore, during the *cognition* step a robot will select a strategy for achieving its goals. If it intends to reach a particular location, then localization may not be enough. The robot may need to acquire or build an environmental model, a *map*, that aids it in planning a path to the goal. Once again, localization means more than simply determining an absolute pose in space; it means building a map, then identifying the robot's position relative to that map.

Clearly, the robot's sensors and effectors play an integral role in all the above forms of localization. It is because of the inaccuracy and incompleteness of these sensors and effectors that localization poses difficult challenges. This section identifies important aspects of this sensor and effector suboptimality.

5.2.1 Sensor noise

Sensors are the fundamental robot input for the process of *perception*, and therefore the degree to which sensors can discriminate the world state is critical. Sensor noise induces a limitation on the consistency of sensor readings in the same environmental state and, therefore, on the number of useful bits available from each sensor reading. Often, the source of sensor noise problems is that some environmental features are not captured by the robot's representation and are thus overlooked.

For example, a vision system used for indoor navigation in an office building may use the color values detected by its color CCD camera. When the sun is hidden by clouds, the illumination of the building's interior changes because of the windows throughout the building. As a result, hue values are not constant. The color CCD appears noisy from the robot's perspective as if subject to random error, and the hue values obtained from the CCD camera will be unusable, unless the robot is able to note the position of the sun and clouds in its representation.

Illumination dependence is only one example of the apparent noise in a vision-based sensor system. Picture jitter, signal gain, blooming, and blurring are all additional sources of noise, potentially reducing the useful content of a color video image.

Consider the noise level (i.e., apparent random error) of ultrasonic range-measuring sensors (e.g., sonars) as discussed in section 4.1.2.3. When a sonar transducer emits sound toward a relatively smooth and angled surface, much of the signal will coherently reflect away, failing to generate a return echo. Depending on the material characteristics, a small amount of energy may return nonetheless. When this level is close to the gain threshold of the sonar sensor, then the sonar will, at times, succeed and, at other times, fail to detect the object. From the robot's perspective, a virtually unchanged environmental state will result in two different possible sonar readings: one short and one long.

The poor signal-to-noise ratio of a sonar sensor is further confounded by interference between multiple sonar emitters. Often, research robots have between twelve and forty-eight sonars on a single platform. In acoustically reflective environments, multipath interference is possible between the sonar emissions of one transducer and the echo detection circuitry of another transducer. The result can be dramatically large errors (i.e., underestimation) in ranging values due to a set of coincidental angles. Such errors occur rarely, less than 1% of the time, and are virtually random from the robot's perspective.

In conclusion, sensor noise reduces the useful information content of sensor readings. Clearly, the solution is to take multiple readings into account, employing temporal fusion or multisensor fusion to increase the overall information content of the robot's inputs.

5.2.2 Sensor aliasing

A second shortcoming of mobile robot sensors causes them to yield little information content, further exacerbating the problem of perception and, thus, localization. The problem, known as *sensor aliasing*, is a phenomenon that humans rarely encounter. The human sensory system, particularly the visual system, tends to receive unique inputs in each unique local state. In other words, every different place looks different. The power of this unique mapping is only apparent when one considers situations where this fails to hold. Consider moving through an unfamiliar building that is completely dark. When the visual system sees only black, one's localization system quickly degrades. Another useful example is that of a human-sized maze made from tall hedges. Such mazes have been created for centuries, and humans find them extremely difficult to solve without landmarks or clues because, without visual uniqueness, human localization competence degrades rapidly.

In robots, the nonuniqueness of sensor readings, or *sensor aliasing*, is the norm and not the exception. Consider a narrow-beam rangefinder such as an ultrasonic or infrared rangefinder. This sensor provides range information in a single direction without any additional data regarding material composition such as color, texture, and hardness. Even for a robot with several such sensors in an array, there are a variety of environmental states that would trigger the same sensor values across the array. Formally, there is a many-to-one mapping from environmental states to the robot's perceptual inputs. Thus, the robot's percepts cannot distinguish from among these many states. A classic problem with sonar-based robots involves distinguishing between humans and inanimate objects in an indoor setting. When facing an apparent obstacle in front of itself, should the robot say "Excuse me" because the obstacle may be a moving human, or should the robot plan a path around the object because it may be a cardboard box? With sonar alone, these states are aliased and differentiation is impossible.

The problem posed to navigation because of sensor aliasing is that, even with noise-free sensors, the amount of information is generally insufficient to identify the robot's position from a single-percept reading. Thus techniques must be employed by the robot programmer that base the robot's localization on a series of readings and, thus, sufficient information to recover the robot's position over time.

5.2.3 Effector noise

The challenges of localization do not lie with sensor technologies alone. Just as robot sensors are noisy, limiting the information content of the signal, so robot effectors are also noisy. In particular, a single action taken by a mobile robot may have several different possible results, even though from the robot's point of view the initial state before the action was taken is well known.

In short, mobile robot effectors introduce uncertainty about future state. Therefore the simple act of moving tends to increase the uncertainty of a mobile robot. There are, of course, exceptions. Using *cognition,* the motion can be carefully planned so as to minimize this effect, and indeed sometimes to actually result in more certainty. Furthermore, when the robot's actions are taken in concert with careful interpretation of sensory feedback, it can compensate for the uncertainty introduced by noisy actions using the information provided by the sensors.

First, however, it is important to understand the precise nature of the effector noise that impacts mobile robots. It is important to note that, from the robot's point of view, this error in motion is viewed as an error in odometry, or the robot's inability to estimate its own position over time using knowledge of its kinematics and dynamics. The true source of error generally lies in an incomplete model of the environment. For instance, the robot does not model the fact that the floor may be sloped, the wheels may slip, and a human may push the robot. All of these unmodeled sources of error result in inaccuracy between the physical motion of the robot, the intended motion of the robot, and the proprioceptive sensor estimates of motion.

In odometry (wheel sensors only) and dead reckoning (also heading sensors) the position update is based on *proprioceptive* sensors. The movement of the robot, sensed with wheel encoders or heading sensors or both, is integrated to compute position. Because the sensor measurement errors are integrated, the position error accumulates over time. Thus the position has to be updated from time to time by other localization mechanisms. Otherwise the robot is not able to maintain a meaningful position estimate in the long run.

In the following we concentrate on odometry based on the wheel sensor readings of a differential-drive robot only (see also [4, 57, 58]). Using additional heading sensors (e.g., gyroscope) can help to reduce the cumulative errors, but the main problems remain the same.

There are many sources of odometric error, from environmental factors to resolution:

- Limited resolution during integration (time increments, measurement resolution, etc.);
- Misalignment of the wheels (deterministic);
- Uncertainty in the wheel diameter and in particular unequal wheel diameter (deterministic);
- Variation in the contact point of the wheel;

- Unequal floor contact (slipping, nonplanar surface, etc.).

Some of the errors might be *deterministic (systematic)*, thus they can be eliminated by proper calibration of the system. However, there are still a number of *nondeterministic (random)* errors which remain, leading to uncertainties in position estimation over time. From a geometric point of view one can classify the errors into three types:

1. Range error: integrated path length (distance) of the robot's movement
   → sum of the wheel movements

2. Turn error: similar to range error, but for turns
   → difference of the wheel motions

3. Drift error: difference in the error of the wheels leads to an error in the robot's angular orientation

Over long periods of time, turn and drift errors far outweigh range errors, since their contribution to the overall position error is nonlinear. Consider a robot whose position is initially perfectly well-known, moving forward in a straight line along the x-axis. The error in the y-position introduced by a move of d meters will have a component of $d \sin \Delta\theta$, which can be quite large as the angular error $\Delta\theta$ grows. Over time, as a mobile robot moves about the environment, the rotational error between its internal reference frame and its original reference frame grows quickly. As the robot moves away from the origin of these reference frames, the resulting linear error in position grows quite large. It is instructive to establish an error model for odometric accuracy and see how the errors propagate over time.

5.2.4 An error model for odometric position estimation

Generally the pose (position) of a robot is represented by the vector

$$p = \begin{bmatrix} x \\ y \\ \theta \end{bmatrix} \tag{5.1}$$

For a differential-drive robot the position can be estimated starting from a known position by integrating the movement (summing the incremental travel distances). For a discrete system with a fixed sampling interval Δt the incremental travel distances $(\Delta x; \Delta y; \Delta\theta)$ are

$$\Delta x = \Delta s \cos(\theta + \Delta\theta / 2) \tag{5.2}$$

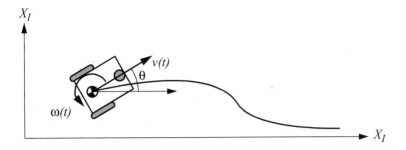

Figure 5.3
Movement of a differential-drive robot.

$$\Delta y = \Delta s \sin(\theta + \Delta\theta/2) \tag{5.3}$$

$$\Delta\theta = \frac{\Delta s_r - \Delta s_l}{b} \tag{5.4}$$

$$\Delta s = \frac{\Delta s_r + \Delta s_l}{2} \tag{5.5}$$

where

$(\Delta x; \Delta y; \Delta\theta)$ = path traveled in the last sampling interval;

$\Delta s_r; \Delta s_l$ = traveled distances for the right and left wheel respectively;

b = distance between the two wheels of differential-drive robot.

Thus we get the updated position p' :

$$p' = \begin{bmatrix} x' \\ y' \\ \theta' \end{bmatrix} = p + \begin{bmatrix} \Delta s \cos(\theta + \Delta\theta/2) \\ \Delta s \sin(\theta + \Delta\theta/2) \\ \Delta\theta \end{bmatrix} = \begin{bmatrix} x \\ y \\ \theta \end{bmatrix} + \begin{bmatrix} \Delta s \cos(\theta + \Delta\theta/2) \\ \Delta s \sin(\theta + \Delta\theta/2) \\ \Delta\theta \end{bmatrix} \tag{5.6}$$

By using the relation for $(\Delta s; \Delta\theta)$ of equations (5.4) and (5.5) we further obtain the basic equation for odometric position update (for differential drive robots):

$$p' = f(x, y, \theta, \Delta s_r, \Delta s_l) = \begin{bmatrix} x \\ y \\ \theta \end{bmatrix} + \begin{bmatrix} \dfrac{\Delta s_r + \Delta s_l}{2} \cos\left(\theta + \dfrac{\Delta s_r - \Delta s_l}{2b}\right) \\[2ex] \dfrac{\Delta s_r + \Delta s_l}{2} \sin\left(\theta + \dfrac{\Delta s_r - \Delta s_l}{2b}\right) \\[2ex] \dfrac{\Delta s_r - \Delta s_l}{b} \end{bmatrix} \qquad (5.7)$$

As we discussed earlier, odometric position updates can give only a very rough estimate of the actual position. Owing to integration errors of the uncertainties of p and the motion errors during the incremental motion $(\Delta s_r; \Delta s_l)$ the position error based on odometry integration grows with time.

In the next step we will establish an error model for the integrated position p' to obtain the covariance matrix $\Sigma_{p'}$ of the odometric position estimate. To do so, we assume that at the starting point the initial covariance matrix Σ_p is known. For the motion increment $(\Delta s_r; \Delta s_l)$ we assume the following covariance matrix Σ_Δ:

$$\Sigma_\Delta = covar(\Delta s_r, \Delta s_l) = \begin{bmatrix} k_r |\Delta s_r| & 0 \\ 0 & k_l |\Delta s_l| \end{bmatrix} \qquad (5.8)$$

where Δs_r and Δs_l are the distances traveled by each wheel, and k_r, k_l are error constants representing the nondeterministic parameters of the motor drive and the wheel-floor interaction. As you can see, in equation (5.8) we made the following assumptions:

- The two errors of the individually driven wheels are independent[5];

- The variance of the errors (left and right wheels) are proportional to the absolute value of the traveled distances $(\Delta s_r; \Delta s_l)$.

These assumptions, while not perfect, are suitable and will thus be used for the further development of the error model. The *motion errors* are due to imprecise movement because of deformation of wheel, slippage, unequal floor, errors in encoders, and so on. The values for the error constants k_r and k_l depend on the robot and the environment and should be experimentally established by performing and analyzing representative movements.

If we assume that p and $\Delta_{rl} = (\Delta s_r; \Delta s_l)$ are uncorrelated and the derivation of f [equation (5.7)] is reasonably approximated by the first-order Taylor expansion (linearization), we conclude, using the error propagation law (see section 4.2.2),

---

5. If there is more knowledge regarding the actual robot kinematics, the correlation terms of the covariance matrix could also be used.

$$\Sigma_{p'} = \nabla_p f \cdot \Sigma_p \cdot \nabla_p f^T + \nabla_{\Delta_{rl}} f \cdot \Sigma_\Delta \cdot \nabla_{\Delta_{rl}} f^T \qquad (5.9)$$

The covariance matrix Σ_p is, of course, always given by the $\Sigma_{p'}$ of the previous step, and can thus be calculated after specifying an initial value (e.g., 0).

Using equation (5.7) we can develop the two *Jacobians*, $F_p = \nabla_p f$ and $F_{\Delta_{rl}} = \nabla_{\Delta_{rl}} f$:

$$F_p = \nabla_p f = \nabla_p (f^T) = \left[\frac{\partial f}{\partial x} \ \frac{\partial f}{\partial y} \ \frac{\partial f}{\partial \theta} \right] = \begin{bmatrix} 1 & 0 & -\Delta s \sin(\theta + \Delta\theta/2) \\ 0 & 1 & \Delta s \cos(\theta + \Delta\theta/2) \\ 0 & 0 & 1 \end{bmatrix} \qquad (5.10)$$

$$F_{\Delta_{rl}} = \begin{bmatrix} \frac{1}{2}\cos\left(\theta + \frac{\Delta\theta}{2}\right) - \frac{\Delta s}{2b}\sin\left(\theta + \frac{\Delta\theta}{2}\right) & \frac{1}{2}\cos\left(\theta + \frac{\Delta\theta}{2}\right) + \frac{\Delta s}{2b}\sin\left(\theta + \frac{\Delta\theta}{2}\right) \\ \frac{1}{2}\sin\left(\theta + \frac{\Delta\theta}{2}\right) + \frac{\Delta s}{2b}\cos\left(\theta + \frac{\Delta\theta}{2}\right) & \frac{1}{2}\sin\left(\theta + \frac{\Delta\theta}{2}\right) - \frac{\Delta s}{2b}\cos\left(\theta + \frac{\Delta\theta}{2}\right) \\ \frac{1}{b} & -\frac{1}{b} \end{bmatrix} \qquad (5.11)$$

The details for arriving at equation (5.11) are

$$F_{\Delta_{rl}} = \nabla_{\Delta_{rl}} f = \left[\frac{\partial f}{\partial \Delta s_r} \ \frac{\partial f}{\partial \Delta s_l} \right] = \dots \qquad (5.12)$$

$$\begin{bmatrix} \frac{\partial \Delta s}{\partial \Delta s_r}\cos\left(\theta + \frac{\Delta\theta}{2}\right) + \frac{\Delta s}{2} - \sin\left(\theta + \frac{\Delta\theta}{2}\right)\frac{\partial \Delta\theta}{\partial \Delta s_r} & \frac{\partial \Delta s}{\partial \Delta s_l}\cos\left(\theta + \frac{\Delta\theta}{2}\right) + \frac{\Delta s}{2} - \sin\left(\theta + \frac{\Delta\theta}{2}\right)\frac{\partial \Delta\theta}{\partial \Delta s_l} \\ \frac{\partial \Delta s}{\partial \Delta s_r}\sin\left(\theta + \frac{\Delta\theta}{2}\right) + \frac{\Delta s}{2}\cos\left(\theta + \frac{\Delta\theta}{2}\right)\frac{\partial \Delta\theta}{\partial \Delta s_r} & \frac{\partial \Delta s}{\partial \Delta s_l}\sin\left(\theta + \frac{\Delta\theta}{2}\right) + \frac{\Delta s}{2}\cos\left(\theta + \frac{\Delta\theta}{2}\right)\frac{\partial \Delta\theta}{\partial \Delta s_l} \\ \frac{\partial \Delta\theta}{\partial \Delta s_r} & \frac{\partial \Delta\theta}{\partial \Delta s_l} \end{bmatrix}$$

$$(5.13)$$

and with

$$\Delta s = \frac{\Delta s_r + \Delta s_l}{2} \ ; \qquad \Delta\theta = \frac{\Delta s_r - \Delta s_l}{b} \qquad (5.14)$$

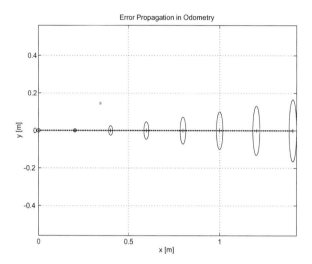

Figure 5.4
Growth of the pose uncertainty for straight-line movement: Note that the uncertainty in y grows much faster than in the direction of movement. This results from the integration of the uncertainty about the robot's orientation. The ellipses drawn around the robot positions represent the uncertainties in the x,y direction (e.g. 3σ). The uncertainty of the orientation θ is not represented in the picture although its effect can be indirectly observed.

$$\frac{\partial \Delta s}{\partial \Delta s_r} = \frac{1}{2} \ ; \ \frac{\partial \Delta s}{\partial \Delta s_l} = \frac{1}{2} \ ; \ \frac{\partial \Delta \theta}{\partial \Delta s_r} = \frac{1}{b} \ ; \ \frac{\partial \Delta \theta}{\partial \Delta s_l} = -\frac{1}{b} \qquad (5.15)$$

we obtain equation (5.11).

Figures 5.4 and 5.5 show typical examples of how the position errors grow with time. The results have been computed using the error model presented above.

Once the error model has been established, the error parameters must be specified. One can compensate for deterministic errors properly calibrating the robot. However the error parameters specifying the nondeterministic errors can only be quantified by statistical (repetitive) measurements. A detailed discussion of odometric errors and a method for calibration and quantification of deterministic and nondeterministic errors can be found in [5]. A method for on-the-fly odometry error estimation is presented in [105].

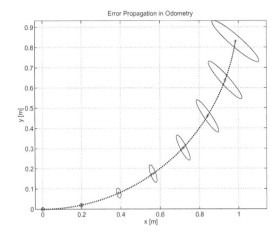

Figure 5.5
Growth of the pose uncertainty for circular movement (r = const): Again, the uncertainty perpendicular to the movement grows much faster than that in the direction of movement. Note that the main axis of the uncertainty ellipse does not remain perpendicular to the direction of movement.

5.3 To Localize or Not to Localize: Localization-Based Navigation versus Programmed Solutions

Figure 5.6 depicts a standard indoor environment that a mobile robot navigates. Suppose that the mobile robot in question must deliver messages between two specific rooms in this environment: rooms A and B. In creating a navigation system, it is clear that the mobile robot will need sensors and a motion control system. Sensors are absolutely required to avoid hitting moving obstacles such as humans, and some motion control system is required so that the robot can deliberately move.

It is less evident, however, whether or not this mobile robot will require a *localization system*. Localization may seem mandatory in order to successfully navigate between the two rooms. It is through localizing on a map, after all, that the robot can hope to recover its position and detect when it has arrived at the goal location. It is true that, at the least, the robot must have a way of detecting the goal location. However, explicit localization with reference to a map is not the only strategy that qualifies as a goal detector.

An alternative, espoused by the behavior-based community, suggests that, since sensors and effectors are noisy and information-limited, one should avoid creating a geometric map for localization. Instead, this community suggests designing sets of behaviors that together result in the desired robot motion. Fundamentally, this approach avoids explicit reasoning about localization and position, and thus generally avoids explicit path planning as well.

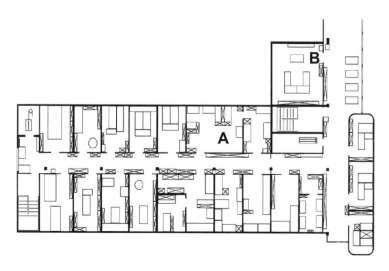

Figure 5.6
A sample environment.

   This technique is based on a belief that there exists a procedural solution to the particular navigation problem at hand. For example, in figure 5.6, the behavioralist approach to navigating from room *A* to room *B* might be to design a left-wall following behavior and a detector for room *B* that is triggered by some unique queue in room *B*, such as the color of the carpet. Then the robot can reach room *B* by engaging the left-wall follower with the room *B* detector as the termination condition for the program.

   The architecture of this solution to a specific navigation problem is shown in figure 5.7. The key advantage of this method is that, when possible, it may be implemented very quickly for a single environment with a small number of goal positions. It suffers from some disadvantages, however. First, the method does not directly scale to other environments or to larger environments. Often, the navigation code is location-specific, and the same degree of coding and debugging is required to move the robot to a new environment. Second, the underlying procedures, such as *left-wall-follow,* must be carefully designed to produce the desired behavior. This task may be time-consuming and is heavily dependent on the specific robot hardware and environmental characteristics.

   Third, a behavior-based system may have multiple active behaviors at any one time. Even when individual behaviors are tuned to optimize performance, this fusion and rapid switching between multiple behaviors can negate that fine-tuning. Often, the addition of each new incremental behavior forces the robot designer to retune all of the existing behaviors again to ensure that the new interactions with the freshly introduced behavior are all stable.

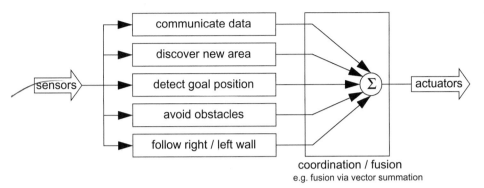

Figure 5.7
An architecture for behavior-based navigation.

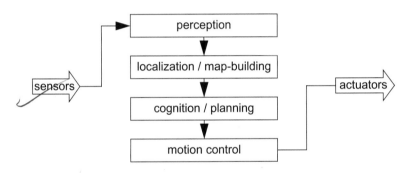

Figure 5.8
An architecture for map-based (or model-based) navigation.

In contrast to the behavior-based approach, the map-based approach includes both *localization* and *cognition* modules (see figure 5.8). In map-based navigation, the robot explicitly attempts to localize by collecting sensor data, then updating some belief about its position with respect to a map of the environment. The key advantages of the map-based approach for navigation are as follows:

The explicit, map-based concept of position makes the system's belief about position transparently available to the human operators.

The existence of the map itself represents a medium for communication between human and robot: the human can simply give the robot a new map if the robot goes to a new environment.

- The map, if created by the robot, can be used by humans as well, achieving two uses.

The map-based approach will require more up-front development effort to create a navigating mobile robot. The hope is that the development effort results in an architecture that can successfully map and navigate a variety of environments, thereby amortizing the up-front design cost over time.

Of course the key risk of the map-based approach is that an internal representation, rather than the real world itself, is being constructed and *trusted* by the robot. If that model diverges from reality (i.e., if the map is wrong), then the robot's behavior may be undesirable, even if the raw sensor values of the robot are only transiently incorrect.

In the remainder of this chapter, we focus on a discussion of map-based approaches and, specifically, the localization component of these techniques. These approaches are particularly appropriate for study given their significant recent successes in enabling mobile robots to navigate a variety of environments, from academic research buildings, to factory floors, and to museums around the world.

5.4   Belief Representation

The fundamental issue that differentiates various map-based localization systems is the issue of *representation*. There are two specific concepts that the robot must represent, and each has its own unique possible solutions. The robot must have a representation (a model) of the environment, or a map. What aspects of the environment are contained in this map? At what level of fidelity does the map represent the environment? These are the design questions for *map representation.*

The robot must also have a representation of its belief regarding its position on the map. Does the robot identify a single unique position as its current position, or does it describe its position in terms of a set of possible positions? If multiple possible positions are expressed in a single belief, how are those multiple positions ranked, if at all? These are the design questions for *belief representation.*

Decisions along these two design axes can result in varying levels of architectural complexity, computational complexity, and overall localization accuracy. We begin by discussing belief representation. The first major branch in a taxonomy of belief representation systems differentiates between single-hypothesis and multiple-hypothesis belief systems. The former covers solutions in which the robot postulates its unique position, whereas the latter enables a mobile robot to describe the degree to which it is uncertain about its position. A sampling of different belief and map representations is shown in figure 5.9.

5.4.1   Single-hypothesis belief

The single-hypothesis belief representation is the most direct possible postulation of mobile robot position. Given some environmental map, the robot's belief about position is

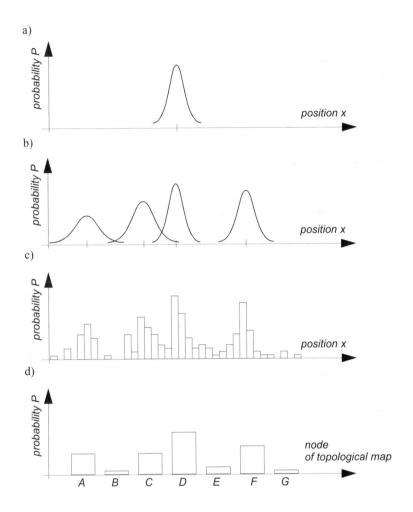

Figure 5.9
Belief representation regarding the robot position (1D) in continuous and discretized (tessellated) maps. (a) Continuous map with single-hypothesis belief, e.g., single Gaussian centered at a single continuous value. (b) Continuous map with multiple-hypothesis belief, e.g;. multiple Gaussians centered at multiple continuous values. (c) Discretized (decomposed) grid map with probability values for all possible robot positions, e.g.; Markov approach. (d) Discretized topological map with probability value for all possible nodes (topological robot positions), e.g.; Markov approach.

expressed as a single unique point on the map. In figure 5.10, three examples of a single-hypothesis belief are shown using three different map representations of the same actual environment (figure 5.10a). In figure 5.10b, a single point is geometrically annotated as the robot's position in a continuous 2D geometric map. In figure 5.10c, the map is a discrete, tessellated map, and the position is noted at the same level of fidelity as the map cell size. In figure 5.10d, the map is not geometric at all but abstract and topological. In this case, the single hypothesis of position involves identifying a single node i in the topological graph as the robot's position.

The principal advantage of the single-hypothesis representation of position stems from the fact that, given a unique belief, there is no position ambiguity. The unambiguous nature of this representation facilitates decision-making at the robot's cognitive level (e.g., path planning). The robot can simply assume that its belief is correct, and can then select its future actions based on its unique position.

Just as decision-making is facilitated by a single-position hypothesis, so updating the robot's belief regarding position is also facilitated, since the single position must be updated by definition to a new, single position. The challenge with this position update approach, which ultimately is the principal disadvantage of single-hypothesis representation, is that robot motion often induces uncertainty due to effector and sensor noise. Therefore, forcing the position update process to always generate a *single* hypothesis of position is challenging and, often, impossible.

5.4.2 Multiple-hypothesis belief

In the case of multiple-hypothesis beliefs regarding position, the robot tracks not just a single possible position but a possibly infinite set of positions.

In one simple example originating in the work of Jean-Claude Latombe [21, 99], the robot's position is described in terms of a convex polygon positioned in a 2D map of the environment. This multiple-hypothesis representation communicates the set of possible robot positions geometrically, with no preference ordering over the positions. Each point in the map is simply either contained by the polygon and, therefore, in the robot's belief set, or outside the polygon and thereby excluded. Mathematically, the position polygon serves to partition the space of possible robot positions. Such a polygonal representation of the multiple-hypothesis belief can apply to a continuous, geometric map of the environment [35] or, alternatively, to a tessellated, discrete approximation to the continuous environment.

It may be useful, however, to incorporate some ordering on the possible robot positions, capturing the fact that some robot positions are likelier than others. A strategy for representing a continuous multiple-hypothesis belief state along with a preference ordering over possible positions is to model the belief as a mathematical distribution. For example, [50, 142] notate the robot's position belief using an $\{X, Y\}$ point in the 2D environment as the

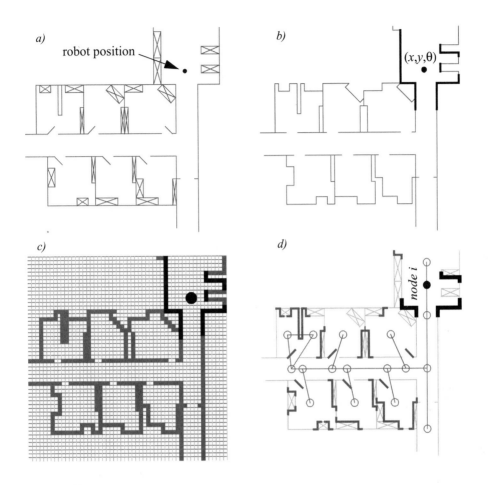

Figure 5.10
Three examples of single hypotheses of position using different map representations: (a) real map
with walls, doors and furniture; (b) line-based map $\rightarrow$ around 100 lines with two parameters; (c)
occupancy grid-based map $\rightarrow$ around 3000 grid cells size 50 x 50 cm; (d) topological map using line
features (Z/S lines) and doors $\rightarrow$ around 50 features and 18 nodes.

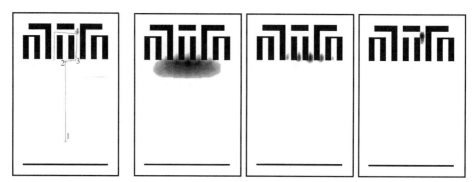

Path of the robot   Belief states at positions 2, 3, and 4

Figure 5.11
Example of multiple-hypothesis tracking (courtesy of W. Burgard [49]). The belief state that is largely distributed becomes very certain after moving to position 4. Note that darker coloring represents higher probability.

mean μ plus a standard deviation parameter σ, thereby defining a Gaussian distribution. The intended interpretation is that the distribution at each position represents the probability assigned to the robot being at that location. This representation is particularly amenable to mathematically defined tracking functions, such as the Kalman filter, that are designed to operate efficiently on Gaussian distributions.

An alternative is to represent the set of possible robot positions, not using a single Gaussian probability density function, but using discrete markers for each possible position. In this case, each possible robot position is individually noted along with a confidence or probability parameter (see figure 5.11). In the case of a highly tessellated map this can result in thousands or even tens of thousands of possible robot positions in a single-belief state.

The key advantage of the multiple-hypothesis representation is that the robot can explicitly maintain uncertainty regarding its position. If the robot only acquires partial information regarding position from its sensors and effectors, that information can conceptually be incorporated in an updated belief.

A more subtle advantage of this approach revolves around the robot's ability to explicitly measure its own degree of uncertainty regarding position. This advantage is the key to a class of localization and navigation solutions in which the robot not only reasons about reaching a particular goal but reasons about the future trajectory of its own belief state. For instance, a robot may choose paths that minimize its future position uncertainty. An example of this approach is [141], in which the robot plans a path from point A to point B that takes it near a series of landmarks in order to mitigate localization difficulties. This type of explicit reasoning about the effect that trajectories will have on the quality of localization requires a multiple-hypothesis representation.

One of the fundamental disadvantages of multiple-hypothesis approaches involves decision-making. If the robot represents its position as a region or set of possible positions, then how shall it decide what to do next? Figure 5.11 provides an example. At position 3, the robot's belief state is distributed among five hallways separately. If the goal of the robot is to travel down one particular hallway, then given this belief state, what action should the robot choose?

The challenge occurs because some of the robot's possible positions imply a motion trajectory that is inconsistent with some of its other possible positions. One approach that we will see in the case studies below is to assume, for decision-making purposes, that the robot is physically at the most probable location in its belief state, then to choose a path based on that current position. But this approach demands that each possible position have an associated probability.

In general, the right approach to such decision-making problems would be to decide on trajectories that eliminate the ambiguity explicitly. But this leads us to the second major disadvantage of multiple-hypothesis approaches. In the most general case, they can be computationally very expensive. When one reasons in a 3D space of discrete possible positions, the number of possible belief states in the single-hypothesis case is limited to the number of possible positions in the 3D world. Consider this number to be N. When one moves to an arbitrary multiple-hypothesis representation, then the number of possible belief states is the power set of N, which is far larger: 2^N. Thus explicit reasoning about the possible trajectory of the belief state over time quickly becomes computationally untenable as the size of the environment grows.

There are, however, specific forms of multiple-hypothesis representations that are somewhat more constrained, thereby avoiding the computational explosion while allowing a limited type of multiple-hypothesis belief. For example, if one assumes a Gaussian distribution of probability centered at a single position, then the problem of representation and tracking of belief becomes equivalent to Kalman filtering, a straightforward mathematical process described below. Alternatively, a highly tessellated map representation combined with a limit of ten possible positions in the belief state, results in a discrete update cycle that is, at worst, only ten times more computationally expensive than a single-hypothesis belief update. And other ways to cope with the complexity problem, still being precise and computationally cheap, are hybrid metric-topological approaches [145, 147] or multi-Gaussian position estimation [35, 60, 81].

In conclusion, the most critical benefit of the multiple-hypothesis belief state is the ability to maintain a sense of position while explicitly annotating the robot's uncertainty about its own position. This powerful representation has enabled robots with limited sensory information to navigate robustly in an array of environments, as we shall see in the case studies below.

5.5   Map Representation

The problem of representing the environment in which the robot moves is a dual of the problem of representing the robot's possible position or positions. Decisions made regarding the environmental representation can have impact on the choices available for robot position representation. Often the fidelity of the position representation is bounded by the fidelity of the map.

Three fundamental relationships must be understood when choosing a particular map representation:

1. The precision of the map must appropriately match the precision with which the robot needs to achieve its goals.

2. The precision of the map and the type of features represented must match the precision and data types returned by the robot's sensors.

3. The complexity of the map representation has direct impact on the computational complexity of reasoning about mapping, localization, and navigation.

In the following sections, we identify and discuss critical design choices in creating a map representation. Each such choice has great impact on the relationships listed above and on the resulting robot localization architecture. As we shall see, the choice of possible map representations is broad. Selecting an appropriate representation requires understanding all of the trade-offs inherent in that choice as well as understanding the specific context in which a particular mobile robot implementation must perform localization. In general, the environmental representation and model can be roughly classified as presented in chapter 4, section 4.3.

5.5.1   Continuous representations

A continuous-valued map is one method for *exact* decomposition of the environment. The position of environmental features can be annotated precisely in continuous space. Mobile robot implementations to date use continuous maps only in 2D representations, as further dimensionality can result in computational explosion.

A common approach is to combine the exactness of a continuous representation with the compactness of the *closed-world assumption*. This means that one assumes that the representation will specify all environmental objects in the map, and that any area in the map that is devoid of objects has no objects in the corresponding portion of the environment. Thus, the total storage needed in the map is proportional to the density of objects in the environment, and a sparse environment can be represented by a low-memory map.

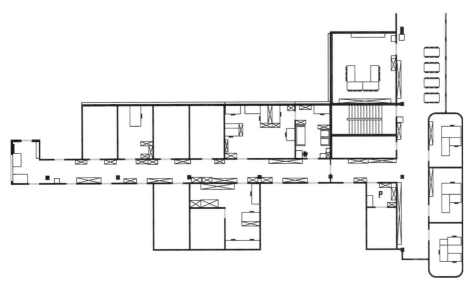

Figure 5.12
A continuous representation using polygons as environmental obstacles.

One example of such a representation, shown in figure 5.12, is a 2D representation in which polygons represent all obstacles in a continuous-valued coordinate space. This is similar to the method used by Latombe [21, 98] and others to represent environments for mobile robot path-planning techniques.

In the case of [21, 98], most of the experiments are in fact simulations run exclusively within the computer's memory. Therefore, no real effort would have been expended to attempt to use sets of polygons to describe a real-world environment, such as a park or office building.

In other work in which real environments must be captured by the maps, one sees a trend toward selectivity and abstraction. The human map maker tends to capture on the map, for localization purposes, only objects that can be detected by the robot's sensors and, furthermore, only a subset of the features of real-world objects.

It should be immediately apparent that geometric maps can capably represent the physical locations of objects without referring to their texture, color, elasticity, or any other such secondary features that do not relate directly to position and space. In addition to this level of simplification, a mobile robot map can further reduce memory usage by capturing only aspects of object geometry that are immediately relevant to localization. For example, all objects may be approximated using very simple convex polygons, sacrificing map felicity for the sake of computational speed.

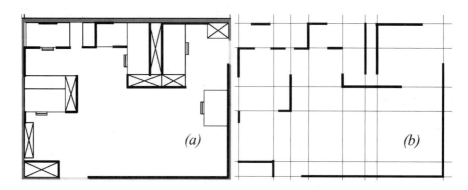

Figure 5.13
Example of a continuous-valued line representation of EPFL. (a) Real map. (b) Representation with
a set of infinite lines.

One excellent example involves line extraction. Many indoor mobile robots rely upon
laser rangefinding devices to recover distance readings to nearby objects. Such robots can
automatically extract best-fit lines from the dense range data provided by thousands of
points of laser strikes. Given such a line extraction sensor, an appropriate continuous mapping approach is to populate the map with a set of infinite lines. The continuous nature of
the map guarantees that lines can be positioned at arbitrary positions in the plane and at
arbitrary angles. The abstraction of real environmental objects such as walls and intersections captures only the information in the map representation that matches the type of information recovered by the mobile robot's rangefinding sensor.

Figure 5.13 shows a map of an indoor environment at EPFL using a continuous line representation. Note that the only environmental features captured by the map are straight
lines, such as those found at corners and along walls. This represents not only a sampling
of the real world of richer features but also a simplification, for an actual wall may have
texture and relief that is not captured by the mapped line.

The impact of continuous map representations on position representation is primarily
positive. In the case of single-hypothesis position representation, that position may be specified as any continuous-valued point in the coordinate space, and therefore extremely high
accuracy is possible. In the case of multiple-hypothesis position representation, the continuous map enables two types of multiple position representation.

In one case, the possible robot position may be depicted as a geometric shape in the
hyperplane, such that the robot is known to be within the bounds of that shape. This is
shown in figure 5.29, in which the position of the robot is depicted by an oval bounding
area.

Yet, the continuous representation does not disallow representation of position in the form of a discrete set of possible positions. For instance, in [62] the robot position belief state is captured by sampling nine continuous-valued positions from within a region near the robot's best-known position. This algorithm captures, within a continuous space, a discrete sampling of possible robot positions.

In summary, the key advantage of a continuous map representation is the potential for high accuracy and expressiveness with respect to the environmental configuration as well as the robot position within that environment. The danger of a continuous representation is that the map may be computationally costly. But this danger can be tempered by employing abstraction and capturing only the most relevant environmental features. Together with the use of the *closed-world assumption*, these techniques can enable a continuous-valued map to be no more costly, and sometimes even less costly, than a standard discrete representation.

5.5.2 Decomposition strategies

In the section above, we discussed one method of simplification, in which the continuous map representation contains a set of infinite lines that approximate real-world environmental lines based on a 2D slice of the world. Basically this transformation from the real world to the map representation is a filter that removes all nonstraight data and furthermore extends line segment data into infinite lines that require fewer parameters.

A more dramatic form of simplification is *abstraction*: a general decomposition and selection of environmental features. In this section, we explore decomposition as applied in its more extreme forms to the question of map representation.

Why would one radically decompose the real environment during the design of a map representation? The immediate disadvantage of decomposition and abstraction is the loss of fidelity between the map and the real world. Both qualitatively, in terms of overall structure, and quantitatively, in terms of geometric precision, a highly abstract map does not compare favorably to a high-fidelity map.

Despite this disadvantage, decomposition and abstraction may be useful if the abstraction can be planned carefully so as to capture the relevant, *useful* features of the world while discarding all other features. The advantage of this approach is that the map representation can potentially be minimized. Furthermore, if the decomposition is hierarchical, such as in a pyramid of recursive abstraction, then reasoning and planning with respect to the map representation may be computationally far superior to planning in a fully detailed world model.

A standard, lossless form of *opportunistic decomposition* is termed *exact cell decomposition*. This method, introduced by Latombe [21], achieves decomposition by selecting boundaries between discrete cells based on geometric criticality.

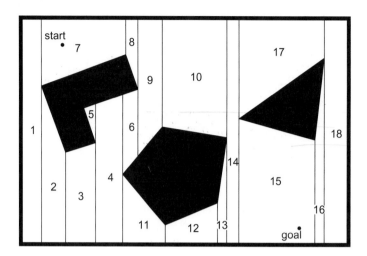

Figure 5.14
Example of exact cell decomposition.

Figure 5.14 depicts an exact decomposition of a planar workspace populated by polygonal obstacles. The map representation tessellates the space into areas of free space. The
representation can be extremely compact because each such area is actually stored as a
single node, resulting in a total of only eighteen nodes in this example.

The underlying assumption behind this decomposition is that the particular position of
a robot within each area of free space does not matter. What matters is the robot's ability
to traverse from each area of free space to the adjacent areas. Therefore, as with other representations we will see, the resulting graph captures the adjacency of map locales. If
indeed the assumptions are valid and the robot does not care about its precise position
within a single area, then this can be an effective representation that nonetheless captures
the connectivity of the environment.

Such an exact decomposition is not always appropriate. Exact decomposition is a function of the particular environment obstacles and free space. If this information is expensive
to collect or even unknown, then such an approach is not feasible.

An alternative is *fixed decomposition*, in which the world is tessellated, transforming the
continuous real environment into a discrete approximation for the map. Such a transformation is demonstrated in figure 5.15, which depicts what happens to obstacle-filled and free
areas during this transformation. The key disadvantage of this approach stems from its *inexact* nature. It is possible for narrow passageways to be lost during such a transformation, as
shown in figure 5.15. Formally, this means that fixed decomposition is sound but not complete. Yet another approach is adaptive cell decomposition, as presented in figure 5.16.

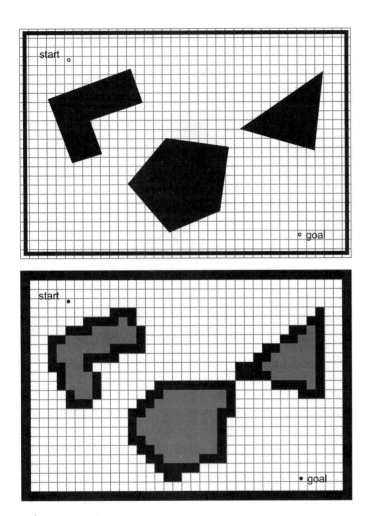

Figure 5.15
Fixed decomposition of the same space (narrow passage disappears).

The concept of fixed decomposition is extremely popular in mobile robotics; it is perhaps the single most common map representation technique currently utilized. One very popular version of fixed decomposition is known as the *occupancy grid* representation [112]. In an occupancy grid, the environment is represented by a discrete grid, where each cell is either filled (part of an obstacle) or empty (part of free space). This method is of particular value when a robot is equipped with range-based sensors because the range values

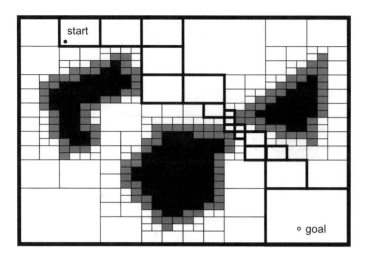

Figure 5.16
Example of adaptive (approximate variable-cell) decomposition of an environment [21]. The rectangle, bounding the free space, is decomposed into four identical rectangles. If the interior of a rectangle lies completely in free space or in the configuration space obstacle, it is not decomposed further. Otherwise, it is recursively decomposed into four rectangles until some predefined resolution is attained. The white cells lie outside the obstacles, the black inside, and the gray are part of both regions.

of each sensor, combined with the absolute position of the robot, can be used directly to update the filled or empty value of each cell.

In the occupancy grid, each cell may have a counter, whereby the value 0 indicates that the cell has not been "hit" by any ranging measurements and, therefore, it is likely free space. As the number of ranging strikes increases, the cell's value is incremented and, above a certain threshold, the cell is deemed to be an obstacle. The values of cells are commonly discounted when a ranging strike travels *through* the cell, striking a further cell. By also discounting the values of cells over time, both hysteresis and the possibility of transient obstacles can be represented using this occupancy grid approach. Figure 5.17 depicts an occupancy grid representation in which the darkness of each cell is proportional to the value of its counter. One commercial robot that uses a standard occupancy grid for mapping and navigation is the Cye robot [163].

There remain two main disadvantages of the occupancy grid approach. First, the size of the map in robot memory grows with the size of the environment and if a small cell size is used, this size can quickly become untenable. This occupancy grid approach is not compatible with the *closed-world assumption*, which enabled continuous representations to have potentially very small memory requirements in large, sparse environments. In contrast, the

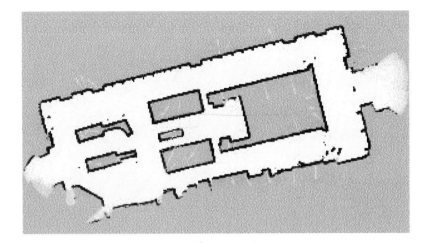

Figure 5.17
Example of an occupancy grid map representation (courtesy of S. Thrun [145]).

occupancy grid must have memory set aside for every cell in the matrix. Furthermore, any fixed decomposition method such as this imposes a geometric grid on the world *a priori*, regardless of the environmental details. This can be inappropriate in cases where geometry is not the most salient feature of the environment.

For these reasons, an alternative, called *topological* decomposition, has been the subject of some exploration in mobile robotics. Topological approaches avoid direct measurement of geometric environmental qualities, instead concentrating on characteristics of the environment that are most relevant to the robot for localization.

Formally, a topological representation is a graph that specifies two things: *nodes* and the *connectivity* between those nodes. Insofar as a topological representation is intended for the use of a mobile robot, nodes are used to denote areas in the world and arcs are used to denote adjacency of pairs of nodes. When an arc connects two nodes, then the robot can traverse from one node to the other without requiring traversal of any other intermediary node.

Adjacency is clearly at the heart of the topological approach, just as adjacency in a cell decomposition representation maps to geometric adjacency in the real world. However, the topological approach diverges in that the nodes are not of fixed size or even specifications of free space. Instead, nodes document an area based on any sensor discriminant such that the robot can recognize entry and exit of the node.

Figure 5.18 depicts a topological representation of a set of hallways and offices in an indoor environment. In this case, the robot is assumed to have an intersection detector, perhaps using sonar and vision to find intersections between halls and between halls and

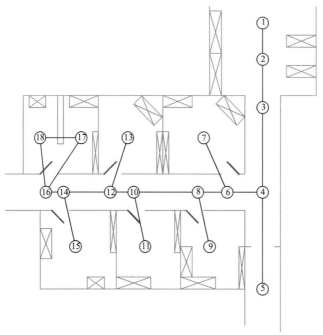

Figure 5.18
A topological representation of an indoor office area.

rooms. Note that nodes capture geometric space, and arcs in this representation simply represent connectivity.

Another example of topological representation is the work of Simhon and Dudek [134], in which the goal is to create a mobile robot that can capture the most interesting aspects of an area for human consumption. The nodes in their representation are visually striking locales rather than route intersections.

In order to navigate using a topological map robustly, a robot must satisfy two constraints. First, it must have a means for detecting its current position in terms of the nodes of the topological graph. Second, it must have a means for traveling between nodes using robot motion. The node sizes and particular dimensions must be optimized to match the sensory discrimination of the mobile robot hardware. This ability to "tune" the representation to the robot's particular sensors can be an important advantage of the topological approach. However, as the map representation drifts further away from true geometry, the expressiveness of the representation for accurately and precisely describing a robot position is lost. Therein lies the compromise between the discrete cell-based map representations and the topological representations. Interestingly, the continuous map representation has

Figure 5.19
An artificial landmark used by Chips during autonomous docking.

the potential to be both compact like a topological representation and precise as with all direct geometric representations.

Yet, a chief motivation of the topological approach is that the environment may contain important nongeometric features – features that have no ranging relevance but are useful for localization. In chapter 4 we described such whole-image vision-based features.

In contrast to these whole-image feature extractors, often spatially localized landmarks are artificially placed in an environment to impose a particular visual-topological connectivity upon the environment. In effect, the artificial landmark can impose artificial structure. Examples of working systems operating with this landmark-based strategy have also demonstrated success. Latombe's landmark-based navigation research [99] has been implemented on real-world indoor mobile robots that employ paper landmarks attached to the ceiling as the locally observable features. Chips, the museum robot, is another robot that uses man-made landmarks to obviate the localization problem. In this case, a bright pink square serves as a landmark with dimensions and color signature that would be hard to accidentally reproduce in a museum environment [118]. One such museum landmark is shown in figure 5.19.

In summary, range is clearly not the only measurable and useful environmental value for a mobile robot. This is particularly true with the advent of color vision, as well as laser rangefinding, which provides reflectance information in addition to range information. Choosing a map representation for a particular mobile robot requires, first, understanding the sensors available on the mobile robot, and, second, understanding the mobile robot's functional requirements (e.g., required goal precision and accuracy).

5.5.3 State of the art: current challenges in map representation

The sections above describe major design decisions in regard to map representation choices. There are, however, fundamental real-world features that mobile robot map representations do not yet represent well. These continue to be the subject of open research, and several such challenges are described below.

The real world is dynamic. As mobile robots come to inhabit the same spaces as humans, they will encounter moving people, cars, strollers, and the transient obstacles placed and moved by humans as they go about their activities. This is particularly true when one considers the home environment with which domestic robots will someday need to contend.

The map representations described above do not, in general, have explicit facilities for identifying and distinguishing between permanent obstacles (e.g., walls, doorways, etc.) and transient obstacles (e.g., humans, shipping packages, etc.). The current state of the art in terms of mobile robot sensors is partly to blame for this shortcoming. Although vision research is rapidly advancing, robust sensors that discriminate between moving animals and static structures *from a moving reference frame* are not yet available. Furthermore, estimating the motion vector of transient objects remains a research problem.

Usually, the assumption behind the above map representations is that all objects on the map are effectively static. Partial success can be achieved by discounting mapped objects over time. For example, occupancy grid techniques can be more robust to dynamic settings by introducing temporal discounting, effectively treating transient obstacles as noise. The more challenging process of map creation is particularly fragile to environmental dynamics; most mapping techniques generally require that the environment be free of moving objects during the mapping process. One exception to this limitation involves topological representations. Because precise geometry is not important, transient objects have little effect on the mapping or localization process, subject to the critical constraint that the transient objects must not change the topological connectivity of the environment. Still, neither the occupancy grid representation nor a topological approach is actively recognizing and representing transient objects as distinct from both sensor error and permanent map features.

As vision sensing provides more robust and more informative content regarding the transience and motion details of objects in the world, mobile roboticists will in time propose representations that make use of that information. A classic example involves occlusion by human crowds. Museum tour guide robots generally suffer from an extreme amount of occlusion. If the robot's sensing suite is located along the robot's body, then the robot is effectively blind when a group of human visitors completely surround the robot. This is because its map contains only environmental features that are, at that point, fully hidden from the robot's sensors by the wall of people. In the best case, the robot should recognize its occlusion and make no effort to localize using these invalid sensor readings. In the worst case, the robot will localize with the fully occluded data, and will update its location incorrectly. A vision sensor that can discriminate the local conditions of the robot (e.g,. we are surrounded by people) can help eliminate this error mode.

A second open challenge in mobile robot localization involves the traversal of open spaces. Existing localization techniques generally depend on local measures such as range, thereby demanding environments that are somewhat densely filled with objects that the sensors can detect and measure. Wide-open spaces such as parking lots, fields of grass, and indoor atriums such as those found in convention centers pose a difficulty for such systems because of their relative sparseness. Indeed, when populated with humans, the challenge is exacerbated because any mapped objects are almost certain to be occluded from view by the people.

Once again, more recent technologies provide some hope of overcoming these limitations. Both vision and state-of-the-art laser rangefinding devices offer outdoor performance with ranges of up to a hundred meters and more. Of course, GPS performs even better. Such long-range sensing may be required for robots to localize using distant features.

This trend teases out a hidden assumption underlying most topological map representations. Usually, topological representations make assumptions regarding spatial locality: a node contains objects and features that are themselves within that node. The process of map creation thus involves making nodes that are, in their own self-contained way, recognizable by virtue of the objects contained within the node. Therefore, in an indoor environment, each room can be a separate node, and this is reasonable because each room will have a layout and a set of belongings that are unique to that room.

However, consider the outdoor world of a wide-open park. Where should a single node end and the next node begin? The answer is unclear because objects that are far away from the current node, or position, can yield information for the localization process. For example, the hump of a hill at the horizon, the position of a river in the valley, and the trajectory of the sun all are nonlocal features that have great bearing on one's ability to infer current position. The spatial locality assumption is violated and, instead, replaced by a visibility criterion: the node or cell may need a mechanism for representing objects that are measurable and visible from that cell. Once again, as sensors improve and, in this case, as outdoor locomotion mechanisms improve, there will be greater urgency to solve problems associated with localization in wide-open settings, with and without GPS-type global localization sensors.

We end this section with one final open challenge that represents one of the fundamental academic research questions of robotics: sensor fusion. A variety of measurement types are possible using off-the-shelf robot sensors, including heat, range, acoustic and light-based reflectivity, color, texture, friction, and so on. Sensor fusion is a research topic closely related to map representation. Just as a map must embody an environment in sufficient detail for a robot to perform localization and reasoning, sensor fusion demands a representation of the world that is sufficiently general and expressive that a variety of sensor types can have their data correlated appropriately, strengthening the resulting percepts well beyond that of any individual sensor's readings.

Perhaps the only general implementation of sensor fusion to date is that of neural network classifier. Using this technique, any number and any type of sensor values may be jointly combined in a network that will use whatever means necessary to optimize its classification accuracy. For the mobile robot that must use a human-readable internal map representation, no equally general sensor fusion scheme has yet been born. It is reasonable to expect that, when the sensor fusion problem is solved, integration of a large number of disparate sensor types may easily result in sufficient discriminatory power for robots to achieve real-world navigation, even in wide-open and dynamic circumstances such as a public square filled with people.

5.6   Probabilistic Map-Based Localization

5.6.1   Introduction

As stated earlier, multiple-hypothesis position representation is advantageous because the robot can explicitly track its own beliefs regarding its possible positions in the environment. Ideally, the robot's *belief state* will change, over time, as is consistent with its motor outputs and perceptual inputs. One geometric approach to multiple-hypothesis representation, mentioned earlier, involves identifying the possible positions of the robot by specifying a polygon in the environmental representation [98]. This method does not provide any indication of the relative chances between various possible robot positions.

Probabilistic techniques differ from this because they explicitly identify probabilities with the possible robot positions, and for this reason these methods have been the focus of recent research. In the following sections we present two classes of probabilistic localization. The first class, *Markov localization*, uses an explicitly specified probability distribution across all possible robot positions. The second method, *Kalman filter localization*, uses a Gaussian probability density representation of robot position and scan matching for localization. Unlike Markov localization, Kalman filter localization does not independently consider each possible pose in the robot's configuration space. Interestingly, the Kalman filter localization process results from the Markov localization axioms if the robot's position uncertainty is assumed to have a Gaussian form [3, pp. 43-44].

Before discussing each method in detail, we present the general robot localization problem and solution strategy. Consider a mobile robot moving in a known environment. As it starts to move, say from a precisely known location, it can keep track of its motion using odometry. Due to odometry uncertainty, after some movement the robot will become very uncertain about its position (see section 5.2.4). To keep position uncertainty from growing unbounded, the robot must localize itself in relation to its environment map. To localize, the robot might use its on-board sensors (ultrasonic, range sensor, vision) to make observations of its environment. The information provided by the robot's odometry, plus the information provided by such exteroceptive observations, can be combined to enable the robot to localize as well as possible with respect to its map. The processes of updating based on proprioceptive sensor values and exteroceptive sensor values are often separated logically, leading to a general two-step process for robot position update.

Action update represents the application of some action model Act to the mobile robot's proprioceptive encoder measurements o_t and prior belief state s_{t-1} to yield a new belief state representing the robot's belief about its current position. Note that throughout this chapter we assume that the robot's proprioceptive encoder measurements are used as the best possible measure of its actions over time. If, for instance, a differential-drive robot had motors without encoders connected to its wheels and employed open-loop control, then instead of encoder measurements the robot's highly uncertain estimates of wheel spin would need to be incorporated. We ignore such cases and therefore have a simple formula:

$$s'_t = Act(o_t, s_{t-1}).$$ (5.16)

Perception update represents the application of some perception model *See* to the mobile robot's exteroceptive sensor inputs i_t and updated belief state s'_t to yield a refined belief state representing the robot's current position:

$$s_t = See(i_t, s'_t)$$ (5.17)

The perception model *See* and sometimes the action model Act are abstract functions of both the map and the robot's physical configuration (e.g., sensors and their positions, kinematics, etc.).

In general, the action update process contributes uncertainty to the robot's belief about position: encoders have error and therefore motion is somewhat nondeterministic. By contrast, perception update generally refines the belief state. Sensor measurements, when compared to the robot's environmental model, tend to provide clues regarding the robot's possible position.

In the case of Markov localization, the robot's belief state is usually represented as separate probability assignments for every possible robot pose in its map. The action update and perception update processes must update the probability of every cell in this case. Kalman filter localization represents the robot's belief state using a single, well-defined

Gaussian probability density function, and thus retains just a μ and σ parameterization of the robot's belief about position with respect to the map. Updating the parameters of the Gaussian distribution is all that is required. This fundamental difference in the representation of belief state leads to the following advantages and disadvantages of the two methods, as presented in [73]:

• Markov localization allows for localization starting from any unknown position and can thus recover from ambiguous situations because the robot can track multiple, completely disparate possible positions. However, to update the probability of all positions within the whole state space at any time requires a discrete representation of the space, such as a geometric grid or a topological graph (see section 5.5.2). The required memory and computational power can thus limit precision and map size.

• Kalman filter localization tracks the robot from an initially known position and is inherently both precise and efficient. In particular, Kalman filter localization can be used in continuous world representations. However, if the uncertainty of the robot becomes too large (e.g., due to a robot collision with an object) and thus not truly unimodal, the Kalman filter can fail to capture the multitude of possible robot positions and can become irrevocably lost.

In recent research projects improvements are achieved or proposed by either only updating the state space of interest within the Markov approach [49] or by tracking multiple hypotheses with Kalman filters [35], or by combining both methods to create a hybrid localization system [73, 147]. In the next two sections we will each approach in detail.

5.6.2 Markov localization

Markov localization tracks the robot's belief state using an arbitrary probability density function to represent the robot's position (see also [50, 88, 116, 119]). In practice, all known Markov localization systems implement this generic belief representation by first tessellating the robot configuration space into a finite, discrete number of possible robot poses in the map. In actual applications, the number of possible poses can range from several hundred to millions of positions.

Given such a generic conception of robot position, a powerful update mechanism is required that can compute the belief state that results when new information (e.g., encoder values and sensor values) is incorporated into a prior belief state with arbitrary probability density. The solution is born out of probability theory, and so the next section describes the foundations of probability theory that apply to this problem, notably the Bayes formula. Then, two subsequent sections provide case studies, one robot implementing a simple feature-driven topological representation of the environment [88, 116, 119] and the other using a geometric grid-based map [49, 50].

5.6.2.1 Introduction: applying probability theory to robot localization

Given a discrete representation of robot positions, in order to express a belief state we wish to assign to each possible robot position a probability that the robot is indeed at that position. From probability theory we use the term $p(A)$ to denote the probability that A is true. This is also called the *prior probability* of A because it measures the probability that A is true independent of any additional knowledge we may have. For example we can use $p(r_t = l)$ to denote the prior probability that the robot r is at position l at time t.

In practice, we wish to compute the probability of each individual robot position given the encoder and sensor evidence the robot has collected. In probability theory, we use the term $p(A|B)$ to denote the *conditional* probability of A given that we know B. For example, we use $p(r_t = l|i_t)$ to denote the probability that the robot is at position l given that the robot's sensor inputs i.

The question is, how can a term such as $p(r_t = l|i_t)$ be simplified to its constituent parts so that it can be computed? The answer lies in the product rule, which states

$$p(A \wedge B) = p(A|B)p(B) \tag{5.18}$$

Equation (5.18) is intuitively straightforward, as the probability of both A and B being true is being related to B being true *and* the other being conditionally true. But you should be able to convince yourself that the alternate equation is equally correct:

$$p(A \wedge B) = p(B|A)p(A) \tag{5.19}$$

Using equations (5.18) and (5.19) together, we can derive the Bayes formula for computing $p(A|B)$:

$$p(A|B) = \frac{p(B|A)p(A)}{p(B)} \tag{5.20}$$

We use the Bayes rule to compute the robot's new belief state as a function of its sensory inputs and its former belief state. But to do this properly, we must recall the basic goal of the Markov localization approach: a discrete set of possible robot positions L are represented. The belief state of the robot must assign a probability $p(r_t = l)$ for each location l in L.

The *See* function described in equation (5.17) expresses a mapping from a belief state and sensor input to a refined belief state. To do this, we must update the probability associated with each position l in L, and we can do this by directly applying the Bayes formula to every such l. In denoting this, we will stop representing the temporal index t for simplicity and will further use $p(l)$ to mean $p(r = l)$:

$$p(l|i) = \frac{p(i|l)p(l)}{p(i)} \tag{5.21}$$

The value of $p(i|l)$ is key to equation (5.21), and this probability of a sensor input at each robot position must be computed using some model. An obvious strategy would be to consult the robot's map, identifying the probability of particular sensor readings with each possible map position, given knowledge about the robot's sensor geometry and the mapped environment. The value of $p(l)$ is easy to recover in this case. It is simply the probability $p(r = l)$ associated with the belief state before the perceptual update process. Finally, note that the denominator $p(i)$ does not depend upon l; that is, as we apply equation (5.21) to all positions l in L, the denominator never varies. Because it is effectively constant, in practice this denominator is usually dropped and, at the end of the perception update step, all probabilities in the belief state are re-normalized to sum at 1.0.

Now consider the *Act* function of equation (5.16). *Act* maps a former belief state and encoder measurement (i.e., robot action) to a new belief state. In order to compute the probability of position l in the new belief state, one must integrate over all the possible ways in which the robot may have reached l according to the potential positions expressed in the former belief state. This is subtle but fundamentally important. The same location l can be reached from multiple source locations with the same encoder measurement o because the encoder measurement is uncertain. Temporal indices are required in this update equation:

$$p(l_t|o_t) = \int p(l_t|l'_{t-1}, o_t)p(l'_{t-1})dl'_{t-1} \tag{5.22}$$

Thus, the total probability for a specific position l is built up from the individual contributions from every location l' in the former belief state given encoder measurement o.

Equations (5.21) and (5.22) form the basis of Markov localization, and they incorporate the *Markov assumption*. Formally, this means that their output is a function only of the robot's previous state and its most recent actions (odometry) and perception. In a general, non-Markovian situation, the state of a system depends upon all of its history. After all, the values of a robot's sensors at time t do not really depend only on its position at time t. They depend to some degree on the trajectory of the robot over time; indeed, on the entire history of the robot. For example, the robot could have experienced a serious collision recently that has biased the sensor's behavior. By the same token, the position of the robot at time t does not really depend only on its position at time $t - 1$ and its odometric measurements. Due to its history of motion, one wheel may have worn more than the other, causing a left-turning bias over time that affects its current position.

So the Markov assumption is, of course, not a valid assumption. However the Markov assumption greatly simplifies tracking, reasoning, and planning and so it is an approximation that continues to be extremely popular in mobile robotics.

Figure 5.20
Dervish exploring its environment.

5.6.2.2 Case study 1: Markov localization using a topological map

A straightforward application of Markov localization is possible when the robot's environment representation already provides an appropriate decomposition. This is the case when the environmental representation is purely topological.

Consider a contest in which each robot is to receive a topological description of the environment. The description would include only the connectivity of hallways and rooms, with no mention of geometric distance. In addition, this supplied *map* would be imperfect, containing several false arcs (e.g., a closed door). Such was the case for the 1994 American Association for Artificial Intelligence (AAAI) National Robot Contest, at which each robot's mission was to use the supplied map and its own sensors to navigate from a chosen starting position to a target room.

Dervish, the winner of this contest, employed probabilistic Markov localization and used a multiple-hypothesis belief state over a topological environmental representation. We now describe Dervish as an example of a robot with a discrete, topological representation and a probabilistic localization algorithm.

Dervish, shown in figure 5.20, includes a sonar arrangement custom-designed for the 1994 AAAI National Robot Contest. The environment in this contest consisted of a rectilinear indoor office space filled with real office furniture as obstacles. Traditional sonars were arranged radially around the robot in a ring. Robots with such sensor configurations are subject to both tripping over short objects below the ring and to decapitation by tall objects (such as ledges, shelves, and tables) that are above the ring.

Dervish's answer to this challenge was to arrange one pair of sonars diagonally upward to detect ledges and other overhangs. In addition, the diagonal sonar pair also proved to ably detect tables, enabling the robot to avoid wandering underneath tall tables. The remaining sonars were clustered in sets of sonars, such that each individual transducer in the set would be at a slightly varied angle to minimize specularity. Finally, two sonars near the robot's base were positioned to detect low obstacles, such as paper cups, on the floor.

We have already noted that the representation provided by the contest organizers was purely topological, noting the connectivity of hallways and rooms in the office environment. Thus, it would be appropriate to design Dervish's perceptual system to detect matching perceptual events: the detection and passage of connections between hallways and offices.

This *abstract* perceptual system was implemented by viewing the trajectory of sonar strikes to the left and right sides of Dervish over time. Interestingly, this perceptual system would use time alone and no concept of encoder value to trigger perceptual events. Thus, for instance, when the robot detects a 7 to 17 cm indentation in the width of the hallway for more than 1 second continuously, a *closed door* sensory event is triggered. If the sonar strikes jump well beyond 17 cm for more than 1 second, an *open door* sensory event triggers.

To reduce coherent reflection sensor noise (see section 4.1.6) associated with Dervish's sonars, the robot would track its angle relative to the hallway centerline and completely suppress sensor events when its angle to the hallway exceeded 9 degrees. Interestingly, this would result in a conservative perceptual system that frequently misses features, particularly when the hallway is crowded with obstacles that Dervish must negotiate. Once again, the conservative nature of the perceptual system, and in particular its tendency to issue false negatives, would point to a probabilistic solution to the localization problem so that a complete trajectory of perceptual inputs could be considered.

Dervish's environmental representation was a discrete topological map, identical in abstraction and information to the map provided by the contest organizers. Figure 5.21 depicts a geometric representation of a typical office environment overlaid with the topological map for the same office environment. Recall that for a topological representation the key decision involves assignment of nodes and connectivity between nodes (see section 5.5.2). As shown on the left in figure 5.21 Dervish uses a topology in which node boundaries are marked primarily by doorways (and hallways and foyers). The topological graph shown on the right depicts the information captured in the example shown.

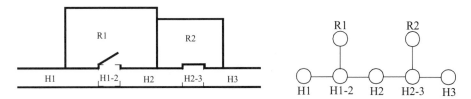

Figure 5.21
A geometric office environment (left) and its topological analog (right).

Note that in this particular topological model arcs are zero-length while nodes have spatial expansiveness and together cover the entire space. This particular topological representation is particularly apt for Dervish given its task of navigating through hallways into a specific room and its perceptual capability of recognizing discontinuities in hallway walls.

In order to represent a specific belief state, Dervish associated with each topological node n a probability that the robot is at a physical position within the boundaries of n: $p(r_t = n)$. As will become clear below, the probabilistic update used by Dervish was approximate, therefore technically one should refer to the resulting values as *likelihoods* rather than probabilities.

Table 5.1
Dervish's certainty matrix.

	Wall	Closed door	Open door	Open hallway	Foyer
Nothing detected	0.70	0.40	0.05	0.001	0.30
Closed door detected	0.30	0.60	0	0	0.05
Open door detected	0	0	0.90	0.10	0.15
Open hallway detected	0	0	0.001	0.90	0.50

The perception update process for Dervish functions precisely as in equation (5.21). Perceptual events are generated asynchronously, each time the feature extractor is able to recognize a large scale feature (e.g., doorway, intersection) based on recent ultrasonic values. Each perceptual event consists of a percept-pair (a feature on one side of the robot or two features on both sides).

Given a specific percept-pair i, equation (5.21) enables the likelihood of each possible position n to be updated using the formula:

$$p(n|i) = p(i|n)p(n) \tag{5.23}$$

The value of $p(n)$ is already available from the current belief state of Dervish, and so the challenge lies in computing $p(i|n)$. The key simplification for Dervish is based upon the realization that, because the feature extraction system only extracts four total features and because a node contains (on a single side) one of five total features, every possible combination of node type and extracted feature can be represented in a 4 x 5 table.

Dervish's *certainty matrix* (show in table 5.1) is just this lookup table. Dervish makes the simplifying assumption that the performance of the feature detector (i.e., the probability that it is correct) is only a function of the feature extracted and the actual feature in the node. With this assumption in hand, we can populate the *certainty matrix* with confidence estimates for each possible pairing of perception and node type. For each of the five world features that the robot can encounter (wall, closed door, open door, open hallway-and foyer) this matrix assigns a likelihood for each of the three one-sided percepts that the sensory system can issue. In addition, this matrix assigns a likelihood that the sensory system will fail to issue a perceptual event altogether (*nothing detected*).

For example, using the specific values in table 5.1, if Dervish is next to an open hallway, the likelihood of mistakenly recognizing it as an open door is 0.10. This means that for any node n that is of type *open hallway* and for the sensor value $i =open\ door, p(i|n) = 0.10$. Together with a specific topological map, the certainty matrix enables straightforward computation of $p(i|n)$ during the perception update process.

For Dervish's particular sensory suite and for any specific environment it intends to navigate, humans generate a specific certainty matrix that loosely represents its perceptual confidence, along with a global measure for the probability that any given door will be closed versus opened in the real world.

Recall that Dervish has no encoders and that perceptual events are triggered asynchronously by the feature extraction processes. Therefore, Dervish has no action update step as depicted by equation (5.22). When the robot does detect a perceptual event, multiple perception update steps will need to be performed to update the likelihood of every possible robot position given Dervish's former belief state. This is because there is a chance that the robot has traveled *multiple* topological nodes since its previous perceptual event (i.e., false-negative errors). Formally, the perception update formula for Dervish is in reality a combination of the general form of action update and perception update. The likelihood of position n given perceptual event i is calculated as in equation (5.22):

$$p(n_t|i_t) = \int p(n_t|n'_{t-i}, i_t)p(n'_{t-i})dn'_{t-i} \tag{5.24}$$

The value of $p(n'_{t-i})$ denotes the likelihood of Dervish being at position n' as represented by Dervish's former belief state. The temporal subscript $t-i$ is used in lieu of $t-1$

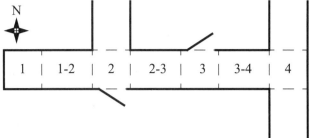

Figure 5.22
A realistic indoor topological environment.

because for each possible position n' the discrete topological distance from n' to n can vary depending on the specific topological map. The calculation of $p(n_t | n'_{t-i}, i_t)$ is performed by multiplying the probability of generating perceptual event i at position n by the probability of having failed to generate perceptual events at all nodes between n' and n:

$$p(n_t | n'_{t-i}, i_t) = p(i_t, n_t) \cdot p(\emptyset, n_{t-1}) \cdot p(\emptyset, n_{t-2}) \cdot \; ... \; \cdot p(\emptyset, n_{t-i+1}) \qquad (5.25)$$

For example (figure 5.22), suppose that the robot has only two nonzero nodes in its belief state, {1-2, 2-3}, with likelihoods associated with each possible position: $p(1-2) = 1.0$ and $p(2-3) = 0.2$. For simplicity assume the robot is facing east with certainty. Note that the likelihoods for nodes 1-2 and 2-3 do not sum to 1.0. These values are not formal probabilities, and so computational effort is minimized in Dervish by avoiding normalization altogether. Now suppose that a perceptual event is generated: the robot detects an open hallway on its left and an open door on its right simultaneously.

State 2-3 will progress potentially to states 3, 3-4, and 4. But states 3 and 3-4 can be eliminated because the likelihood of detecting an open door when there is only wall is zero. The likelihood of reaching state 4 is the product of the initial likelihood for state 2-3, 0.2, the likelihood of not detecting anything at node 3, (a), and the likelihood of detecting a hallway on the left and a door on the right at node 4, (b). Note that we assume the likelihood of detecting nothing at node 3-4 is 1.0 (a simplifying approximation).

(a) occurs only if Dervish fails to detect the door on its left at node 3 (either closed or open), $[0.6 \cdot 0.4 + (1 - 0.6) \cdot 0.05]$, and correctly detects nothing on its right, 0.7.

(b) occurs if Dervish correctly identifies the open hallway on its left at node 4, 0.90, and mistakes the right hallway for an open door, 0.10.

The final formula, $0.2 \cdot [0.6 \cdot 0.4 + 0.4 \cdot 0.05] \cdot 0.7 \cdot [0.9 \cdot 0.1]$, yields a likelihood of 0.003 for state 4. This is a partial result for $p(4)$ following from the prior belief state node 2-3.

Turning to the other node in Dervish's prior belief state, 1-2 will potentially progress to states 2, 2-3, 3, 3-4, and 4. Again, states 2-3, 3, and 3-4 can all be eliminated since the likelihood of detecting an open door when a wall is present is zero. The likelihood of state 2 is the product of the prior likelihood for state 1-2, (1.0), the likelihood of detecting the door on the right as an open door, $[0.6 \cdot 0 + 0.4 \cdot 0.9]$, and the likelihood of correctly detecting an open hallway to the left, 0.9. The likelihood for being at state 2 is then $1.0 \cdot 0.4 \cdot 0.9 \cdot 0.9 = 0.3$. In addition, 1-2 progresses to state 4 with a certainty factor of $4.3 \cdot 10^{-6}$, which is added to the certainty factor above to bring the total for state 4 to 0.00328. Dervish would therefore track the new belief state to be {2, 4}, assigning a very high likelihood to position 2 and a low likelihood to position 4.

Empirically, Dervish's map representation and localization system have proved to be sufficient for navigation of four indoor office environments: the artificial office environment created explicitly for the 1994 National Conference on Artificial Intelligence; and the psychology, history, and computer science departments at Stanford University. All of these experiments were run while providing Dervish with no notion of the distance between adjacent nodes in its topological map. It is a demonstration of the power of probabilistic localization that, in spite of the tremendous lack of action and encoder information, the robot is able to navigate several real-world office buildings successfully.

One open question remains with respect to Dervish's localization system. Dervish was not just a localizer but also a navigator. As with all multiple hypothesis systems, one must ask the question, how does the robot decide how to move, given that it has multiple possible robot positions in its representation? The technique employed by Dervish is a common technique in the mobile robotics field: plan the robot's actions by assuming that the robot's actual position is its most likely node in the belief state. Generally, the most likely position is a good measure of the robot's actual world position. However, this technique has shortcomings when the highest and second highest most likely positions have similar values. In the case of Dervish, it nonetheless goes with the highest-likelihood position at all times, save at one critical juncture. The robot's goal is to enter a target room and remain there. Therefore, from the point of view of its goal, it is critical that Dervish finish navigating only when the robot has strong confidence in being at the correct final location. In this particular case, Dervish's execution module refuses to enter a room if the gap between the most likely position and the second likeliest position is below a preset threshold. In such a case, Dervish will actively plan a path that causes it to move further down the hallway in an attempt to collect more sensor data and thereby increase the relative likelihood of one position in the multiple-hypothesis belief state.

Although computationally unattractive, one can go further, imagining a planning system for robots such as Dervish for which one specifies a *goal belief state* rather than a goal position. The robot can then reason and plan in order to achieve a goal confidence level, thus explicitly taking into account not only robot position but also the measured likelihood of each position. An example of just such a procedure is the sensory uncertainty field of Latombe [141], in which the robot must find a trajectory that reaches its goal while maximizing its localization confidence on-line.

5.6.2.3 Case study 2: Markov localization using a grid map
The major weakness of a purely topological decomposition of the environment is the resolution limitation imposed by such a granular representation. The position of the robot is usually limited to the resolution of a single node in such cases, and this may be undesirable for certain applications.

In this case study, we examine the work of Burgard and colleagues [49, 50] in which far more precise navigation is made possible using a grid-based representation while still employing the Markov localization technique.

The robot used by this research, Rhino, is an RWI B24 robot with twenty-four sonars and two Sick laser rangefinders. Clearly, at the sensory level this robot accumulates greater and more accurate range data than is possible with the handful of sonar sensors mounted on Dervish. In order to make maximal use of these fine-grained sensory data, Rhino uses a 2D geometric environmental representation of free and occupied space. This metric map is tessellated regularly into a *fixed decomposition* grid with each cell occupying 4 to 64 cm in various instantiations.

Like Dervish, Rhino uses multiple-hypothesis belief representation. In line with the far improved resolution of the environmental representation, the belief state representation of Rhino consists of a $15 \times 15 \times 15$ 3D array representing the probability of 15^3 possible robot positions (see figure 5.23). The resolution of the array is 15 cm $\times$ 15 cm $\times 1°$ (Note that unlike Dervish, which assumes its orientation is approximate and known, Rhino explicitly represents fine-grained alternative orientations, and so its belief state formally represents three degrees of freedom. As we have stated before, the resolution of the belief state representation must match the environmental representation in order for the overall system to function well.

Whereas Dervish made use of only perceptual events, ignoring encoder inputs and therefore metric distance altogether, Rhino uses the complete Markov probabilistic localization approach summarized in section 5.6.2.1, including both an explicit action update phase and a perception update phase at every cycle.

The discrete Markov chain version of action update is performed because of the tessellated representation of position. Given encoder measurements o at time t, each updated position probability in the belief state is expressed as a sum over previous possible positions and the motion model:

$$P(l_t | o_t) = \sum_{l'} P(l_t | l'_{t-1}, o_t) \cdot p(l'_{t-1}) \tag{5.26}$$

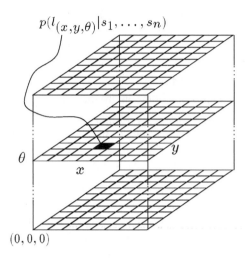

$p(l_{(x,y,\theta)}|s_1,\ldots,s_n)$

θ

x

y

$(0,0,0)$

Figure 5.23
The belief state representation 3D array used by Rhino (courtesy of W. Burgard and S. Thrun).

Note that equation (5.26) is simply a discrete version of equation (5.22). The specific motion model used by Rhino represents the result of motion as a Gaussian that is bounded (i.e., the tails of the distribution are finite). Rhino's kinematic configuration is a three-wheel synchro-drive rather than a differential-drive robot. Nevertheless, the error ellipses depicted in figures 5.4 and 5.5 are similar to the Gaussian bounds that result from Rhino's motion model.

The perception model follows the Bayes formula precisely, as in equation (5.21). Given a range perception i the probability of the robot being at each location l is updated as follows:

$$p(l|i) = \frac{p(i|l)p(l)}{p(i)} \tag{5.27}$$

Note that a denominator is used by Rhino, although the denominator is constant for varying values of l. This denominator acts as a normalizer to ensure that the probability measures in the belief state continue to sum to 1.

The critical challenge is, of course, the calculation of $p(i|l)$. In the case of Dervish, the number of possible values for i and l were so small that a simple table could suffice. However, with the fine-grained metric representation of Rhino, the number of possible sensor readings and environmental geometric contexts is extremely large. Thus, Rhino computes

$p(i|l)$ directly using a model of the robot's sensor behavior, its position l, and the local environmental metric map around l.

The sensor model must calculate the probability of a specific perceptual measurement given that its likelihood is justified by known errors of the sonar or laser rangefinder sensors. Three key assumptions are used to construct this sensor model:

1. If an object in the metric map is detected by a range sensor, the measurement error can be described with a distribution that has a mean at the correct reading.

2. There should always be a nonzero chance that a range sensor will read any measurement value, even if this measurement disagrees sharply with the environmental geometry.

3. In contrast to the generic error described in (2), there is a specific failure mode in ranging sensors whereby the signal is absorbed or coherently reflected, causing the sensor's range measurement to be maximal. Therefore, there is a local peak in the probability density distribution at the maximal reading of a range sensor.

By validating these assumptions using empirical sonar trials in multiple environments, the research group has delivered to Rhino a conservative and powerful sensor model for its particular sensors.

Figure 5.24 provides a simple 1D example of the grid-based Markov localization algorithm. The robot begins with a flat probability density function for its possible location. In other words, it initially has no bias regarding position. As the robot encounters first one door and then a second door, the probability density function over possible positions becomes first multimodal and finally unimodal and sharply defined. The ability of a Markov localization system to *localize* the robot from an initially lost belief state is its key distinguishing feature.

The resulting robot localization system has been part of a navigation system that has demonstrated great success both at the University of Bonn (Germany) and at a public museum in Bonn. This is a challenging application because of the dynamic nature of the environment, as the robot's sensors are frequently subject to occlusion due to humans gathering around the robot. Rhino's ability to function well in this setting is a demonstration of the power of the Markov localization approach.

Reducing computational complexity: randomized sampling. A great many steps are taken in real-world implementations such as Rhino in order to effect computational gains. These are valuable because, with an exact cell decomposition representation and use of raw sensor values rather than abstraction to features, such a robot has a massive computational effort associated with each perceptual update.

One class of techniques deserves mention because it can significantly reduce the computational overhead of techniques that employ fixed-cell decomposition representations.

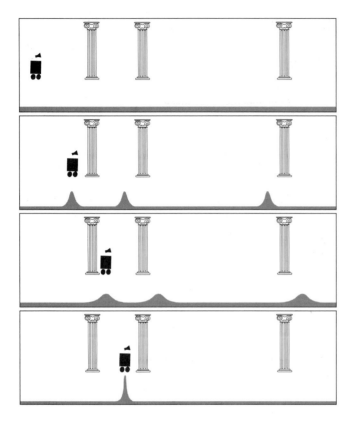

Figure 5.24
Improving belief state by moving.

The basic idea, which we call *randomized sampling,* is known alternatively as particle filter algorithms, condensation algorithms, and Monte Carlo algorithms [68, 144].

Irrespective of the specific technique, the basic algorithm is the same in all these cases. Instead of representing *every* possible robot position by representing the complete and correct belief state, an approximate belief state is constructed by representing only a *subset* of the complete set of possible locations that should be considered.

For example, consider a robot with a complete belief state of 10,000 possible locations at time t. Instead of tracking and updating all 10,000 possible locations based on a new sensor measurement, the robot can select only 10% of the stored locations and update only those locations. By weighting this sampling process with the probability values of the locations, one can bias the system to generate more samples at local peaks in the probability density function. So the resulting 1000 locations will be concentrated primarily at the highest probability locations. This biasing is desirable, but only to a point.

We also wish to ensure that *some* less likely locations are tracked, as otherwise, if the robot does indeed receive unlikely sensor measurements, it will fail to localize. This *randomization* of the sampling process can be performed by adding additional samples from a flat distribution, for example. Further enhancements of these randomized methods enable the number of statistical samples to be varied on the fly, based, for instance, on the ongoing localization confidence of the system. This further reduces the number of samples required on average while guaranteeing that a large number of samples will be used when necessary [68].

These sampling techniques have resulted in robots that function indistinguishably as compared to their full belief state set ancestors, yet use computationally a fraction of the resources. Of course, such sampling has a penalty: completeness. The probabilistically complete nature of Markov localization is violated by these sampling approaches because the robot is failing to update *all* the nonzero probability locations, and thus there is a danger that the robot, due to an unlikely but correct sensor reading, could become truly lost. Of course, recovery from a lost state is feasible just as with all Markov localization techniques.

5.6.3 Kalman filter localization

The Markov localization model can represent any probability density function over robot position. This approach is very general but, due to its generality, inefficient. Consider instead the key demands on a robot localization system. One can argue that it is not the exact replication of a probability density curve but the *sensor fusion* problem that is key to robust localization. Robots usually include a large number of heterogeneous sensors, each providing clues as to robot position and, critically, each suffering from its own failure modes. Optimal localization should take into account the information provided by all of these sensors. In this section we describe a powerful technique for achieving this sensor fusion, called the Kalman filter. This mechanism is in fact more efficient than Markov localization because of key simplifications when representing the probability density function of the robot's belief state and even its individual sensor readings, as described below. But the benefit of this simplification is a resulting *optimal recursive data-processing algorithm*. It incorporates all information, regardless of precision, to estimate the current value of the variable of interest (i.e., the robot's position). A general introduction to Kalman filters can be found in [106] and a more detailed treatment is presented in [3].

Figure 5.25 depicts the general scheme of Kalman filter estimation, where a system has a control signal and system error sources as inputs. A measuring device enables measuring some system states with errors. The Kalman filter is a mathematical mechanism for producing an optimal estimate of the system state based on the knowledge of the *system* and the *measuring device*, the description of the system noise and measurement errors and the

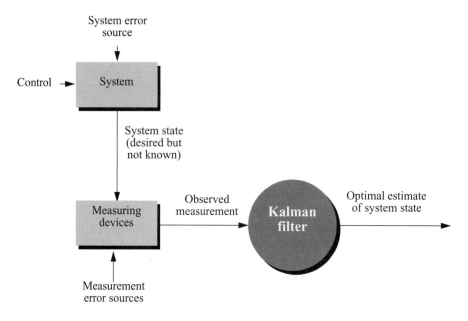

Figure 5.25
Typical Kalman filter application [106].

uncertainty in the dynamics models. Thus the Kalman filter *fuses* sensor signals and system knowledge in an optimal way. Optimality depends on the criteria chosen to evaluate the performance and on the assumptions. Within the Kalman filter theory the system is assumed to be *linear* and *white* with *Gaussian* noise. As we have discussed earlier, the assumption of Gaussian error is invalid for our mobile robot applications but, nevertheless, the results are extremely useful. In other engineering disciplines, the Gaussian error assumption has in some cases been shown to be quite accurate [106].

We begin with a section that introduces Kalman filter theory, then we present an application of that theory to the problem of mobile robot localization (5.6.3.2). Finally, section 5.6.3.2 presents a case study of a mobile robot that navigates indoor spaces by virtue of Kalman filter localization.

5.6.3.1 Introduction to Kalman filter theory

The basic Kalman filter method allows multiple measurements to be incorporated optimally into a single estimate of state. In demonstrating this, first we make the simplifying assumption that the state does not change (e.g., the robot does not move) between the acquisition of the first and second measurement. After presenting this static case, we can introduce *dynamic prediction* readily.

Static estimation. Suppose that our robot has two sensors, an ultrasonic range sensor and a laser rangefinding sensor. The laser rangefinder provides far richer and more accurate data for localization, but it will suffer from failure modes that differ from that of the sonar ranger. For instance, a glass wall will be transparent to the laser but, when measured head-on, the sonar will provide an accurate reading. Thus we wish to combine the information provided by the two sensors, recognizing that such sensor fusion, when done in a principled way, can only result in information gain.

The Kalman filter enables such fusion extremely efficiently, as long as we are willing to approximate the error characteristics of these sensors with unimodal, zero-mean, Gaussian noise. Specifically, assume we have taken two measurements, one with the sonar sensor at time k and one with the laser rangefinder at time $k+1$. Based on each measurement individually we can estimate the robot's position. Such an estimate derived from the sonar is q_1 and the estimate of position based on the laser is q_2. As a simplified way of characterizing the error associated with each of these estimates, we presume a (unimodal) Gaussian probability density curve and thereby associate one variance with each measurement: σ_1^2 and σ_2^2. The two dashed probability densities in figure 5.26 depict two such measurements. In summary, this yields two robot position estimates:

$$\hat{q}_1 = q_1 \text{ with variance } \sigma_1^2 \tag{5.28}$$

$$\hat{q}_2 = q_2 \text{ with variance } \sigma_2^2. \tag{5.29}$$

The question is, how do we *fuse* (combine) these data to get the best estimate $\hat{q}$ for the robot position? We are assuming that there was no robot motion between time k and time $k+1$, and therefore we can directly apply the same weighted least-squares technique of equation (5.26) in section 4.3.1.1. Thus we write

$$S = \sum_{i=1}^{n} w_i (\hat{q} - q_i)^2 \tag{5.30}$$

with w_i being the weight of measurement i. To find the minimum error we set the derivative of S equal to zero.

$$\frac{\partial S}{\partial \hat{q}} = \frac{\partial}{\partial \hat{q}} \sum_{i=1}^{n} w_i (\hat{q} - q_i)^2 = 2 \sum_{i=1}^{n} w_i (\hat{q} - q_i) = 0 \tag{5.31}$$

$$\sum_{i=1}^{n} w_i \hat{q} - \sum_{i=1}^{n} w_i q_i = 0 \tag{5.32}$$

$$\hat{q} = \frac{\sum_{i=1}^{n} w_i q_i}{\sum_{i=1}^{n} w_i} \tag{5.33}$$

If we take as the weight w_i

$$w_i = \frac{1}{\sigma_i^2} \tag{5.34}$$

then the value of $\hat{q}$ in terms of two measurements can be defined as follows:

$$\hat{q} = \frac{\frac{1}{\sigma_1^2} q_1 + \frac{1}{\sigma_2^2} q_2}{\frac{1}{\sigma_1^2} + \frac{1}{\sigma_2^2}} = \frac{\sigma_2^2}{\sigma_1^2 + \sigma_2^2} q_1 + \frac{\sigma_1^2}{\sigma_1^2 + \sigma_2^2} q_2 \tag{5.35}$$

$$\frac{1}{\sigma^2} = \frac{1}{\sigma_1^2} + \frac{1}{\sigma_2^2} = \frac{\sigma_2^2 + \sigma_1^2}{\sigma_1^2 \sigma_2^2} \quad ; \quad \sigma^2 = \frac{\sigma_1^2 \sigma_2^2}{\sigma_2^2 + \sigma_1^2} \tag{5.36}$$

Note that from equation (5.36) we can see that the resulting variance σ^2 is less than all the variances σ_i^2 of the individual measurements. Thus the uncertainty of the position estimate has been decreased by combining the two measurements. The solid probability density curve represents the result of the Kalman filter in figure 5.26, depicting this result. Even poor measurements, such as are provided by the sonar, will only increase the precision of an estimate. This is a result that we expect based on information theory.

Equation (5.35) can be rewritten as

$$\hat{q} = q_1 + \frac{\sigma_1^2}{\sigma_1^2 + \sigma_2^2} (q_2 - q_1) \tag{5.37}$$

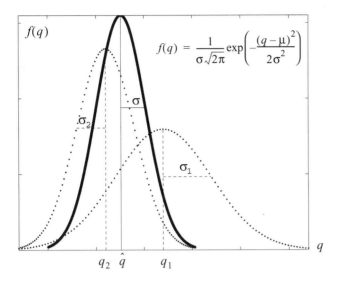

Figure 5.26
Fusing probability density of two estimates [106].

or, in the final form that is used in Kalman filter implementation,

$$\hat{x}_{k+1} = \hat{x}_k + K_{k+1}(z_{k+1} - \hat{x}_k)$$

(5.38)

where

$$K_{k+1} = \frac{\sigma_k^2}{\sigma_k^2 + \sigma_z^2} \quad ; \quad \sigma_k^2 = \sigma_1^2 \quad ; \quad \sigma_z^2 = \sigma_2^2$$

(5.39)

Equation (5.38) tells us, that the best estimate $\hat{x}_{k+1}$ of the state x_{k+1} at time $k+1$ is equal to the best prediction of the value $\hat{x}_k$ before the new measurement z_{k+1} is taken, plus a correction term of an optimal weighting value times the difference between z_{k+1} and the best prediction $\hat{x}_k$ at time $k+1$. The updated variance of the state $\hat{x}_{k+1}$ is given using equation (5.36)

$$\sigma_{k+1}^2 = \sigma_k^2 - K_{k+1}\sigma_k^2$$

(5.40)

The new, fused estimate of robot position provided by the Kalman filter is again subject to a Gaussian probability density curve. Its mean and variance are simply functions of the inputs' means and variances. Thus the Kalman filter provides both a compact, simplified representation of uncertainty and an extremely efficient technique for combining heterogeneous estimates to yield a new estimate for our robot's position.

Dynamic estimation. Next, consider a robot that moves between successive sensor measurements. Suppose that the motion of the robot between times k and $k+1$ is described by the velocity u and the noise w which represents the uncertainty of the actual velocity:

$$\frac{dx}{dt} = u + w \tag{5.41}$$

If we now start at time k, knowing the variance σ_k^2 of the robot position at this time and knowing the variance σ_w^2 of the motion, we obtain for the time k' just when the measurement is taken,

$$\hat{x}_{k'} = \hat{x}_k + u(t_{k+1} - t_k) \tag{5.42}$$

$$\sigma_{k'}^2 = \sigma_k^2 + \sigma_w^2[t_{k+1} - t_k] \tag{5.43}$$

where

$$t_{k'} = t_{k+1};$$

t_{k+1} and t_k are the time in seconds at $k+1$ and k respectively.

Thus $\hat{x}_{k'}$ is the optimal prediction of the robot's position just as the measurement is taken at time $k+1$. It describes the growth of position error until a new measurement is taken (figure 5.27).

We can now rewrite equations (5.38) and (5.39) using equations (5.42) and (5.43).

$$\hat{x}_{k+1} = \hat{x}_{k'} + K_{k+1}(z_{k+1} - \hat{x}_{k'})$$

$$= [\hat{x}_k + u(t_{k+1} - t_k)] + K_{k+1}[z_{k+1} - \hat{x}_k - u(t_{k+1} - t_k)] \tag{5.44}$$

$$K_{k+1} = \frac{\sigma_{k'}^2}{\sigma_{k'}^2 + \sigma_z^2} = \frac{\sigma_k^2 + \sigma_w^2[t_{k+1} - t_k]}{\sigma_k^2 + \sigma_w^2[t_{k+1} - t_k] + \sigma_z^2} \tag{5.45}$$

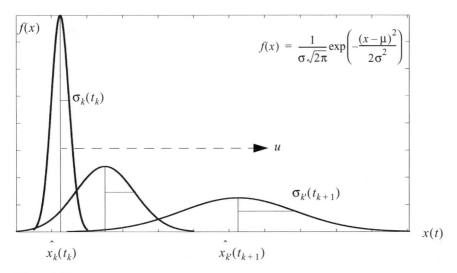

$$f(x) = \frac{1}{\sigma\sqrt{2\pi}}\exp\left(-\frac{(x-\mu)^2}{2\sigma^2}\right)$$

Figure 5.27
Propagation of probability density of a moving robot [106].

The optimal estimate at time $k+1$ is given by the last estimate at k and the estimate of the robot motion including the estimated movement errors.

By extending the above equations to the vector case and allowing time-varying parameters in the system and a description of noise, we can derive the Kalman filter localization algorithm.

5.6.3.2 Application to mobile robots: Kalman filter localization
The Kalman filter is an optimal and efficient sensor fusion technique. Application of the Kalman filter to localization requires posing the robot localization problem as a sensor fusion problem. Recall that the basic probabilistic update of robot belief state can be segmented into two phases, *perception update* and *action update,* as specified by equations (5.21) and (5.22).

The key difference between the Kalman filter approach and our earlier Markov localization approach lies in the perception update process. In Markov localization, the entire perception, that is, the robot's set of instantaneous sensor measurements, is used to update each possible robot position in the belief state individually using the Bayes formula. In some cases, the perception is abstract, having been produced by a feature extraction mechanism, as in Dervish. In other cases, as with Rhino, the perception consists of raw sensor readings.

By contrast, perception update using a Kalman filter is a multistep process. The robot's total sensory input is treated not as a monolithic whole but as a set of extracted features that

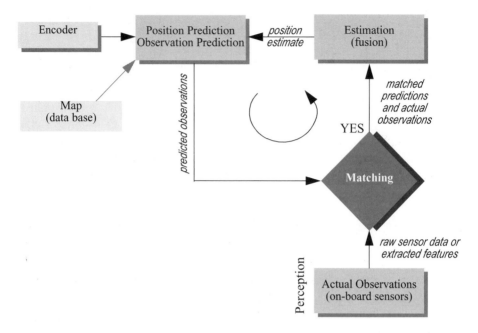

Figure 5.28
Schematic for Kalman filter mobile robot localization (see [23]).

each relate to objects in the environment. Given a set of possible features, the Kalman filter is used to fuse the distance estimate from each feature to a matching object in the map. Instead of carrying out this matching process for many possible robot locations individually as in the Markov approach, the Kalman filter accomplishes the same probabilistic update by treating the whole, unimodal, and Gaussian belief state at once. Figure 5.28 depicts the particular schematic for Kalman filter localization.

The first step is action update or *position prediction*, the straightforward application of a Gaussian error motion model to the robot's measured encoder travel. The robot then collects actual sensor data and extracts appropriate features (e.g., lines, doors, or even the value of a specific sensor) in the *observation* step. At the same time, based on its predicted position in the map, the robot generates a *measurement prediction* which identifies the features that the robot expects to find and the positions of those features. In *matching* the robot identifies the best pairings between the features actually extracted during observation and the expected features due to measurement prediction. Finally, the Kalman filter can fuse the information provided by all of these matches to update the robot belief state in *estimation*.

In the following sections these five steps are described in greater detail. The presentation is based on the work of Leonard and Durrant-Whyte [23, pp. 61–65].

1. Robot position prediction. The robot's position at timestep $k+1$ is predicted based on its old location (at timestep k) and its movement due to the control input $u(k)$:

$$\hat{p}(k+1|k) = f(\hat{p}(k|k), u(k)) \tag{5.46}$$

For the differential-drive robot, $\hat{p}(k+1|k) = p'$ is derived in equations (5.6) and (5.7) respectively.

Knowing the plant and error model, we can also compute the variance $\Sigma_p(k+1|k)$ associated with this prediction [see equation. (5.9), section 5.2.4]:

$$\Sigma_p(k+1|k) = \nabla_p f \cdot \Sigma_p(k|k) \cdot \nabla_p f^T + \nabla_u f \cdot \Sigma_u(k) \cdot \nabla_u f^T \tag{5.47}$$

This allows us to predict the robot's position and its uncertainty after a movement specified by the control input $u(k)$. Note that the belief state is assumed to be Gaussian, and so we can characterize the belief state with just the two parameters $\hat{p}(k+1|k)$ and $\Sigma_p(k+1|k)$.

2. Observation. The second step it to obtain sensor measurements $Z(k+1)$ from the robot at time $k+1$. In this presentation, we assume that the observation is the result of a feature extraction process executed on the raw sensor data. Therefore, the observation consists of a set n_0 of single observations $z_j(k+1)$ extracted from various sensors. Formally, each single observation can represent an extracted feature such as a line or door, or even a single, raw sensor value.

The parameters of the features are usually specified in the sensor frame and therefore in a local reference frame of the robot. However, for matching we need to represent the observations and measurement predictions in the same frame $\{S\}$. In our presentation we will transform the measurement predictions from the global coordinate frame to the sensor frame $\{S\}$. This transformation is specified in the function h_i discussed in the next paragraph.

3. Measurement prediction. We use the predicted robot position $\hat{p}(k+1|k)$ and the map $M(k)$ to generate multiple predicted feature observations z_t. Each predicted feature has its position transformed into the sensor frame:

$$\hat{z}_i(k+1) = h_i(z_t, \hat{p}(k+1|k)) \tag{5.48}$$

We can define the measurement prediction as the set containing all n_t predicted feature observations:

$$\hat{Z}(k+1) = \{\hat{z}_i(k+1) | (1 \le i \le n_t)\} \tag{5.49}$$

The predicted state estimate $\hat{p}(k+1|k)$ is used to compute the measurement Jacobian ∇h_i for each prediction. As you will see in the example below, the function h_i is mainly a coordinate transformation between the world frame and the sensor frame.

4. Matching. At this point we have a set of actual, single observations, which are features in sensor space, and we also have a set of predicted features, also positioned in sensor space. The matching step has the purpose of identifying all of the single observations that match specific predicted features well enough to be used during the estimation process. In other words, we will, for a subset of the observations and a subset of the predicted features, find pairings that intuitively say "this observation is the robot's measurement of this predicted feature based on the map."

Formally, the goal of the matching procedure is to produce an assignment from observations $z_j(k+1)$ to the targets z_t (stored in the map). For each measurement prediction for which a corresponding observation is found we calculate the innovation $v_{ij}(k+1)$. *Innovation* is a measure of the difference between the predicted and observed measurements:

$$v_{ij}(k+1) = [z_j(k+1) - \hat{z}_i(k+1)]$$
$$= [z_j(k+1) - h_i(z_t, \hat{p}(k+1|k))] \tag{5.50}$$

The innovation covariance $\Sigma_{IN,\,ij}(k+1)$ can be found by applying the error propagation law [section 4.2.2, equation (4.60)]:

$$\Sigma_{IN,\,ij}(k+1) = \nabla h_i \cdot \Sigma_p(k+1|k) \cdot \nabla h_i^T + \Sigma_{R,\,i}(k+1) \tag{5.51}$$

where $\Sigma_{R,\,i}(k+1)$ represents the covariance (noise) of the measurement $z_i(k+1)$.

To determine the validity of the correspondence between measurement prediction and observation, a *validation gate* has to be specified. A possible definition of the validation gate is the Mahalanobis distance:

$$v_{ij}^T(k+1) \cdot \Sigma_{IN,\,ij}^{-1}(k+1) \cdot v_{ij}(k+1) \le g^2 \tag{5.52}$$

However, dependent on the application, the sensors, and the environment models, more sophisticated validation gates might be employed.

The validation equation is used to test observation $z_j(k+1)$ for membership in the validation gate for each predicted measurement. When a single observation falls in the validation gate, we get a successful match. If one observation falls in multiple validation gates, the best matching candidate is selected or multiple hypotheses are tracked. Observations that do not fall in the validation gate are simply ignored for localization. Such observations could have resulted from objects not in the map, such as new objects (e.g., someone places a large box in the hallway) or transient objects (e.g., humans standing next to the robot may form a line feature). One approach is to take advantage of such unmatched observations to populate the robot's map.

5. Estimation: applying the Kalman filter. Next we compute the best estimate $\hat{p}(k+1|k+1)$ of the robot's position based on the position prediction and all the observations at time $k+1$. To do this position update, we first stack the validated observations $z_j(k+1)$ into a single vector to form $z(k+1)$ and designate the composite innovation $v(k+1)$. Then we stack the measurement Jacobians ∇h_i for each validated measurement together to form the composite Jacobian ∇h and the measurement error (noise) vector $\Sigma_R(k+1) = diag[\Sigma_{R,i}(k+1)]$. We can then compute the composite innovation covariance $\Sigma_{IN}(k+1)$ according to equation (5.51) and by utilizing the well-known result [3] that the Kalman gain can be written as

$$K(k+1) = \Sigma_p(k+1|k) \cdot \nabla h^T \cdot \Sigma_{IN}^{-1}(k+1) \tag{5.53}$$

we can update the robot's position estimate

$$\hat{p}(k+1|k+1) = \hat{p}(k+1|k) + K(k+1) \cdot v(k+1) \tag{5.54}$$

with the associated variance

$$\Sigma_p(k+1|k+1) = \Sigma_p(k+1|k) - K(k+1) \cdot \Sigma_{IN}(k+1) \cdot K^T(k+1) \tag{5.55}$$

For the 1D case and with $h_i(z_t, \hat{p}(k+1|k)) = z_t$ we can show that this formula corresponds to the 1D case derived earlier

Equation (5.53) is simplified to

$$K(k+1) = \frac{\sigma_p^2(k+1|k)}{\sigma_{IN}^2(k+1)} = \frac{\sigma_p^2(k+1|k)}{\sigma_p^2(k+1|k) + \sigma_R^2(k+1)} \tag{5.56}$$

corresponding to equation (5.45), and equation (5.54) simplifies to

$$\hat{p}(k+1|k+1) = \hat{p}(k+1|k) + K(k+1) \cdot v(k+1)$$
$$= \hat{p}(k+1|k) + K(k+1) \cdot [z_j(k+1) - h_i(z_t, \hat{p}(k+1|k))]$$
$$= \hat{p}(k+1|k) + K(k+1) \cdot [z_j(k+1) - z_t] \qquad (5.57)$$

corresponding to equation (5.44).

5.6.3.3 Case study: Kalman filter localization with line feature extraction

The Pygmalion robot at EPFL is a differential-drive robot that uses a laser rangefinder as its primary sensor [37, 38]. In contrast to both Dervish and Rhino, the environmental representation of Pygmalion is continuous and abstract: the map consists of a set of infinite lines describing the environment. Pygmalion's belief state is, of course, represented as a Gaussian distribution since this robot uses the Kalman filter localization algorithm. The value of its mean position μ is represented to a high level of precision, enabling Pygmalion to localize with very high precision when desired. Below, we present details for Pygmalion's implementation of the five Kalman filter localization steps. For simplicity we assume that the sensor frame $\{S\}$ is equal to the robot frame $\{R\}$. If not specified all the vectors are represented in the world coordinate system $\{W\}$.

1. Robot position prediction. At the time increment k the robot is at position $p(k) = \begin{bmatrix} x(k) & y(k) & \theta(k) \end{bmatrix}^T$ and its best position estimate is $\hat{p}(k|k)$. The control input $u(k)$ drives the robot to the position $p(k+1)$ (figure 5.29).

The robot position prediction $\hat{p}(k+1)$ at the time increment $k+1$ can be computed from the previous estimate $\hat{p}(k|k)$ and the odometric integration of the movement. For the differential drive that Pygmalion has we can use the model (odometry) developed in section 5.2.4:

$$\hat{p}(k+1|k) = \hat{p}(k|k) + u(k) = \hat{p}(k|k) + \begin{bmatrix} \dfrac{\Delta s_r + \Delta s_l}{2} \cos\left(\theta + \dfrac{\Delta s_r - \Delta s_l}{2b}\right) \\ \dfrac{\Delta s_r + \Delta s_l}{2} \sin\left(\theta + \dfrac{\Delta s_r - \Delta s_l}{2b}\right) \\ \dfrac{\Delta s_r - \Delta s_l}{b} \end{bmatrix} \qquad (5.58)$$

with the updated covariance matrix

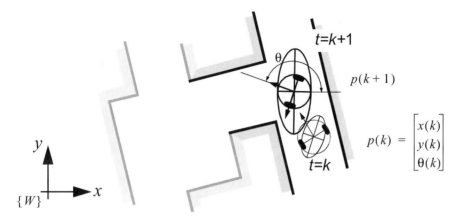

Figure 5.29
Prediction of the robot's position (thick) based on its former position (thin) and the executed movement. The ellipses drawn around the robot positions represent the uncertainties in the x,y direction
(e.g.; 3σ). The uncertainty of the orientation θ is not represented in the picture.

$$\Sigma_p(k+1|k) = \nabla_p f \cdot \Sigma_p(k|k) \cdot \nabla_p f^T + \nabla_u f \cdot \Sigma_u(k) \cdot \nabla_u f^T \qquad (5.59)$$

where

$$\Sigma_u = cov(\Delta s_r, \Delta s_l) = \begin{bmatrix} k_r|\Delta s_r| & 0 \\ 0 & k_l|\Delta s_l| \end{bmatrix} \qquad (5.60)$$

2. Observation. For line-based localization, each single observation (i.e., a line feature) is
extracted from the raw laser rangefinder data and consists of the two line parameters $\beta_{0,j}$,
$\beta_{1,j}$ or α_j, r_j (figure 4.36) respectively. For a rotating laser rangefinder, a representation
in the polar coordinate frame is more appropriate and so we use this coordinate frame here:

$$z_j(k+1) = {}^R\begin{bmatrix} \alpha_j \\ r_j \end{bmatrix} \qquad (5.61)$$

After acquiring the raw data at time $k+1$, lines and their uncertainties are extracted (figure 5.30a, b). This leads to n_0 observed lines with $2n_0$ line parameters (figure 5.30c) and
a covariance matrix for each line that can be calculated from the uncertainties of all the

measurement points contributing to each line as developed for line extraction in section 4.3.1.1:

$$\Sigma_{R,j} = \begin{bmatrix} \sigma_{\alpha\alpha} & \sigma_{\alpha r} \\ \sigma_{r\alpha} & \sigma_{rr} \end{bmatrix}_j \tag{5.62}$$

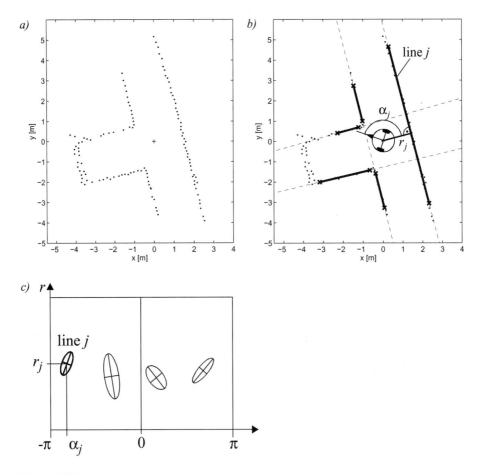

Figure 5.30
Observation: From the raw data (a) acquired by the laser scanner at time $k + 1$, lines are extracted (b). The line parameters α_j and r_j and its uncertainties can be represented in the model space (c).

3. Measurement prediction. Based on the stored map and the predicted robot position $\hat{p}(k|k)$, the measurement predictions of expected features $z_{t,\,i}$ are generated (figure 5.31). To reduce the required calculation power, there is often an additional step that first selects the possible features, in this case lines, from the whole set of features in the map. These lines are stored in the map and specified in the world coordinate system $\{W\}$. Therefore they need to be transformed to the robot frame $\{R\}$:

$$
{}^{W}z_{t,\,i} = {}^{W}\begin{bmatrix} \alpha_{t,\,i} \\ r_{t,\,i} \end{bmatrix} \rightarrow {}^{R}z_{t,\,i} = {}^{R}\begin{bmatrix} \alpha_{t,\,i} \\ r_{t,\,i} \end{bmatrix}
\tag{5.63}
$$

According to figure (5.31), the transformation is given by

$$
\hat{z}_i(k+1) = {}^{R}\begin{bmatrix} \alpha_{t,\,i} \\ r_{t,\,i} \end{bmatrix} = h_i(z_{t,\,i},\,\hat{p}(k+1|k))
$$

$$
= \begin{bmatrix} {}^{W}\alpha_{t,\,i} - {}^{W}\hat{\theta}(k+1|k) \\ {}^{W}r_{t,\,i} - ({}^{W}\hat{x}(k+1|k)\cos({}^{W}\alpha_{t,\,i}) + {}^{W}\hat{y}(k+1|k)\sin({}^{W}\alpha_{t,\,i})) \end{bmatrix}
\tag{5.64}
$$

and its Jacobian ∇h_i by

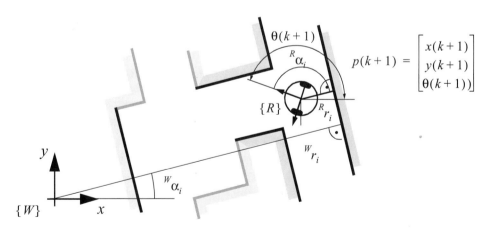

Figure 5.31
Representation of the target position in the world coordinate frame $\{W\}$ and robot coordinate frame $\{R\}$.

$$\nabla h_i = \begin{bmatrix} \dfrac{\partial \alpha_{t,i}}{\partial \hat{x}} & \dfrac{\partial \alpha_{t,i}}{\partial \hat{y}} & \dfrac{\partial \alpha_{t,i}}{\partial \hat{\theta}} \\[2ex] \dfrac{\partial r_{t,i}}{\partial \hat{x}} & \dfrac{\partial r_{t,i}}{\partial \hat{y}} & \dfrac{\partial r_{t,i}}{\partial \hat{\theta}} \end{bmatrix} = \begin{bmatrix} 0 & 0 & -1 \\ -\cos{}^W\alpha_{t,i} & -\sin{}^W\alpha_{t,i} & 0 \end{bmatrix} \tag{5.65}$$

The measurement prediction results in predicted lines represented in the robot coordinate frame (figure 5.32). They are uncertain, because the prediction of robot position is uncertain.

4. Matching. For matching, we must find correspondence (or a pairing) between predicted and observed features (figure 5.33). In our case we take the Mahalanobis distance

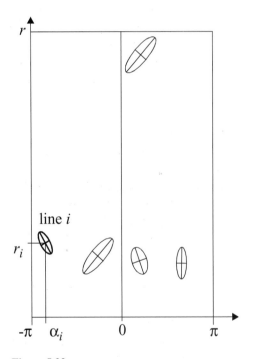

Figure 5.32
Measurement predictions: Based on the map and the estimated robot position the targets (visible lines) are predicted. They are represented in the model space similar to the observations.

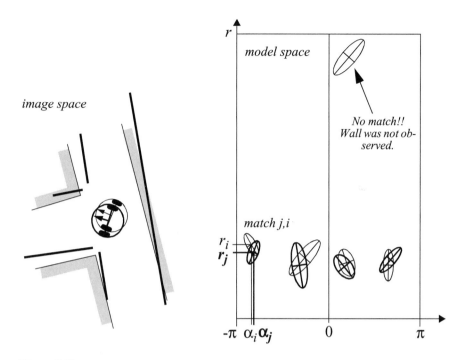

Figure 5.33
Matching: The observations (thick) and measurement prediction (thin) are matched and the innovation and its uncertainties are calculated.

$$v_{ij}^T(k+1) \cdot \Sigma_{IN, ij}^{-1}(k+1) \cdot v_{ij}(k+1) \leq g^2 \tag{5.66}$$

with

$$v_{ij}(k+1) = [z_j(k+1) - h_i(z_t, \hat{p}(k+1|k))]$$

$$= \begin{bmatrix} \alpha_j \\ r_j \end{bmatrix} - \begin{bmatrix} {}^W\alpha_{t, i} - {}^W\hat{\theta}(k+1|k) \\ {}^Wr_{t, i} - ({}^W\hat{x}(k+1|k) \cos({}^W\alpha_{t, i}) + {}^W\hat{y}(k+1|k) \sin({}^W\alpha_{t, i})) \end{bmatrix} \tag{5.67}$$

$$\Sigma_{IN, ij}(k+1) = \nabla h_i \cdot \Sigma_p(k+1|k) \cdot \nabla h_i^T + \Sigma_{R, i}(k+1) \tag{5.68}$$

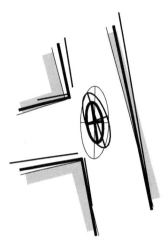

Figure 5.34
Kalman filter estimation of the new robot position: By fusing the prediction of robot position (thin) with the innovation gained by the measurements (thick) we get the updated estimate $\hat{p}(k|k)$ of the robot position (very thick).

to enable finding the best matches while eliminating all other remaining observed and predicted unmatched features.

5. Estimation. Applying the Kalman filter results in a final pose estimate corresponding to the weighted sum of (figure 5.34)

- the pose estimates of each matched pairing of observed and predicted features;

- the robot position estimation based on odometry and observation positions.

5.7   Other Examples of Localization Systems

Markov localization and Kalman filter localization have been two extremely popular strategies for research mobile robot systems navigating indoor environments. They have strong formal bases and therefore well-defined behavior. But there are a large number of other localization techniques that have been used with varying degrees of success on commercial and research mobile robot platforms. We will not explore the space of all localization systems in detail. Refer to surveys such as [5] for such information.

There are, however, several categories of localization techniques that deserve mention. Not surprisingly, many implementations of these techniques in commercial robotics

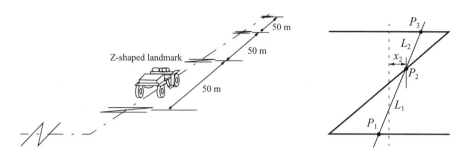

Figure 5.35
Z-shaped landmarks on the ground. Komatsu Ltd., Japan [5 pp. 179-180]

employ modifications of the robot's environment, something that the Markov localization and Kalman filter localization communities eschew. In the following sections, we briefly identify the general strategy incorporated by each category and reference example systems, including, as appropriate, those that modify the environment and those that function without environmental modification.

5.7.1 Landmark-based navigation

Landmarks are generally defined as passive objects in the environment that provide a high degree of localization accuracy when they are within the robot's field of view. Mobile robots that make use of landmarks for localization generally use artificial markers that have been placed by the robot's designers to make localization easy.

The control system for a landmark-based navigator consists of two discrete phases. When a landmark is in view, the robot localizes frequently and accurately, using action update and perception update to track its position without cumulative error. But when the robot is in no landmark "zone," then only action update occurs, and the robot accumulates position uncertainty until the next landmark enters the robot's field of view.

The robot is thus effectively *dead-reckoning* from landmark zone to landmark zone. This in turn means the robot must consult its map carefully, ensuring that each motion between landmarks is sufficiently short, given its motion model, that it will be able to localize successfully upon reaching the next landmark.

Figure 5.35 shows one instantiation of landmark-based localization. The particular shape of the landmarks enables reliable and accurate pose estimation by the robot, which must travel using *dead reckoning* between the landmarks.

One key advantage of the landmark-based navigation approach is that a strong formal theory has been developed for this general system architecture [98]. In this work, the authors have shown precise assumptions and conditions which, when satisfied, guarantee that the robot will always be able to localize successfully. This work also led to a real-world demonstration of landmark-based localization. Standard sheets of paper were placed on the ceiling of the Robotics Laboratory at Stanford University, each with a unique checkerboard pattern. A Nomadics 200 mobile robot was fitted with a monochrome CCD camera aimed vertically up at the ceiling. By recognizing the paper landmarks, which were placed approximately 2 m apart, the robot was able to localize to within several centimeters, then move, using dead reckoning, to another landmark zone.

The primary disadvantage of landmark-based navigation is that in general it requires significant environmental modification. Landmarks are local, and therefore a large number are usually required to cover a large factory area or research laboratory. For example, the Robotics Laboratory at Stanford made use of approximately thirty discrete landmarks, all affixed individually to the ceiling.

5.7.2 Globally unique localization

The landmark-based navigation approach makes a strong general assumption: when the landmark is in the robot's field of view, localization is essentially perfect. One way to reach the Holy Grail of mobile robotic localization is to effectively enable such an assumption to be valid no matter *where* the robot is located. It would be revolutionary if a look at the robot's sensors immediately identified its particular location, uniquely and repeatedly.

Such a strategy for localization is surely aggressive, but the question of whether it can be done is primarily a question of sensor technology and sensing software. Clearly, such a localization system would need to use a sensor that collects a very large amount of information. Since vision does indeed collect far more information than previous sensors, it has been used as the sensor of choice in research toward globally unique localization.

Figure 4.49 depicts the image taken by a catadioptric camera system. If humans were able to look at an individual such picture and identify the robot's location in a well-known environment, then one could argue that the information for globally unique localization does exist within the picture; it must simply be teased out.

One such approach has been attempted by several researchers and involves constructing one or more image histograms to represent the information content of an image stably (see e.g., figure 4.50 and section 4.3.2.2). A robot using such an image-histogramming system has been shown to uniquely identify individual rooms in an office building as well as individual sidewalks in an outdoor environment. However, such a system is highly sensitive to external illumination and provides only a level of localization resolution equal to the visual footprint of the camera optics.

The angular histogram depicted in figure 4.39 of the previous chapter is another example in which the robot's sensor values are transformed into an identifier of location. However, due to the limited information content of sonar ranging strikes, it is likely that two *places* in the robot's environment may have angular histograms that are too similar to be differentiated successfully.

One way of attempting to gather sufficient sonar information for global localization is to allow the robot time to gather a large amount of sonar data into a local evidence grid (i.e., occupancy grid) first, then match the local evidence grid with a global metric map of the environment. In [129] the researchers demonstrate such a system as able to localize on the fly even as significant changes are made to the environment, degrading the fidelity of the map. Most interesting is that the local evidence grid represents information well enough that it can be used to correct and update the map over time, thereby leading to a localization system that provides corrective feedback to the environmental representation directly. This is similar in spirit to the idea of taking rejected observed features in the Kalman filter localization algorithm and using them to create new features in the map.

A most promising, new method for globally unique localization is called *mosaic-based localization* [83]. This fascinating approach takes advantage of an environmental feature that is rarely used by mobile robots: fine-grained floor texture. This method succeeds primarily because of the recent ubiquity of very fast processors, very fast cameras, and very large storage media.

The robot is fitted with a high-quality high-speed CCD camera pointed toward the floor, ideally situated between the robot's wheels, and illuminated by a specialized light pattern off the camera axis to enhance floor texture. The robot begins by collecting images of the entire floor in the robot's workspace using this camera. Of course, the memory requirements are significant, requiring a 10 GB drive in order to store the complete image library of a 300 x 300 area.

Once the complete image mosaic is stored, the robot can travel any trajectory on the floor while tracking its own position without difficulty. Localization is performed by simply recording one image, performing action update, then performing perception update by matching the image to the mosaic database using simple techniques based on image database matching. The resulting performance has been impressive: such a robot has been shown to localize repeatedly with 1 mm precision while moving at 25 km/hr.

The key advantage of globally unique localization is that, when these systems function correctly, they greatly simplify robot navigation. The robot can move to any point and will always be assured of localizing by collecting a sensor scan.

But the main disadvantage of globally unique localization is that it is likely that this method will *never* offer a complete solution to the localization problem. There will always be cases where local sensory information is truly ambiguous and, therefore, globally unique localization using only current sensor information is unlikely to succeed. Humans often have excellent *local positioning systems*, particularly in nonrepeating and well-known environments such as their homes. However, there are a number of environments in which such immediate localization is challenging even for humans: consider hedge mazes and

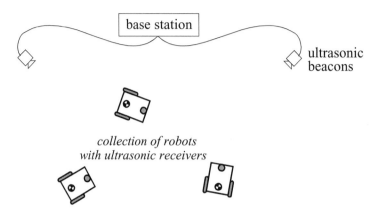

Figure 5.36
Active ultrasonic beacons.

large new office buildings with repeating halls that are identical. Indeed, the mosaic-based localization prototype described above encountered such a problem in its first implementation. The floor of the factory floor had been freshly painted and was thus devoid of sufficient micro fractures to generate texture for correlation. Their solution was to modify the environment after all, painting random texture onto the factory floor.

5.7.3 Positioning beacon systems

One of the most reliable solutions to the localization problem is to design and deploy an active beacon system specifically for the target environment. This is the preferred technique used by both industry and military applications as a way of ensuring the highest possible reliability of localization. The GPS system can be considered as just such a system (see section 4.1.5.1).

Figure 5.36 depicts one such beacon arrangement for a collection of robots. Just as with GPS, by designing a system whereby the robots localize passively while the beacons are active, any number of robots can simultaneously take advantage of a single beacon system. As with most beacon systems, the design depicted depends foremost upon geometric principles to effect localization. In this case the robots must know the positions of the two active ultrasonic beacons in the global coordinate frame in order to localize themselves to the global coordinate frame.

A popular type of beacon system in industrial robotic applications is depicted in figure 5.37. In this case beacons are retroreflective markers that can be easily detected by a mobile robot based on their reflection of energy back to the robot. Given known positions for the optical retroreflectors, a mobile robot can identify its position whenever it has three such

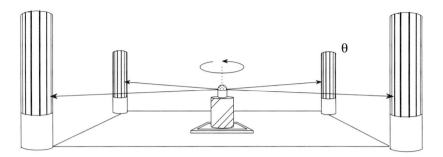

Figure 5.37
Passive optical beacons.

beacons in sight simultaneously. Of course, a robot with encoders can localize over time as well, and does not need to measure its angle to all three beacons at the same instant.

The advantage of such beacon-based systems is usually extremely high engineered reliability. By the same token, significant engineering usually surrounds the installation of such a system in a specific commercial setting. Therefore, moving the robot to a different factory floor will be both, time consuming and expensive. Usually, even changing the routes used by the robot will require serious re-engineering.

5.7.4 Route-based localization

Even more reliable than beacon-based systems are route-based localization strategies. In this case, the route of the robot is explicitly marked so that it can determine its position, not relative to some global coordinate frame but relative to the specific path it is allowed to travel. There are many techniques for marking such a route and the subsequent intersections. In all cases, one is effectively creating a railway system, except that the railway system is somewhat more flexible and certainly more human-friendly than a physical rail. For example, high ultraviolet-reflective, optically transparent paint can mark the route such that only the robot, using a specialized sensor, easily detects it. Alternatively, a guidewire buried underneath the hall can be detected using inductive coils located on the robot chassis.

In all such cases, the robot localization problem is effectively trivialized by forcing the robot to always follow a prescribed path. To be fair, there are new industrial *unmanned guided vehicles* that do deviate briefly from their route in order to avoid obstacles. Nevertheless, the cost of this extreme reliability is obvious: the robot is much more inflexible given such localization means, and therefore any change to the robot's behavior requires significant engineering and time.

5.8   Autonomous Map Building

All of the localization strategies we have discussed require human effort to install the robot
into a space. Artificial environmental modifications may be necessary. Even if this not be
case, a map of the environment must be created for the robot. But a robot that localizes successfully has the right sensors for detecting the environment, and so the robot ought to build
its own map. This ambition goes to the heart of autonomous mobile robotics. In prose, we
can express our eventual goal as follows:

Starting from an arbitrary initial point, a mobile robot should be able to autonomously
explore the environment with its on-board sensors, gain knowledge about it, interpret the
scene, build an appropriate map, and localize itself relative to this map.

Accomplishing this goal robustly is probably years away, but an important subgoal is
the invention of techniques for autonomous creation and modification of an environmental
map. Of course a mobile robot's sensors have only a limited range, and so it must physically
explore its environment to build such a map. So, the robot must not only create a map but
it must do so while moving and localizing to explore the environment. In the robotics community, this is often called the simultaneous localization and mapping (SLAM) problem,
arguably the most difficult problem specific to mobile robot systems.

The reason that SLAM is difficult is born precisely from the interaction between the
robot's position updates as it localizes and its mapping actions. If a mobile robot updates
its position based on an observation of an imprecisely known feature, the resulting position
estimate becomes correlated with the feature location estimate. Similarly, the map becomes
correlated with the position estimate if an observation taken from an imprecisely known
position is used to update or add a feature to the map. The general problem of map-building
is thus an example of the chicken-and-egg problem. For localization the robot needs to
know where the features are, whereas for map-building the robot needs to know where it is
on the map.

The only path to a complete and optimal solution to this joint problem is to consider all
the correlations between position estimation and feature location estimation. Such cross-
correlated maps are called *stochastic* maps, and we begin with a discussion of the theory
behind this approach in the following section [55].

Unfortunately, implementing such an optimal solution is computationally prohibitive. In
response a number of researchers have offered other solutions that have functioned well in
limited circumstances. Section 5.8.2 characterizes these alternative partial solutions.

5.8.1   The stochastic map technique

Figure 5.38 shows a general schematic incorporating map building and maintenance into
the standard localization loop depicted by figure 5.28 during the discussion of Kalman filter

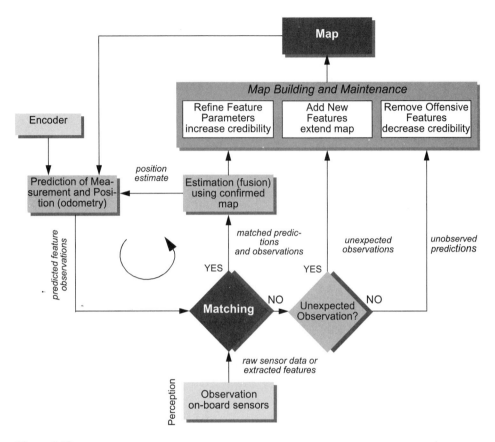

Figure 5.38
General schematic for concurrent localization and map building (see [23]).

localization [23]. The added arcs represent the additional flow of information that occurs when there is an imperfect match between observations and measurement predictions.

Unexpected observations will effect the creation of new features in the map, whereas unobserved measurement predictions will effect the removal of features from the map. As discussed earlier, each specific prediction or observation has an unknown exact value and so it is represented by a distribution. The uncertainties of all of these quantities must be considered throughout this process.

The new type of map we are creating not only has features in it, as did previous maps, but it also has varying degrees of probability that each feature is indeed part of the environment. We represent this new map M with a set n of probabilistic feature locations $\hat{z}_t$, each

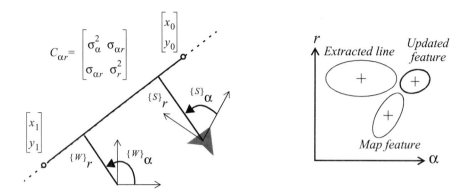

Figure 5.39
Uncertainties in the map.

with the covariance matrix Σ_t and an associated *credibility factor* c_t between 0 and 1 quantifying the belief in the existence of the feature in the environment (see figure 5.39):

$$M = \{\hat{z}_t, \Sigma_t, c_t | (1 \le t \le n)\} \tag{5.69}$$

In contrast to the map used for Kalman filter localization previously, the map M is not assumed to be precisely known because it will be created by an uncertain robot over time. This is why the features $\hat{z}_t$ are described with associated covariance matrices Σ_t.

Just as with Kalman filter localization, the matching step yields has three outcomes in regard to measurement predictions and observations: *matched prediction and observations*, *unexpected observations,* and *unobserved predictions*. Localization, or the position update of the robot, proceeds as before. However, the map is also updated now, using all three outcomes and complete propagation of all the correlated uncertainties (see [23] for more details).

An interesting variable is the credibility factor c_t, which governs the likelihood that the mapped feature is indeed in the environment. How should the robot's failure to match observed features to a particular map feature reduce that map feature's credibility? And also, how should the robot's success at matching a mapped feature increase the chance that the mapped feature is "correct?" In [23] the following function is proposed for calculating credibility:

$$c_t(k) = 1 - e^{-\left(\frac{n_s}{a} - \frac{n_u}{b}\right)} \tag{5.70}$$

where a and b define the learning and forgetting rate and n_s and n_u are the number of matched and unobserved predictions up to time k, respectively. The update of the covariance matrix Σ_t can be done similarly to the position update seen in the previous section. In map-building the feature positions and the robot's position are strongly correlated. This forces us to use a *stochastic map*, in which all cross-correlations must be updated in each cycle [55, 113, 136].

The stochastic map consists of a stacked system state vector:

$$X = \begin{bmatrix} x_r(k) & x_1(k) & x_2(k) & \dots & x_n(k) \end{bmatrix}^T \tag{5.71}$$

and a system state covariance matrix:

$$\Sigma = \begin{bmatrix} C_{rr} & C_{r1} & C_{r2} & \dots & C_{rn} \\ C_{1r} & C_{11} & \dots & \dots & C_{1n} \\ C_{2r} & \dots & \dots & \dots & C_{2n} \\ \dots & \dots & \dots & \dots & \dots \\ C_{nr} & C_{n1} & C_{n2} & \dots & C_{nn} \end{bmatrix} \tag{5.72}$$

where the index r stands for the robot and the index $i = 1$ to n for the features in the map.

In contrast to localization based on an a priori accurate map, in the case of a stochastic map the cross-correlations must be maintained and updated as the robot is performing automatic map-building. During each localization cycle, the cross-correlations robot-to-feature and feature-to-robot are also updated. In short, this optimal approach requires every value in the map to depend on every other value, and therein lies the reason that such a complete solution to the automatic mapping problem is beyond the reach of even today's computational resources.

5.8.2 Other mapping techniques

The mobile robotics research community has spent significant research effort on the problem of automatic mapping, and has demonstrated working systems in many environments without having solved the complete stochastic map problem described earlier. This field of mobile robotics research is extremely large, and this text will not present a comprehensive survey of the field. Instead, we present below two key considerations associated with automatic mapping, together with brief discussions of the approaches taken by several automatic mapping solutions to overcome these challenges.

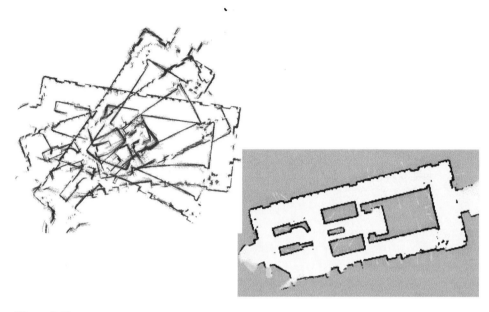

Figure 5.40
Cyclic environments: A naive, local mapping strategy with small local error leads to global maps that
have a significant error, as demonstrated by this real-world run on the left. By applying topological
correction, the grid map on the right is extracted (courtesy of S. Thrun [142]).

5.8.2.1 Cyclic environments

Possibly the single hardest challenge for automatic mapping to be conquered is to correctly
map cyclic environments. The problem is simple: given an environment that has one or
more loops or cycles (e.g., four hallways that intersect to form a rectangle), create a globally consistent map for the whole environment.

This problem is hard because of the fundamental behavior of automatic mapping systems; the maps they create are not perfect. And, given any local imperfection, accumulating
such imperfections over time can lead to arbitrarily large *global* errors between a map, at
the macrolevel, and the real world, as shown in figure 5.40. Such global error is usually
irrelevant to mobile robot localization and navigation. After all, a warped map will still
serve the robot perfectly well so long as the local error is bounded. However, an extremely
large loop still eventually returns to the same spot, and the robot must be able to note this
fact in its map. Therefore, global error does indeed matter in the case of cycles.

In some of the earliest work attempting to solve the cyclic environment problem,
Kuipers and Byun [94] used a purely topological representation of the environment, reasoning that the topological representation only captures the most abstract, most important

features and avoids a great deal of irrelevant detail. When the robot arrives at a topological node that could be the same as a previously visited and mapped node (e.g., similar distinguishing features), then the robot postulates that it has indeed returned to the same node. To check this hypothesis, the robot explicitly plans and moves to adjacent nodes to see if its perceptual readings are consistent with the cycle hypothesis.

With the recent popularity of metric maps, such as fixed decomposition grid representations, the cycle detection strategy is not as straightforward. Two important features are found in most autonomous mapping systems that claim to solve the cycle detection problem. First, as with many recent systems, these mobile robots tend to accumulate recent perceptual history to create small-scale local *submaps* [51, 74, 157]. Each submap is treated as a single sensor during the robot's position update. The advantage of this approach is twofold. Because odometry is relatively accurate over small distances, the relative registration of features and raw sensor strikes in a local submap will be quite accurate. In addition to this, the robot will have created a virtual sensor system with a significantly larger horizon than its actual sensor system's range. In a sense, this strategy at the very least defers the problem of very large cyclic environments by increasing the map scale that can be handled well by the robot.

The second recent technique for dealing with cycle environments is in fact a return to the topological representation. Some recent automatic mapping systems will attempt to identify cycles by associating a topology with the set of metric submaps, explicitly identifying the loops first at the topological level. In the case of [51], for example, the topological level loop is identified by a human who pushes a button at a known landmark position. In the case of [74], the topological level loop is determined by performing correspondence tests between submaps, postulating that two submaps represent the same place in the environment when the correspondence is good.

One could certainly imagine other augmentations based on known topological methods. For example, the globally unique localization methods described in section 5.7 could be used to identify topological correctness. It is notable that the automatic mapping research of the present has, in many ways, returned to the basic topological correctness question that was at the heart of some of the earliest automatic mapping research in mobile robotics more than a decade ago. Of course, unlike that early work, today's automatic mapping results boast correct cycle detection combined with high-fidelity geometric maps of the environment.

5.8.2.2 Dynamic environments

A second challenge extends not just to existing autonomous mapping solutions but to the basic formulation of the stochastic map approach. All of these strategies tend to assume that the environment is either unchanging or changes in ways that are virtually insignificant. Such assumptions are certainly valid with respect to some environments, such as, for example, the computer science department of a university at 3 AM. However, in a great many cases this assumption is incorrect. In the case of wide-open spaces that are popular gathering places for humans, there is rapid change in the free space and a vast majority of sensor strikes represent detection of transient humans rather than fixed surfaces such as the perimeter wall. Another class of dynamic environments are spaces such as factory floors and warehouses, where the objects being stored redefine the topology of the pathways on a day-to-day basis as shipments are moved in and out.

In all such dynamic environments, an automatic mapping system should capture the *salient* objects detected by its sensors and, furthermore, the robot should have the flexibility to modify its map as to the positions of these salient objects changes. The subject of *continuous mapping*, or mapping of dynamic environments, is to some degree a direct outgrowth of successful strategies for automatic mapping of unfamiliar environments. For example, in the case of stochastic mapping using the credibility factor c_t mechanism, the credibility equation can continue to provide feedback regarding the probability of the existence of various mapped features after the initial map creation process is ostensibly complete. Thus, a mapping system can become a map-modifying system by simply continuing to operate. This is most effective, of course, if the mapping system is real-time and incremental. If map construction requires off-line global optimization, then the desire to make small-grained, incremental adjustments to the map is more difficult to satisfy.

Earlier we stated that a mapping system should capture only the *salient* objects detected by its sensors. One common argument for handling the detection of, for instance, humans in the environment is that mechanisms such as c_t can take care of all features that did not deserve to be mapped in the first place. For example, in [157] the authors develop a system based on a set of local occupancy grids (called *evidence grids*) and a global occupancy grid. Each time the robot's most recent local evidence grid is used to update a region of the global occupancy grid, extraneous occupied cells in the global occupancy grid are freed if the local occupancy grid detected no objects (with high confidence) at those same positions.

The general solution to the problem of detecting salient features, however, begs a solution to the perception problem in general. When a robot's sensor system can reliably detect the difference between a wall and a human, using, for example, a vision system, then the problem of mapping in dynamic environments will become significantly more straightforward.

We have discussed just two important considerations for automatic mapping. There is still a great deal of research activity focusing on the general map-building and localization problem [22, 23, 55, 63, 80, 134, 147, 156]. However, there are few groups working on the general problem of probabilistic map-building (i.e., stochastic maps) and, so far, a consistent and absolutely general solution is yet to be found. This field is certain to produce significant new results in the next several years, and as the perceptual power of robots improves we expect the payoff to be greatest here.

6 Planning and Navigation

6.1 Introduction

This book has focused on the elements of a mobile robot that are critical to robust mobility: the kinematics of locomotion; sensors for determining the robot's environmental context; and techniques for localizing with respect to its map. We now turn our attention to the robot's cognitive level. Cognition generally represents the purposeful decision-making and execution that a system utilizes to achieve its highest-order goals.

In the case of a mobile robot, the specific aspect of cognition directly linked to robust mobility is *navigation competence*. Given partial knowledge about its environment and a goal position or series of positions, navigation encompasses the ability of the robot to act based on its knowledge and sensor values so as to reach its goal positions as efficiently and as reliably as possible. The focus of this chapter is how the tools of the previous chapters can be combined to solve this navigation problem.

Within the mobile robotics research community, a great many approaches have been proposed for solving the navigation problem. As we sample from this research background it will become clear that in fact there are strong similarities between all of these approaches even though they appear, on the surface, quite disparate. The key difference between various navigation architectures is the manner in which they decompose the problem into smaller subunits. In section 6.3 below, we describe the most popular navigation architectures, contrasting their relative strengths and weaknesses.

First, however, in section 6.2 we discuss two key additional competences required for mobile robot navigation. Given a map and a goal location, *path planning* involves identifying a trajectory that will cause the robot to reach the goal location when executed. Path planning is a strategic problem-solving competence, as the robot must decide what to do over the long term to achieve its goals.

The second competence is equally important but occupies the opposite, tactical extreme. Given real-time sensor readings, *obstacle avoidance* means modulating the trajectory of the robot in order to avoid collisions. A great variety of approaches have demonstrated competent obstacle avoidance, and we survey a number of these approaches as well.

6.2   Competences for Navigation: Planning and Reacting

In the artificial intelligence community planning and reacting are often viewed as contrary approaches or even opposites. In fact, when applied to physical systems such as mobile robots, planning and reacting have a strong complementarity, each being critical to the other's success. The navigation challenge for a robot involves executing a course of action (or plan) to reach its goal position. During execution, the robot must react to unforeseen events (e.g., obstacles) in such a way as to still reach the goal. Without reacting, the planning effort will not pay off because the robot will never physically reach its goal. Without planning, the reacting effort cannot guide the overall robot behavior to reach a distant goal – again, the robot will never reach its goal.

An information-theoretic formulation of the navigation problem will make this complementarity clear. Suppose that a robot M at time i has a map M_i and an initial belief state b_i. The robot's goal is to reach a position p while satisfying some temporal constraints: $loc_g(R) = p$; $(g \le n)$. Thus the robot must be at location p at or before timestep n.

Although the goal of the robot is distinctly physical, the robot can only really sense its belief state, not its physical location, and therefore we map the goal of reaching location p to reaching a belief state b_g, corresponding to the belief that $loc_g(R) = p$. With this formulation, a plan q is nothing more than one or more trajectories from b_i to b_g. In other words, plan q will cause the robot's belief state to transition from b_i to b_g if the plan is executed from a world state consistent with both b_i and M_i.

Of course the problem is that the latter condition may not be met. It is entirely possible that the robot's position is not quite consistent with b_i, and it is even likelier that M_i is either incomplete or incorrect. Furthermore, the real-world environment is dynamic. Even if M_i is correct as a single snapshot in time, the planner's model regarding how M changes over time is usually imperfect.

In order to reach its goal nonetheless, the robot must incorporate new information gained during plan execution. As time marches forward, the environment changes and the robot's sensors gather new information. This is precisely where reacting becomes relevant. In the best of cases, reacting will modulate robot behavior locally in order to correct the planned-upon trajectory so that the robot still reaches the goal. At times, unanticipated new information will require changes to the robot's strategic plans, and so ideally the planner also incorporates new information as that new information is received.

Taken to the limit, the planner would incorporate every new piece of information in real time, instantly producing a new plan that in fact reacts to the new information appropriately. This theoretical extreme, at which point the concept of planning and the concept of reacting merge, is called *integrated planning and execution* and is discussed in section 6.3.4.3.

A useful concept throughout this discussion of robot architecture involves whether particular design decisions sacrifice the system's ability to achieve a desired goal whenever a solution exists. This concept is termed *completeness*. More formally, the robot system is *complete* if and only if, for all possible problems (i.e., initial belief states, maps, and goals), when there exists a trajectory to the goal belief state, the system will achieve the goal belief state (see [27] for further details). Thus when a system is incomplete, then there is at least one example problem for which, although there is a solution, the system fails to generate a solution. As you may expect, achieving completeness is an ambitious goal. Often, completeness is sacrificed for computational complexity at the level of representation or reasoning. Analytically, it is important to understand how completeness is compromised by each particular system.

In the following sections, we describe key aspects of planning and reacting as they apply to a mobile robot path planning and obstacle avoidance and describe how representational decisions impact the potential completeness of the overall system. For greater detail, refer to [21, 30, chapter 25].

6.2.1 Path planning

Even before the advent of affordable mobile robots, the field of path-planning was heavily studied because of its applications in the area of industrial manipulator robotics. Interestingly, the path planning problem for a manipulator with, for instance, six degrees of freedom is far more complex than that of a differential-drive robot operating in a flat environment. Therefore, although we can take inspiration from the techniques invented for manipulation, the path-planning algorithms used by mobile robots tend to be simpler approximations owing to the greatly reduced degrees of freedom. Furthermore, industrial robots often operate at the fastest possible speed because of the economic impact of high throughput on a factory line. So, the dynamics and not just the kinematics of their motions are significant, further complicating path planning and execution. In contrast, a number of mobile robots operate at such low speeds that dynamics are rarely considered during path planning, further simplifying the mobile robot instantiation of the problem.

Configuration space. Path planning for manipulator robots and, indeed, even for most mobile robots, is formally done in a representation called *configuration space*. Suppose that a robot arm (e.g., SCARA robot) has k degrees of freedom. Every state or configuration of the robot can be described with k real values: $q_1, ..., q_k$. The k-values can be regarded as a point p in a k-dimensional space called the configuration space C of the robot. This description is convenient because it allows us to describe the complex 3D shape of the robot with a single k-dimensional point.

Now consider the robot arm moving in an environment where the workspace (i.e., its physical space) contains known obstacles. The goal of path planning is to find a path in the

we can generally distinguish b/w global path planning and local obstacle avoidance

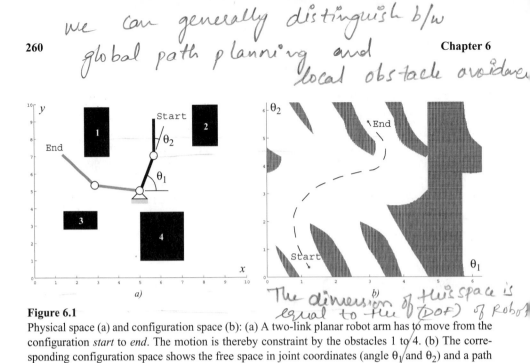

a)

b)

The dimension of this space is equal to the (DOF) of Robot

Figure 6.1
Physical space (a) and configuration space (b): (a) A two-link planar robot arm has to move from the configuration *start* to *end*. The motion is thereby constraint by the obstacles 1 to 4. (b) The corresponding configuration space shows the free space in joint coordinates (angle θ_1 and θ_2) and a path that achieves the goal.

↙Degrees of freedom

physical space from the initial position of the arm to the goal position, avoiding all collisions with the obstacles. This is a difficult problem to visualize and solve in the physical space, particularly as k grows large. But in configuration space the problem is straightforward. If we define the *configuration space obstacle* O as the subspace of C where the robot arm bumps into something, we can compute the free space $F = C - O$ in which the robot can move safely.

Figure 6.1 shows a picture of the physical space and configuration space for a planar robot arm with two links. The robot's goal is to move its end effector from position *start* to *end*. The configuration space depicted is 2D because each of two joints can have any position from 0 to 2π. It is easy to see that the solution in C-space is a line from *start* to *end* that remains always within the free space of the robot arm.

For mobile robots operating on flat ground, we generally represent robot position with three variables (x, y, θ), as in chapter 3. But, as we have seen, most robots are nonholonomic, using differential-drive systems or Ackerman steered systems. For such robots, the nonholonomic constraints limit the robot's velocity $(\dot{x}, \dot{y}, \dot{\theta})$ in each configuration (x, y, θ). For details regarding the construction of the appropriate *free space* to solve such path-planning problems, see [21, p. 405].

In mobile robotics, the most common approach is to assume for path-planning purposes that the robot is in fact holonomic, simplifying the process tremendously. This is especially common for differential-drive robots because they can rotate in place and so a holonomic path can be easily mimicked if the rotational position of the robot is not critical.

Furthermore, mobile roboticists will often plan under the further assumption that the robot is simply a *point*. Thus we can further reduce the configuration space for mobile robot path planning to a 2D representation with just x- and y-axes. The result of all this simplification is that the configuration space looks essentially identical to a 2D (i.e., flat) version of the physical space, with one important difference. Because we have reduced the robot to a point, we must inflate each obstacle by the size of the robot's radius to compensate. With this new, simplified configuration space in mind, we can now introduce common techniques for mobile robot path planning.

global

Path-planning overview. The robot's environment representation can range from a continuous geometric description to a decomposition-based geometric map or even a topological map, as described in section 5.5. The first step of any path-planning system is to transform this possibly continuous environmental model into a discrete map suitable for the chosen path-planning algorithm. Path planners differ as to how they effect this discrete decomposition. We can identify three general strategies for decomposition:

1. Road map: identify a set of routes within the free space.

2. Cell decomposition: discriminate between free and occupied cells.

3. Potential field: impose a mathematical function over the space.

The following sections present common instantiations of the road map and cell decomposition path-planning techniques, noting in each case whether completeness is sacrificed by the particular representation.

6.2.1.1 Road map path planning

Road map approaches capture the connectivity of the robot's free space in a network of 1D curves or lines, called *road maps*. Once a road map is constructed, it is used as a network of road (path) segments for robot motion planning. Path planning is thus reduced to connecting the initial and goal positions of the robot to the road network, then searching for a series of roads from the initial robot position to its goal position.

The road map is a decomposition of the robot's configuration space based specifically on obstacle geometry. The challenge is to construct a set of roads that together enable the robot to go anywhere in its free space, while minimizing the number of total roads. Generally, completeness is preserved in such decompositions as long as the true degrees of freedom of the robot have been captured with appropriate fidelity. We describe two road map approaches below that achieve this result with dramatically different types of roads. In the case of the *visibility graph*, roads come as close as possible to obstacles and resulting paths are minimum-length solutions. In the case of the *Voronoi diagram*, roads stay as far away as possible from obstacles.

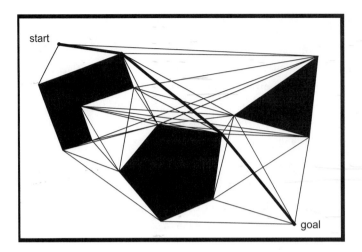

Figure 6.2
Visibility graph [21]. The nodes of the graph are the initial and goal points and the vertices of the configuration space obstacles (polygons). All nodes which are visible from each other are connected by
straight-line segments, defining the road map. This means there are also edges along each polygon's
sides.

Visibility graph. The visibility graph for a polygonal configuration space C consists of
edges joining all pairs of vertices that can see each other (including both the initial and goal
positions as vertices as well). The unobstructed straight lines (roads) joining those vertices
are obviously the shortest distances between them. The task of the path planner is thus to
find the shortest path from the initial position to the goal position along the roads defined
by the visibility graph (figure 6.2).

Visibility graph path planning is moderately popular in mobile robotics, partly because
implementation is quite simple. Particularly when the environmental representation
describes objects in the environment as polygons in either continuous or discrete space, the
visibility graph search can employ the obstacle polygon descriptions readily.

There are, however, two important caveats when employing visibility graph search.
First, the size of the representation and the number of edges and nodes increase with the
number of obstacle polygons. Therefore the method is extremely fast and efficient in sparse
environments, but can be slow and inefficient compared to other techniques when used in
densely populated environments.

The second caveat is a much more serious potential flaw: the solution paths found by
visibility graph planning tend to take the robot as close as possible to obstacles on the way

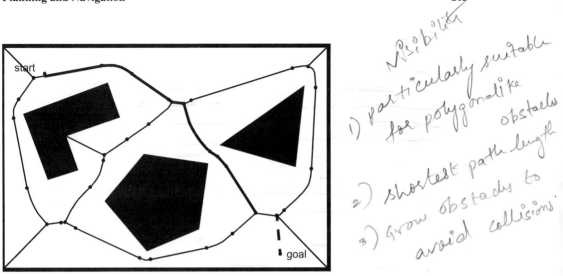

Handwritten annotations in margin:

visibility

1) particularly suitable for polygon-like obstacles

2) shortest path length

3) grow obstacles to avoid collisions

Figure 6.3
Voronoi diagram [21]. The Voronoi diagram consists of the lines constructed from all points that are equidistant from two or more obstacles. The initial q_{init} and goal q_{goal} configurations are mapped into the Voronoi diagram to q'_{init} and q'_{goal}, each by drawing the line along which its distance to the boundary of the obstacles increases the fastest. The direction of movement on the Voronoi diagram is also selected so that the distance to the boundaries increases fastest. The points on the Voronoi diagram represent transitions from line segments (minimum distance between two lines) to parabolic segments (minimum distance between a line and a point).

to the goal. More formally, we can prove that visibility graph planning is *optimal* in terms of the length of the solution path. This powerful result also means that all sense of safety, in terms of staying a reasonable distance from obstacles, is sacrificed for this optimality. The common solution is to grow obstacles by significantly more than the robot's radius, or, alternatively, to modify the solution path after path planning to distance the path from obstacles when possible. Of course such actions sacrifice the optimal-length results of visibility graph path planning.

Voronoi diagram. Contrasting with the visibility graph approach, a Voronoi diagram is a complete road map method that tends to maximize the distance between the robot and obstacles in the map. For each point in the free space, compute its distance to the nearest obstacle. Plot that distance in figure 6.3 as a height coming out of the page. The height increases as you move away from an obstacle. At points that are equidistant from two or more obstacles, such a distance plot has sharp ridges. The Voronoi diagram consists of the edges formed by these sharp ridge points. When the configuration space obstacles are polygons, the Voronoi diagram consists of straight and parabolic segments. Algorithms that

works also for map-building. More on the voronoi edges.

264

Chapter 6

find paths on the Voronoi road map are complete just like visibility graph methods, because the existence of a path in the free space implies the existence of one on the Voronoi diagram as well (i.e., both methods guarantee completeness). However, the path in the Voronoi diagram is usually far from optimal in the sense of total path length.

The Voronoi diagram has an important weakness in the case of limited range localization sensors. Since this path-planning algorithm maximizes the distance between the robot and objects in the environment, any short-range sensor on the robot will be in danger of failing to sense its surroundings. If such short-range sensors are used for localization, then the chosen path will be quite poor from a localization point of view. On the other hand, the visibility graph method can be designed to keep the robot as close as desired to objects in the map.

There is, however, an important subtle advantage that the Voronoi diagram method has over most other obstacle avoidance techniques: *executability*. Given a particular planned path via Voronoi diagram planning, a robot with range sensors, such as a laser rangefinder or ultrasonics, can follow a Voronoi edge in the physical world using simple control rules that match those used to create the Voronoi diagram: the robot maximizes the readings of local minima in its sensor values. This control system will naturally keep the robot on Voronoi edges, so that Voronoi-based motion can mitigate encoder inaccuracy. This interesting physical property of the Voronoi diagram has been used to conduct automatic mapping of an environment by finding and moving on unknown Voronoi edges, then constructing a consistent Voronoi map of the environment [59].

6.2.1.2 Cell decomposition path planning

The idea behind cell decomposition is to discriminate between geometric areas, or cells, that are free and areas that are occupied by objects. The basic cell decomposition path-planning algorithm can be summarized as follows [30]:

- Divide F into simple, connected regions called "cells".

- Determine which opens cells are adjacent and construct a "connectivity graph".

- Find the cells in which the initial and goal configurations lie and search for a path in the connectivity graph to join the initial and goal cell.

- From the sequence of cells found with an appropriate searching algorithm, compute a path within each cell, for example, passing through the midpoints of the cell boundaries or by a sequence of wall-following motions and movements along straight lines.

An important aspect of cell decomposition methods is the placement of the boundaries between cells. If the boundaries are placed as a function of the structure of the environment, such that the decomposition is lossless, then the method is termed *exact cell decomposition*. If the decomposition results in an approximation of the actual map, the system is termed

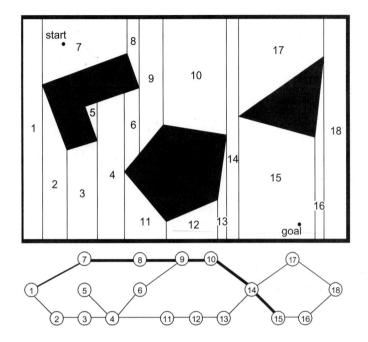

Figure 6.4
Example of exact cell decomposition.

approximate cell decomposition. In section 5.5.2 we described these decomposition strate-gies as they apply to the design of map representation for localization. Here, we briefly summarize these two cell decomposition techniques once again, providing greater detail about their advantages and disadvantages relative to path planning.

Exact cell decomposition. Figure 6.4 depicts exact cell decomposition, whereby the boundary of cells is based on geometric criticality. The resulting cells are each either com-pletely free or completely occupied, and therefore path planning in the network is complete, like the road map based methods above. The basic abstraction behind such a decomposition is that the particular position of the robot within each cell of free space does not matter; what matters is rather the robot's ability to traverse from each free cell to adjacent free cells.

The key disadvantage of exact cell decomposition is that the number of cells and, there-fore, overall path planning computational efficiency depends upon the density and com-plexity of objects in the environment, just as with road mapbased systems. The key advantage is a result of this same correlation. In environments that are extremely sparse, the number of cells will be small, even if the geometric size of the environment is very large. Thus the representation will be efficient in the case of large, sparse environments. Practically speaking, due to complexities in implementation, the exact cell decomposition technique is used relatively rarely in mobile robot applications, although it remains a solid choice when a lossless representation is highly desirable, for instance to preserve completeness fully.

Approximate cell decomposition. By contrast, approximate cell decomposition is one of the most popular techniques for mobile robot path planning. This is partly due to the popularity of grid-based environmental representations. These grid-based representations are themselves fixed grid-size decompositions and so they are identical to an approximate cell decomposition of the environment.

The most popular form of this, shown in figure 5.15 of chapter 5, is the fixed-size cell decomposition. The cell size is not dependent on the particular objects in an environment at all, and so narrow passageways can be lost due to the inexact nature of the tessellation. Practically speaking, this is rarely a problem owing to the very small cell size used (e.g., 5 cm on each side). The great benefit of fixed size cell decomposition is the low computational complexity of path planning.

For example, NF1, often called *grassfire*, is an efficient and simple-to-implement technique for finding routes in such fixed-size cell arrays [96]. The algorithm simply employs wavefront expansion from the goal position outward, marking for each cell its distance to the goal cell [79]. This process continues until the cell corresponding to the initial robot position is reached. At this point, the path planner can estimate the robot's distance to the goal position as well as recover a specific solution trajectory by simply linking together cells that are adjacent and always closer to the goal.

Given that the entire array can be in memory, each cell is only visited once when looking for the shortest discrete path from the initial position to the goal position. So, the search is linear in the number of cells only. Thus complexity does not depend on the sparseness and density of the environment, nor on the complexity of the objects' shapes in the environment. Formally, this grassfire transform is simply breadth-first search implemented in the constrained space of an adjacency array. For more information on breadth-first search and other graph search techniques, refer to [30].

The fundamental cost of the fixed decomposition approach is memory. For a large environment, even when sparse, this grid must be represented in its entirety. Practically, due to the falling cost of computer memory, this disadvantage has been mitigated in recent years. The Cye robot is an example of a commercially available robot that performs all its path planning on a 2D 2 cm fixed-cell decomposition of the environment using a sophisticated grassfire algorithm that avoids known obstacles and prefers known routes [42].

Figure 5.16 of chapter 5 illustrates a variable-size approximate cell decomposition method. The free space is externally bounded by a rectangle and internally bounded by three polygons. The rectangle is recursively decomposed into smaller rectangles. Each decomposition generates four identical new rectangles. At each level of resolution only the cells whose interiors lie entirely in the free space are used to construct the connectivity graph. Path planning in such adaptive representations can proceed in a hierarchical fashion. Starting with a coarse resolution, the resolution is reduced until either the path planner identifies a solution or a limit resolution is attained (e.g, k • size of robot). In contrast to the exact cell decomposition method, the approximate approach can sacrifice completeness, but it is mathematically less involving and thus easier to implement. In contrast to the fixed-size cell decomposition, variable-size cell decomposition will adapt to the complexity of the environment, and therefore sparse environments will contain appropriately fewer cells, consuming dramatically less memory.

6.2.1.3 Potential field path planning

Potential field path planning creates a field, or gradient, across the robot's map that directs the robot to the goal position from multiple prior positions (see [21]). This approach was originally invented for robot manipulator path planning and is used often and under many variants in the mobile robotics community. The potential field method treats the robot as a point under the influence of an artificial potential field $U(q)$. The robot moves by following the field, just as a ball would roll downhill. The goal (a minimum in this space) acts as an attractive force on the robot and the obstacles act as peaks, or repulsive forces. The superposition of all forces is applied to the robot, which, in most cases, is assumed to be a point in the configuration space (see figure 6.5). Such an artificial potential field smoothly guides the robot toward the goal while simultaneously avoiding known obstacles.

It is important to note, though, that this is more than just path planning. The resulting field is also a control law for the robot. Assuming the robot can localize its position with respect to the map and the potential field, it can always determine its next required action based on the field.

The basic idea behind all potential field approaches is that the robot is attracted toward the goal, while being repulsed by the obstacles that are known in advance. If new obstacles appear during robot motion, one could update the potential field in order to integrate this new information. In the simplest case, we assume that the robot is a point, thus the robot's orientation θ is neglected and the resulting potential field is only 2D (x, y). If we assume a differentiable potential field function $U(q)$, we can find the related artificial force $F(q)$ acting at the position $q = (x, y)$.

$$F(q) = -\nabla U(q) \tag{6.1}$$

where $\nabla U(q)$ denotes the gradient vector of U at position q.

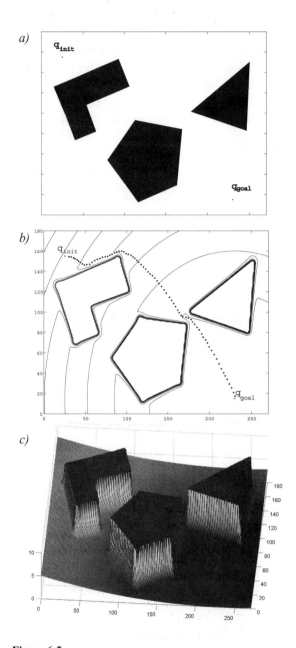

Figure 6.5
Typical potential field generated by the attracting goal and two obstacles (see [21]). (a) Configuration
of the obstacles, start (top left) and goal (bottom right). (b) Equipotential plot and path generated by
the field. (c) Resulting potential field generated by the goal attractor and obstacles.

functions must be differentiable.

$$\nabla U = \begin{bmatrix} \dfrac{\partial U}{\partial x} \\[2mm] \dfrac{\partial U}{\partial y} \end{bmatrix} \tag{6.2}$$

The potential field acting on the robot is then computed as the sum of the attractive field of the goal and the repulsive fields of the obstacles:

$$U(q) = U_{att}(q) + U_{rep}(q) \tag{6.3}$$

Similarly, the forces can also be separated in a attracting and repulsing part:

$$\begin{aligned} F(q) &= F_{att}(q) - F_{rep}(q) \\ &= -\nabla U_{att}(q) - \nabla U_{rep}(q) \end{aligned} \tag{6.4}$$

Attractive potential. An attractive potential can, for example, be defined as a parabolic function.

$$U_{att}(q) = \frac{1}{2} k_{att} \cdot \rho_{goal}^2(q) \tag{6.5}$$

where k_{att} is a positive scaling factor and $\rho_{goal}(q)$ denotes the Euclidean distance $\|q - q_{goal}\|$. This attractive potential is differentiable, leading to the attractive force F_{att}

$$F_{att}(q) = -\nabla U_{att}(q) \tag{6.6}$$

$$= -k_{att} \cdot \rho_{goal}(q) \nabla \rho_{goal}(q) \tag{6.7}$$

$$= -k_{att} \cdot (q - q_{goal}) \tag{6.8}$$

that converges linearly toward 0 as the robot reaches the goal.

Repulsive potential. The idea behind the repulsive potential is to generate a force away from all known obstacles. This repulsive potential should be very strong when the robot is close to the object, but should not influence its movement when the robot is far from the object. One example of such a repulsive field is

(3) At objects are convex

there exists situations where several

minimal distances exist — can result

in oscillations

$$U_{rep}(q) = \begin{cases} \frac{1}{2}k_{rep}\left(\frac{1}{\rho(q)} - \frac{1}{\rho_0}\right)^2 & \text{if } \rho(q) \leq \rho_0 \\ 0 & \text{if } \rho(q) \geq \rho_0 \end{cases} \tag{6.9}$$

where k_{rep} is again a scaling factor, $\rho(q)$ is the minimal distance from q to the object and ρ_0 the distance of influence of the object. The repulsive potential function U_{rep} is positive or zero and tends to infinity as q gets closer to the object.

If the object boundary is convex and piecewise differentiable, $\rho(q)$ is differentiable everywhere in the free configuration space. This leads to the repulsive force F_{rep}:

Cons

1) local minima problem exists

2) problem is getting if the robot

more complex it as a point mass.

is not considered

$$F_{rep}(q) = -\nabla U_{rep}(q) \tag{6.10}$$

$$= \begin{cases} k_{rep}\left(\frac{1}{\rho(q)} - \frac{1}{\rho_0}\right)\frac{1}{\rho^2(q)}\frac{q - q_{obstacle}}{\rho(q)} & \text{if } \rho(q) \leq \rho_0 \\ 0 & \text{if } \rho(q) \geq \rho_0 \end{cases}$$

The resulting force $F(q) = F_{att}(q) + F_{rep}(q)$ acting on a point robot exposed to the attractive and repulsive forces moves the robot away from the obstacles and toward the goal (see figure 6.5). Under ideal conditions, by setting the robot's velocity vector proportional to the field force vector, the robot can be smoothly guided toward the goal, similar to a ball rolling around obstacles and down a hill.

However, there are some limitations with this approach. One is local minima that appear dependent on the obstacle shape and size. Another problem might appear if the objects are concave. This might lead to a situation for which several minimal distances $\rho(q)$ exist, resulting in oscillation between the two closest points to the object, which could obviously sacrifice completeness. For more detailed analyses of potential field characteristics, refer to [21].

The extended potential field method. Khatib and Chatila proposed the extended potential field approach [84]. Like all potential field methods this approach makes use of attractive and repulsive forces that originate from an artificial potential field. However, two additions to the basic potential field are made: the *rotation potential field* and the *task potential field*.

The rotation potential field assumes that the repulsive force is a function of the distance from the obstacle and the orientation of the robot relative to the obstacle. This is done using

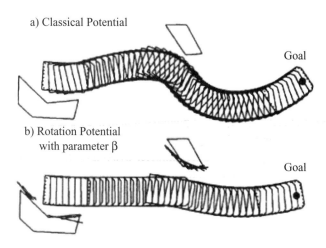

a) Classical Potential

Goal

b) Rotation Potential
   with parameter β

Goal

Figure 6.6
Comparison between a classical potential field and an extended potential field. Image courtesy of
Raja Chatila [84].

a gain factor which reduces the repulsive force when an obstacle is parallel to the robot's
direction of travel, since such an object does not pose an immediate threat to the robot's
trajectory. The result is enhanced wall following, which was problematic for earlier implementations of potential fields methods.

The task potential field considers the present robot velocity and from that it filters out
those obstacles that should not affect the near-term potential based on robot velocity. Again
a scaling is made, this time of all obstacle potentials when there are no obstacles in a sector
named Z in front of the robot. The sector Z is defined as the space which the robot will
sweep during its next movement. The result can be smoother trajectories through space. An
example comparing a classical potential field and an extended potential field is depicted in
figure 6.6.

A great many variations and improvements of the potential field methods have been proposed and implemented by mobile roboticists [67, 111]. In most cases, these variations aim
to improve the behavior of potential fields in local minima while also lowering the chances
of oscillations and instability when a robot must move through a narrow space such as a
doorway.

Potential fields are extremely easy to implement, much like the grassfire algorithm
described in section 6.2.1.2. Thus it has become a common tool in mobile robot applications in spite of its theoretical limitations.

This completes our brief summary of the path-planning techniques that are most popular
in mobile robotics. Of course, as the complexity of a robot increases (e.g., large degree of

"Bug 2" algorithm → 1) head toward goal on the s-line
2) if an obstacle is in the way, follow it until
encountering the s-line again
3) leave obstacle & continue toward goal.

272   Chapter 6

freedom nonholonomics) and, particularly, as environment dynamics becomes more significant, then the path-planning techniques described above become inadequate for grappling
with the full scope of the problem. However, for robots moving in largely flat terrain, the
mobility decision-making techniques roboticists use often fall under one of the above categories.

But a path planner can only take into consideration the environment obstacles that are
known to the robot in *advance*. During path execution the robot's actual sensor values may
disagree with expected values due to map inaccuracy or a dynamic environment. Therefore,
it is critical that the robot modify its path in real time based on actual sensor values. This is
the competence of *obstacle avoidance* which we discuss below.

6.2.2 Obstacle avoidance *local path planning.*

Local obstacle avoidance focuses on changing the robot's trajectory as informed by its sensors during robot motion. The resulting robot motion is both a function of the robot's current or recent sensor readings *and* its goal position and relative location to the goal position.
The obstacle avoidance algorithms presented below depend to varying degrees on the existence of a global map and on the robot's precise knowledge of its location relative to the
map. Despite their differences, all of the algorithms below can be termed obstacle avoidance algorithms because the robot's local sensor readings play an important role in the
robot's future trajectory. We first present the simplest obstacle avoidance systems that are
used successfully in mobile robotics. The Bug algorithm represents such a technique in that
only the most recent robot sensor values are used, and the robot needs, in addition to current
sensor values, only approximate information regarding the direction of the goal. More
sophisticated algorithms are presented afterward, taking into account recent sensor history,
robot kinematics, and even dynamics.

6.2.2.1 Bug algorithm

The Bug algorithm [101, 102] is perhaps the simplest obstacle avoidance algorithm one
could imagine. The basic idea is to follow the contour of each obstacle in the robot's way
and thus circumnavigate it.

With Bug1, the robot fully circles the object first, then departs from the point with the
shortest distance toward the goal (figure 6.7). This approach is, of course, very inefficient
but guarantees that the robot will reach any reachable goal.

With Bug2 the robot begins to follow the object's contour, but departs immediately
when it is able to move directly toward the goal. In general this improved Bug algorithm
will have significantly shorter total robot travel, as shown in figure 6.8. However, one can
still construct situations in which Bug2 is arbitrarily inefficient (i.e., nonoptimal).

A number of variations and extensions of the Bug algorithm exist. We mention one
more, the Tangent Bug [82], which adds range sensing and a local environmental represen-

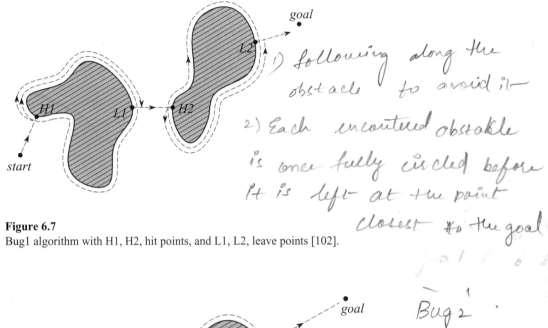

Figure 6.7
Bug1 algorithm with H1, H2, hit points, and L1, L2, leave points [102].

Handwritten notes (Figure 6.7):
1) following along the obstacle to avoid it
2) Each encountered obstacle is once fully circled before it is left at the point closest to the goal

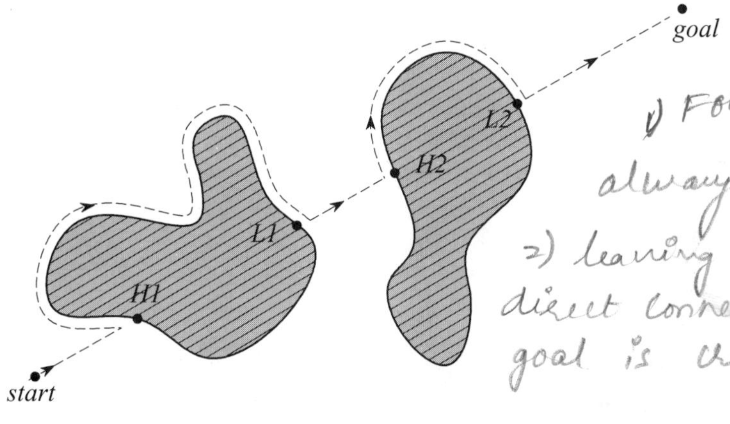

Figure 6.8
Bug2 algorithm with H1, H2, hit points, and L1, L2, leave points [102].

Handwritten notes (Figure 6.8):
Bug2
1) Following the obstacle always on the left or outside
2) leaving the obstacle if the direct connection b/w start and goal is crossed.

tation termed the local tangent graph (LTG). Not only can the robot move more efficiently toward the goal using the LTG, it can also go along shortcuts when contouring obstacles and switch back to goal seeking earlier. In many simple environments, Tangent Bug approaches globally optimal paths.

Practical application: example of Bug2. Because of the popularity and simplicity of Bug2, we present a specific example of obstacle avoidance using a variation of this technique. Consider the path taken by the robot in figure 6.8. One can characterize the robot's motion in terms of two states, one that involves moving toward the goal and a second that involves moving around the contour of an obstacle. We will call the former state GOAL-SEEK and the latter WALLFOLLOW. If we can describe the motion of the robot as a function of its sensor values and the relative direction to the goal for each of these two states, and if we can describe when the robot should switch between them, then we will have a practical implementation of Bug2. The following pseudocode provides the highest-level control code for such a decomposition:

```
public void bug2(position goalPos){
 boolean atGoal = false;

 while( ! atGoal){
    position robotPos = robot.GetPos(&sonars);
    distance goalDist = getDistance(robotPos, goalPos);
    angle goalAngle = Math.atan2(goalPos, robotPos)-robot.GetAngle();
    velocity forwardVel, rotationVel;

    if(goalDist < atGoalThreshold){
      System.out.println("At Goal!");
      forwardVel = 0;
      rotationVel = 0;
      robot.SetState(DONE);
      atGoal = true;
    }
    else{
      forwardVel = ComputeTranslation(&sonars);
      if(robot.GetState() == GOALSEEK){
         rotationVel = ComputeGoalSeekRot(goalAngle);
         if(ObstaclesInWay(goalAngle, &sonars))
            robot.SetState(WALLFOLLOW);
      }
      if(robot.GetState() == WALLFOLLOW){
         rotationVel = ComputeRWFRot(&sonars);
         if( ! ObstaclesInWay(goalAngle, &sonars))
            robot.SetState(GOALSEEK);
      }
    }
    robot.SetVelocity(forwardVel, rotationVel);
 }
}
```

In the ideal case, when encountering an obstacle one would choose between left wall following and right wall following depending on which direction is more promising. In this simple example we have only right wall following, a simplification for didactic purposes that ought not find its way into a real mobile robot program.

Now we consider specifying each remaining function in detail. Consider for our purposes a robot with a ring of sonars placed radially around the robot. This imagined robot will be differential-drive, so that the sonar ring has a clear "front" (aligned with the forward direction of the robot). Furthermore, the robot accepts motion commands of the form shown above, with a rotational velocity parameter and a translational velocity parameter. Mapping these two parameters to individual wheel speeds for each of the two differential drive chassis' drive wheels is a simple matter.

There is one condition we must define in terms of the robot's sonar readings, `Obstacles InWay()`. We define this function to be true whenever any sonar range reading in the direction of the goal (within 45 degrees of the goal direction) is short:

```
private boolean ObstaclesInWay(angle goalAngle, sensorvals sonars) {
    int minSonarValue;
    minSonarValue=MinRange(sonars, goalAngle
                            -(pi/4),goalAngle+(pi/4));
    return (minSonarValue < 200);
} // end ObstaclesInWay() //
```

Note that the function `ComputeTranslation()` computes translational speed whether the robot is wall-following or heading toward the goal. In this simplified example, we define translation speed as being proportional to the largest range readings in the robot's approximate forward direction:

```
private int ComputeTranslation(sensorvals sonars) {
    int minSonarFront;
    minSonarFront = MinRange(sonars, -pi/4.0, pi/4.0);
    if (minSonarFront < 200) return 0;
    else return (Math.min(500, minSonarFront - 200));
} // end ComputeTranslation() //
```

There is a marked similarity between this approach and the potential field approach described in section 6.2.1.3. Indeed, some mobile robots implement obstacle avoidance by treating the current range readings of the robot as force vectors, simply carrying out vector addition to determine the direction of travel and speed. Alternatively, many will consider short-range readings to be repulsive forces, again engaging in vector addition to determine an overall motion command for the robot.

When faced with range sensor data, a popular way of determining rotation direction and speed is to simply subtract left and right range readings of the robot. The larger the difference, the faster the robot will turn in the direction of the longer range readings. The following two rotation functions could be used for our Bug2 implementation:

```
private int ComputeGoalSeekRot(angle goalAngle) {
    if (Math.abs(goalAngle) < pi/10) return 0;
    else return (goalAngle * 100);
} // end ComputeGoalSeekRot() //

private int ComputeRWFRot(sensorvals sonars) {
    int minLeft, minRight, desiredTurn;
    minRight = MinRange(sonars, -pi/2, 0);
    minLeft = MinRange(sonars, 0, pi/2);
    if (Math.max(minRight,minLeft) < 200) return (400);
                                            // hard left turn
    else {
        desiredTurn = (400 - minRight) * 2;
        desiredTurn = Math.inttorange(-400, desiredTurn, 400);
        return desiredTurn;
    } // end else
} // end ComputeRWFRot() //
```

Note that the rotation function for the case of right wall following combines a general avoidance of obstacles with a bias to turn right when there is open space on the right, thereby staying close to the obstacle's contour. This solution is certainly not the best solution for implementation of Bug2. For example, the wall follower could do a far better job by mapping the contour locally and using a PID control loop to achieve and maintain a specific distance from the contour during the right wall following action.

Although such simple obstacle avoidance algorithms are often used in simple mobile robots, they have numerous shortcomings. For example, the Bug2 approach does not take into account robot kinematics, which can be especially important with nonholonomic robots. Furthermore, since only the most recent sensor values are used, sensor noise can have a serious impact on real-world performance. The following obstacle avoidance techniques are designed to overcome one or more of these limitations.

6.2.2.2 Vector field histogram
Borenstein, together with Koren, developed the vector field histogram (VFH) [43]. Their previous work, which was concentrated on potential fields [92], was abandoned due to the method's instability and inability to pass through narrow passages. Later, Borenstein, together with Ulrich, extended the VFH algorithm to yield VFH+ [150] and VFH*[149].

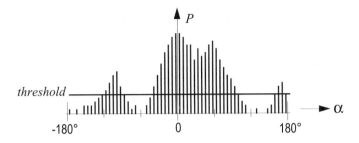

Figure 6.9
Polar histogram [93].

One of the central criticisms of Bug-type algorithms is that the robot's behavior at each instant is generally a function of only its most recent sensor readings. This can lead to undesirable and yet preventable problems in cases where the robot's instantaneous sensor readings do not provide enough information for robust obstacle avoidance. The VFH techniques overcome this limitation by creating a local map of the environment around the robot. This local map is a small occupancy grid, as described in section 5.7 populated only by relatively recent sensor range readings. For obstacle avoidance, VFH generates a polar histogram as shown in figure 6.9. The x-axis represents the angle α at which the obstacle was found and the y-axis represents the probability P that there really is an obstacle in that direction based on the occupancy grid's cell values.

From this histogram a steering direction is calculated. First all openings large enough for the vehicle to pass through are identified. Then a cost function is applied to every such candidate opening. The passage with the lowest cost is chosen. The cost function G has three terms:

$$G = a \cdot \text{target\_direction} + b \cdot \text{wheel\_orientation} + c \cdot \text{previous\_direction} \qquad (6.11)$$

target_direction = alignment of the robot path with the goal;

wheel_orientation = difference between the new direction and the current wheel orientation;

previous_direction = difference between the previously selected direction and the new direction.

The terms are calculated such that a large deviation from the goal direction leads to a big cost in the term "target direction". The parameters a, b, c in the cost function G tune the behavior of the robot. For instance, a strong goal bias would be expressed with a large value for a. For a complete definition of the cost function, refer to [92].

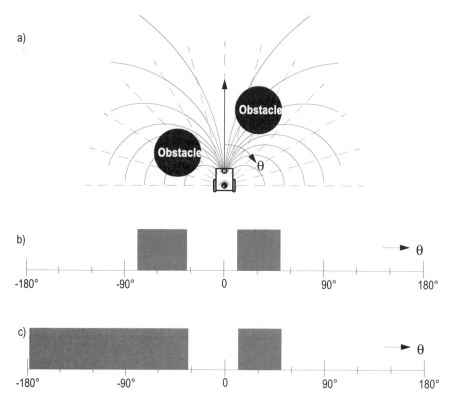

Figure 6.10
Example of blocked directions and resulting polar histograms [54]. (a) Robot and blocking obstacles.
(b) Polar histogram. (b) Masked polar histogram.

In the VFH+ improvement one of the reduction stages takes into account a simplified
model of the moving robot's possible trajectories based on its kinematic limitations (e.g.,
turning radius for an Ackerman vehicle). The robot is modeled to move in arcs or straight
lines. An obstacle thus blocks all of the robot's allowable trajectories which pass through
the obstacle (figure 6.10a). This results in a masked polar histogram where obstacles are
enlarged so that all kinematically blocked trajectories are properly taken into account (figure 6.10c).

6.2.2.3   The bubble band technique
This idea is an extension for nonholonomic vehicles of the elastic band concept suggested
by Khatib and Quinlan [86]. The original elastic band concept applied only to holonomic

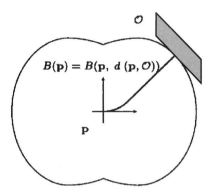

Figure 6.11
Shape of the bubbles around the vehicle (courtesy of Raja Chatila [85]).

vehicles and so we focus only on the bubble band extension made by Khatib, Jaouni, Chatila, and Laumod [85].

A *bubble* is defined as the maximum local subset of the free space around a given configuration of the robot that which can be traveled in any direction without collision. The
bubble is generated using a simplified model of the robot in conjunction with range information available in the robot's map. Even with a simplified model of the robot's geometry,
it is possible to take into account the actual shape of the robot when calculating the bubble's
size (figure 6.11). Given such bubbles, a band or string of bubbles can be used along the
trajectory from the robot's initial position to its goal position to show the robot's expected
free space throughout its path (see figure 6.12).

Clearly, computing the bubble band requires a global map and a global path planner.
Once the path planner's initial trajectory has been computed and the bubble band is calculated, then modification of the planned trajectory ensues. The bubble band takes into
account forces from modeled objects and internal forces. These internal forces try to minimize the "slack" (energy) between adjacent bubbles. This process, plus a final smoothing
operation, makes the trajectory smooth in the sense that the robot's free space will change
as smoothly as possible during path execution.

Of course, so far this is more akin to path optimization than obstacle avoidance. The
obstacle avoidance aspect of the bubble band strategy comes into play during robot motion.
As the robot encounters unforeseen sensor values, the bubble band model is used to deflect
the robot from its originally intended path in a way that minimizes bubble band *tension*.

An advantage of the bubble band technique is that one can account for the actual dimensions of the robot. However, the method is most applicable only when the environment configuration is well-known ahead of time, just as with off-line path-planning techniques.

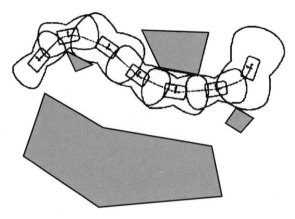

Figure 6.12
A typical bubble band (Courtesy of Raja Chatila [85]).

6.2.2.4 Curvature velocity techniques

The basic curvature velocity approach. The curvature velocity approach (CVM) from
Simmons [135] enables the actual kinematic constraints and even some dynamic constraints of the robot to be taken into account during obstacle avoidance, which is an advantage over more primitive techniques. CVM begins by adding physical constraints from the
robot and the environment to a velocity space. The velocity space consists of rotational
velocity ω and translational velocity v, thus assuming that the robot only travels along arcs
of circles with curvature $c = \omega / v$.

Two types of constraints are identified: those derived from the robot's limitations in
acceleration and speed, typically $-v_{max} < v < v_{max}$, $-\omega_{max} < \omega < \omega_{max}$; and, second, the
constraints from obstacles blocking certain v and ω values due to their positions. The
obstacles begin as objects in a Cartesian grid but are then transformed to the velocity space
by calculating the distance from the robot position to the obstacle following some constant
curvature robot trajectory, as shown in figure 6.13. Only the curvatures that lie within c_{min}
and c_{max} are considered since that curvature space will contain all legal trajectories.

To achieve real-time performance the obstacles are approximated by circular objects
and the contours of the objects are divided into few intervals. The distance from an endpoint
of an interval to the robot is calculated and in between the endpoints the distance function
is assumed to be constant.

The final decision of a new velocity (v and ω) is made by an objective function. This
function is only evaluated on that part of the velocity space that fulfills the kinematic and

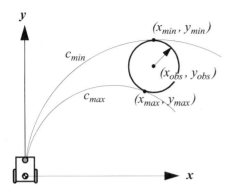

Figure 6.13
Tangent curvatures for an obstacle (from [135]).

dynamic constraints as well as the constraints due to obstacles. The use of a Cartesian grid for initial obstacle representation enables straightforward sensor fusion if, for instance, a robot is equipped with multiple types of ranging sensors.

CVM takes into consideration the dynamics of the vehicle in useful manner. However a limitation of the method is the circular simplification of obstacle shape. In some environments this is acceptable while, in other environments, such a simplification can cause serious problems. The CVM method can also suffer from local minima since no *a priori* knowledge is used by the system.

The lane curvature method. Ko and Simmons presented an improvement of the CVM which they named the lane curvature method, (LCM) [87] based on their experiences with the shortcomings of CVM. CVM had difficulty guiding the robot through intersections of corridors. The problems stemmed from the approximation that the robot moves only along fixed arcs, whereas in practice the robot can change direction many times before reaching an obstacle.

LCM calculates a set of desired lanes, trading off lane length and lane width to the closest obstacle. The lane with the best properties is chosen using an objective function. The local heading is chosen in such way that the robot will transition to the best lane if it is not in that lane already.

Experimental results have demonstrated better performance as compared to CVM. One caveat is that the parameters in the objective function must be chosen carefully to optimize system behavior.

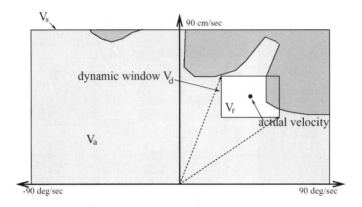

Figure 6.14
The dynamic window approach (courtesy of Dieter Fox [69]). The rectangular window shows the possible speeds (v, ω) and the overlap with obstacles in configuration space.

6.2.2.5 Dynamic window approaches

Another technique for taking into account robot kinematics constraints is the dynamic window obstacle avoidance method. A simple but very effective dynamic model gives this approach its name. Two such approaches are represented in the literature. The dynamic window approach [69] of Fox, Burgard, and Thrun, and the global dynamic window approach [44] of Brock and Khatib.

The local dynamic window approach. In the local dynamic window approach the kinematics of the robot is taken into account by searching a well-chosen velocity space. The velocity space is all possible sets of tuples (v, ω) where v is the velocity and ω is the angular velocity. The approach assumes that robots move only in circular arcs representing each such tuple, at least during one timestamp.

Given the current robot speed, the algorithm first selects a *dynamic window* of all tuples (v, ω) that can be reached within the next sample period, taking into account the acceleration capabilities of the robot and the cycle time. The next step is to reduce the *dynamic window* by keeping only those tuples that ensure that the vehicle can come to a stop before hitting an obstacle. The remaining velocities are called admissible velocities. In figure 6.14, a typical dynamic window is represented. Note that the shape of the dynamic window is rectangular, which follows from the approximation that the dynamic capabilities for translation and rotation are independent.

A new motion direction is chosen by applying an objective function to all the admissible velocity tuples in the dynamic window. The objective function prefers fast forward motion,

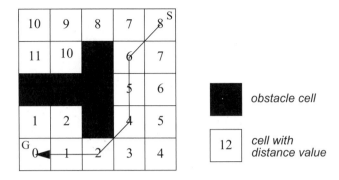

Figure 6.15
An example of the distance transform and the resulting path as it is generated by the NF1 function. S, start; G, goal.

maintenance of large distances to obstacles and alignment to the goal heading. The objective function O has the form

$$O = a \cdot heading(v, \omega) + b \cdot velocity(v, \omega) + c \cdot dist(v, \omega) \tag{6.12}$$

heading = Measure of progress toward the goal location;

velocity = Forward velocity of the robot $\rightarrow$ encouraging fast movements;

dist = Distance to the closest obstacle in the trajectory.

The global dynamic window approach. The global dynamic window approach adds, as the name suggests, global thinking to the algorithm presented above. This is done by adding *NF1*, or grassfire, to the objective function O presented above (see section 6.2.1.2 and figure 6.15). Recall that NF1 labels the cells in the occupancy grid with the total distance L to the goal. To make this faster the global dynamic window approach calculates the NF1 only on a selected rectangular region which is directed from the robot toward the goal. The width of the region is enlarged and recalculated if the goal cannot be reached within the constraints of this chosen region.

This allows the global dynamic window approach to achieve some of the advantages of global path planning without complete a priori knowledge. The occupancy grid is updated from range measurements as the robot moves in the environment. The NF1 is calculated for every new updated version. If the NF1 cannot be calculated due to the fact that the robot is surrounded by obstacles, the method degrades to the dynamic window approach. This keeps the robot moving so that a possible way out may be found and NF1 can resume.

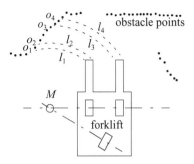

Figure 6.16
Distances l_i resulting from the curvature i_c, when the robot rotates around M (from [128]).

The global dynamic window approach promises real-time, dynamic constraints, global thinking, and minimal free obstacle avoidance at high speed. An implementation has been demonstrated with an omnidirectional robot using a 450 MHz on-board PC. This system produced a cycle frequency of about 15 Hz when the occupancy grid was 30×30 m with a 5 cm resolution. Average robot speed in the tests was greater than 1 m/s.

6.2.2.6 The Schlegel approach to obstacle avoidance
Schlegel [128] presents an approach that considers the dynamics as well as the actual shape of the robot. The approach is adopted for raw laser data measurements and sensor fusion using a Cartesian grid to represent the obstacles in the environment. Real-time performance is achieved by use of precalculated lookup tables.

As with previous methods we have described, the basic assumption is that a robot moves in trajectories built up by circular arcs, defined as curvatures i_c. Given a certain curvature i_c Schlegel calculates the distance l_i to collision between a single obstacle point $[x, y]$ in the Cartesian grid and the robot, depicted in figure 6.16. Since the robot is allowed to be any shape this calculation is time consuming and the result is therefore precalculated and stored in a lookup table.

For example, the search space window V_s is defined for a differential-drive robot to be all the possible speeds of the left and right wheels, v_r, v_l. The dynamic constraints of the robot are taken into account by refining V_s to only those values which are reachable within the next timestep, given the present robot motion. Finally, an objective function chooses the best speed and direction by trading off goal direction, speed, and distance until collision.

During testing Schlegel used a wavefront path planner. Two robot chassis were used, one with synchro-drive kinematics and one with tricycle kinematics. The tricycle-drive

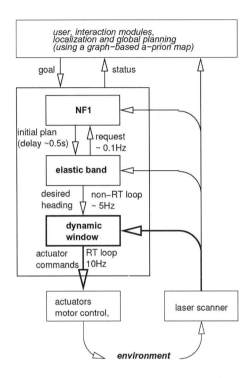

Figure 6.17
Flow diagram of the ASL approach [122].

robot is of particular interest because it was a forklift with a complex shape that had a significant impact on obstacle avoidance. Thus the demonstration of reliable obstacle avoidance with the forklift is an impressive result. Of course, a disadvantage of this approach is the potential memory requirements for the lookup table. In their experiments, the authors used lookup tables of up to 2.5 Mb using a 6×6 m Cartesian grid with a resolution of 10 cm and 323 different curvatures.

6.2.2.7 The ASL approach
The Autonomous Systems Lab (ASL) at the Swiss Federal Institute of Technology developed an obstacle avoidance method [122] for a mass exhibition [132] that required mobile robots to move through dense crowds and also ensure a certain flow of visitors. It merges three approaches in order to have a system that moves smoothly without stopping for replanning and is able to carefully nudge its way through when it is safe to do so. It is a local path-planning and obstacle avoidance method receiving its input in the form of waypoints from higher levels. An overview is given in figure 6.17.

Local path planning is performed by NF1. The resulting path is converted to an elastic band that does not take into account kinematics, taking advantage of the fact that the octagonal robot used in the exhibition can turn on the spot most of the time. This keeps path updates as simple as possible. An enhanced dynamic window then takes care of moving the robot along the path.

6.2.2.8 Nearness diagram

Attempting to close a model fidelity gap in obstacle avoidance methods, the nearness diagram (ND) [107] can be considered to have some similarity to a VFH but solves several of its shortcomings, especially in very cluttered spaces. It was also used in [108] to take into account more precise geometric, kinematic, and dynamic constraints. This was achieved by breaking the problem down into generating the most promising direction of travel with the sole constraint a circular robot, then adapting this to the kinematic and dynamic constraints of the robot, followed by a correction for robot shape if is noncircular (only rectangular shapes were supported in the original publication). Global reasoning was added to the approach and termed the global nearness diagram (GND) in [110], somewhat similar to the GDWA extension to the DWA, but based on a workspace representation (instead of configuration space) and updating free space in addition to obstacle information.

6.2.2.9 Gradient method

Realizing that current computer technology allows fast recalculation of wavefront propagation techniques, the gradient method [89] formulates a grid-based global path planning that takes into account closeness to obstacles and allows generating continuous interpolations of the gradient direction at any given point in the grid. The NF1 is a special case of the proposed algorithm, which calculates a navigation function at each timestep and uses the resulting gradient information to drive the robot toward the goal on a smooth path and not grazing obstacles unless necessary.

6.2.2.10 Adding dynamic constraints

Attempting to address the lack of dynamic models in most of the obstacle avoidance approaches discussed above, a new kind of space representation was proposed by Minguez, Montano, and Khatib in [109]. The ego-dynamic space is equally applicable to workspace and configuration space methods. It transforms obstacles into distances that depend on the braking constraints and sampling time of the underlying obstacle avoidance method. In combination with the proposed spatial window (PF) to represent acceleration capabilities, the approach was tested in conjunction with the ND and PF methods and gives satisfactory results for circular holonomic robots, with plans to extend it to nonholonomic, noncircular architectures.

6.2.2.11 Other approaches

The approaches described above are some of the most popularly referenced obstacle avoidance systems. There are, however, a great many additional obstacle avoidance techniques in the mobile robotics community. For example Tzafestas and Tzafestas [148] provide an overview of fuzzy and neurofuzzy approaches to obstacle avoidance. Inspired by nature, Chen and Quinn [56] present a biological approach in which they replicate the neural network of a cockroach. The network is then applied to a model of a four-wheeled vehicle.

The Liapunov functions form a well known theory that can be used to prove stability for nonlinear systems. In the paper of Vanualailai, Nakagiri, and Ha [153] the Liapunov functions are used to implement a control strategy for two-point masses moving in a known environment. All obstacles are defined as antitargets with an exact position and a circular shape. The antitargets are then used when building up the control laws for the system. However, this complex mathematical model has not been tested on a real-world robot to our knowledge.

6.2.2.12 Overview

Table 6.1 gives an overview on the different approaches for obstacle avoidance.

Table 6.1
Overview of the most popular obstacle avoidance algorithms

method		model fidelity				other requisites			sensors	tested robots	performance		
		shape	kinematics	dynamics	view	local map	global map	path planner			cycle time	architecture	remarks
Bug	Bug1 [101, 102]	point			local				tactile				very inefficient, robust
	Bug2 [101, 102]	point			local				tactile				inefficient, robust
	Tangent Bug [82]	point			local	local tangent graph			range				efficient in many cases, robust

Table 6.1
Overview of the most popular obstacle avoidance algorithms

method		shape	kinematics	dynamics	view	local map	global map	path planner	sensors	tested robots	cycle time	architecture	remarks
Vector Field Histogram (VFH)	VFH [43]	simplistic			local	histogram grid			range	synchro-drive (hexagonal)	27 ms	20 MHz, 386 AT	local minima, oscillating trajectories
	VFH+ [92, 150]	circle	basic	simplistic	local	histogram grid			sonars	nonholonomic (GuideCane)	6 ms	66 MHz, 486 PC	local minima
	VFH* [149]	circle	basic	simplistic	essentially local	histogram grid			sonars	nonholonomic (GuideCane)	6 … 242 ms	66 MHz, 486 PC	fewer local minima
Bubble band	Elastic band [86]	C-space			global		polygonal	required		various			
	Bubble band [85]	C-space	exact		local		polygonal	required		various			

Table 6.1
Overview of the most popular obstacle avoidance algorithms

method	model fidelity			view	other requisites			sensors	tested robots	performance		
	shape	kinematics	dynamics		local map	global map	path planner			cycle time	architecture	remarks
Dynamic window — Global dynamic window [44]	circle	(holonomic)	basic	global	C-space grid		NF1	180° FOV SCK laser scanner	holonomic (circular)	6.7 ms	450 MHz, PC	turning into corridors
Dynamic window — Dynamic window approach [69]	circle	exact	basic	local	obstacle line field			24 sonars ring, 56 infrared ring, stereo camera	synchro-drive (circular)	250 ms	486 PC	local minima
Curvature velocity — Lane curvature method [87]	circle	exact	basic	local	histogram grid			24 sonars ring, 30° FOV laser	synchro-drive (circular)	125 ms	200 MHz, Pentium	local minima
Curvature velocity — Curvature velocity method [135]	circle	exact	basic	local	histogram grid			24 sonars ring, 30° FOV laser	synchro-drive (circular)	125 ms	66 MHz, 486 PC	local minima, turning into corridors

Table 6.1
Overview of the most popular obstacle avoidance algorithms

method	model fidelity			view	other requisites			sensors	tested robots	performance		
	shape	kinematics	dynamics		local map	global map	path planner			cycle time	architecture	remarks
Gradient method [89]	circle	exact	basic	global	local perceptual space	fused	NF1	180° FOV distance sensor	nonholonomic (approx. circle)	100 ms (core algorithm: 10 ms)	266 MHz, Pentium	
Global nearness diagram [110]	circle (but general formulation)	(holonomic)		global	grid		NF1	180° FOV SCK laser scanner	holonomic (circular)			
Nearness diagram [107, 108]	circle (but general formulation)	(holonomic)		local				180° FOV SCK laser scanner	holonomic (circular)			local minima
ASL approach [122]	polygon	exact	basic	local	grid		graph (topological), NF1	2x 180° FOV SCK laser scanner	differential drive (octagonal, rectangular)	100 ms (core algorithm: 22 ms)	380 MHz, G3	turning into corridors
Schlegel [128]	polygon	exact	basic	global		grid	wavefront	360° FOV laser scanner	synchrodrive (circular), tricycle (forklift)			allows shape change

(Category: Other)

6.3   Navigation Architectures

Given techniques for path planning, obstacle avoidance, localization, and perceptual interpretation, how do we combine all of these into one complete robot system for a real-world
application? One way to proceed would be to custom-design an application-specific, monolithic software system that implements everything for a specific purpose. This may be efficient in the case of a trivial mobile robot application with few features and even fewer
planned demonstrations. But for any sophisticated and long-term mobile robot system, the
issue of mobility architecture should be addressed in a principled manner. The study of *navigation architectures* is the study of principled designs for the software modules that con-
stitute a mobile robot navigation system. Using a well-designed navigation architecture has
a number of concrete advantages:

6.3.1   Modularity for code reuse and sharing

Basic software engineering principles embrace software modularity, and the same general
motivations apply equally to mobile robot applications. But modularity is of even greater
importance in mobile robotics because in the course of a single project the mobile robot
hardware or its physical environmental characteristics can change dramatically, a challenge
most traditional computers do not face. For example, one may introduce a Sick laser
rangefinder to a robot that previously used only ultrasonic rangefinders. Or one may test an
existing navigator robot in a new environment where there are obstacles that its sensors
cannot detect, thereby demanding a new path-planning representation.

We would like to change part of the robot's competence without causing a string of side
effects that force us to revisit the functioning of other robot competences. For instance we
would like to retain the obstacle avoidance module intact, even as the particular ranging
sensor suite changes. In a more extreme example, it would be ideal if the nonholonomic
obstacle avoidance module could remain untouched even when the robot's kinematic structure changes from a tricycle chassis to a differential-drive chassis.

6.3.2   Control localization

Localization of robot control is an even more critical issue in mobile robot navigation. The
basic reason is that a robot architecture includes multiple types of control functionality
(e.g., obstacle avoidance, path planning, path execution, etc.). By localizing each functionality to a specific unit in the architecture, we enable individual testing as well as a principled strategy for control composition. For example, consider collision avoidance. For
stability in the face of changing robot software, as well as for focused verification that the
obstacle avoidance system is correctly implemented, it is valuable to localize all software
related to the robot's obstacle avoidance process. At the other extreme, high-level planning
and task-based decision-making are required for robots to perform useful roles in their

environment. It is also valuable to localize such high-level decision-making software, enabling it to be tested exhaustively in simulation and thus verified even without a direct connection to the physical robot. A final advantage of localization is associated with learning. Localization of control can enable a specific learning algorithm to be applied to just one aspect of a mobile robot's overall control system. Such targeted learning is likely to be the first strategy that yields successful integration of learning and traditional mobile robotics.

The advantages of localization and modularity prove a compelling case for the use of principled navigation architectures.

One way to characterize a particular architecture is by its decomposition of the robot's software. There are many favorite robot architectures, especially when one considers the relationship between artificial intelligence level decision making and lower-level robot control. For descriptions of such high-level architectures, refer to [2] and [26]. Here we concentrate on navigation competence. For this purpose, two decompositions are particularly relevant: temporal decomposition and control decomposition. In section 6.3.3 we define these two types of decomposition, then present an introduction to *behaviors*, which are a general tool for implementing control decomposition. Then, in section 6.3.4 we present three types of navigation architectures, describing for each architecture an implemented mobile robot case study.

6.3.3   Techniques for decomposition

Decompositions identify axes along which we can justify discrimination of robot software into distinct modules. Decompositions also serve as a way to classify various mobile robots into a more quantitative taxonomy. *Temporal decomposition* distinguishes between real-time and non real-time demands on mobile robot operation. *Control decomposition* identifies the way in which various control outputs within the mobile robot architecture combine to yield the mobile robot's physical actions. Below we describe each type of decomposition in greater detail.

6.3.3.1   Temporal decomposition

A temporal decomposition of robot software distinguishes between processes that have varying real-time and non real-time demands. Figure 6.18 depicts a generic temporal decomposition for navigation. In this figure, the most real-time processes are shown at the bottom of the *stack*, with the highest category being occupied by processes with no real-time demands.

The lowest level in this example captures functionality that must proceed with a guaranteed fast cycle time, such as a 40 Hz bandwidth. In contrast, a quasi real-time layer may capture processes that require, for example, 0.1 second response time, with large allowable worst-case individual cycle times. A tactical layer can represent decision-making that

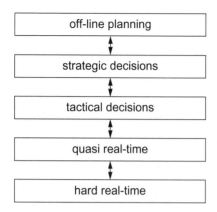

Figure 6.18
Generic temporal decomposition of a navigation architecture.

affects the robot's immediate actions and is therefore subject to some temporal constraints, while a strategic or off-line layer represents decisions that affect the robot's behavior over the long term, with few temporal constraints on the module's response time.

Four important, interrelated trends correlate with temporal decomposition. These are not set in stone; there are exceptions. Nevertheless, these general properties of temporal decompositions are enlightening:

Sensor response time. A particular module's sensor response time can be defined as the amount of time between acquisition of a sensor-based event and a corresponding change in the output of the module. As one moves up the stack in figure 6.18 the sensor response time tends to increase. For the lowest-level modules, the sensor response time is often limited only by the raw processor and sensor speeds. At the highest-level modules, sensor response can be limited by slow and deliberate decision-making processes.

Temporal depth. Temporal depth is a useful concept applying to the temporal window that affects the module's output, both backward and forward in time. *Temporal horizon* describes the amount of look ahead used by the module during the process of choosing an output. *Temporal memory* describes the historical time span of sensor input that is used by the module to determine the next output. Lowest-level modules tend to have very little temporal depth in both directions, whereas the deliberative processes of highest-level modules make use of a large temporal memory and consider actions based on their long-term consequences, making note of large temporal horizons.

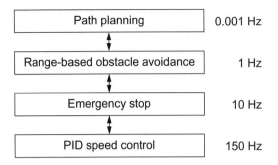

Figure 6.19
Sample four-level temporal decomposition of a simple navigating mobile robot. The column on the right indicates realistic bandwidth values for each module.

Spatial locality. Hand in hand with temporal span, the spatial impact of layers increases dramatically as one moves from low-level modules to high-level modules. Real-time modules tend to control wheel speed and orientation, controlling spatially localized behavior. High-level strategic decision-making has little or no bearing on local position, but informs global position far into the future.

Context specificity. A module makes decisions as a function not only of its immediate inputs but also as a function of the robot's context as captured by other variables, such as the robot's representation of the environment. Lowest-level modules tend to produce outputs directly as a result of immediate sensor inputs, using little context and therefore being relatively context insensitive. Highest-level modules tend to exhibit very high context specificity. For strategic decision-making, given the same sensor values, dramatically different outputs are nevertheless conceivable depending on other contextual parameters.

An example demonstrating these trends is depicted in figure 6.19, which shows a temporal decomposition of a simplistic navigation architecture into four modules. At the lowest level the PID control loop provides feedback to control motor speeds. An emergency stop module uses short-range optical sensors and bumpers to cut current to the motors when it predicts an imminent collision. Knowledge of robot dynamics means that this module by nature has a greater temporal horizon than the PID module. The next module uses longer-range laser rangefinding sensor returns to identify obstacles well ahead of the robot and make minor course deviations. Finally, the path planner module takes the robot's initial and goal positions and produces an initial trajectory for execution, subject to change based on actual obstacles that the robot collects along the way.

Figure 6.20
Example of a pure serial decomposition.

Note that the cycle time, or bandwidth, of the modules changes by orders of magnitude between adjacent modules. Such dramatic differences are common in real navigation architectures, and so temporal decomposition tends to capture a significant axis of variation in a mobile robot's navigation architecture.

6.3.3.2 Control decomposition

Whereas temporal decomposition discriminates based on the time behavior of software modules, control decomposition identifies the way in which each module's output contributes to the overall robot control outputs. Presentation of control decomposition requires the evaluator to understand the basic principles of discrete systems representation and analysis. For a lucid introduction to the theory and formalism of discrete systems, see [17, 71].

Consider the robot algorithm and the physical robot instantiation (i.e., the robot form and its environment) to be members of an overall system whose connectivity we wish to examine. This overall system S is comprised of a set M of modules, each module m connected to other modules via inputs and outputs. The system is *closed*, meaning that the input of every module m is the output of one or more modules in M. Each module has precisely one output and one or more inputs. The one output can be connected to any number of other modules inputs.

We further name a special module r in M to represent the physical robot and environment. Usually by r we represent the physical object on which the robot algorithm is intended to have impact, and from which the robot algorithm derives perceptual inputs. The module r contains one input and one output line. The input of r represents the complete action specification for the physical robot. The output of r represents the complete perceptual output to the robot. Of course the physical robot may have many possible degrees of freedom and, equivalently, many discrete sensors. But for this analysis we simply imagine the entire input/output vector, thus simplifying r to just one input and one output. For simplicity we will refer to the input of r as O and to the robot's sensor readings I. From the point of view of the rest of the control system, the robot's sensor values I are inputs, and the robot's actions O are the outputs, explaining our choice of I and O.

Control decomposition discriminates between different types of control pathways through the portion of this system comprising the robot algorithm. At one extreme, depicted in figure 6.20 we can consider a perfectly linear, or sequential control pathway.

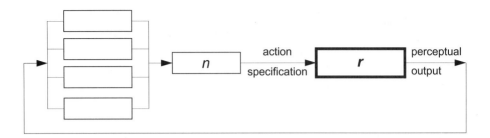

Figure 6.21
Example of a pure parallel decomposition.

Such a serial system uses the internal state of all associated modules and the value of the robot's percept I in a sequential manner to compute the next robot action O. A pure serial architecture has advantages relating to predictability and verifiability. Since the state and outputs of each module depend entirely on the inputs it receives from the module upstream, the entire system, including the robot, is a single well-formed loop. Therefore, the overall behavior of the system can be evaluated using well-known discrete forward simulation methods.

Figure 6.21 depicts the extreme opposite of pure serial control, a fully parallel control architecture. Because we choose to define r as a module with precisely one input, this parallel system includes a special module n that provides a single output for the consumption of r. Intuitively, the fully parallel system distributes responsibility for the system's control output O across multiple modules, possibly simultaneously. In a pure sequential system, the control flow is a linear sequence through a string of modules. Here, the control flow contains a *combination* step at which point the result of multiple modules may impact O in arbitrary ways.

Thus parallelization of control leads to an important question: how will the output of each component module inform the overall decision concerning the value of O? One simple combination technique is temporal switching. In this case, called *switched parallel*, the system has a parallel decomposition but at any particular instant in time the output O can be attributed to one specific module. The value of O can of course depend on a different module at each successive time instant, but the instantaneous value of O can always be determined based on the functions of a single module. For instance, suppose that a robot has an obstacle avoidance module and a path-following module. One switched control implementation may involve execution of the path-following recommendation whenever the robot is more than 50 cm from all sensed obstacles and execution of the obstacle avoidance recommendation when any sensor reports a range closer than 50 cm.

The advantage of such switched control is particularly clear if switching is relatively rare. If the behavior of each module is well understood, then it is easy to characterize the behavior of the switched control robot: it will obstacle avoid at times, and it will path-follow other times. If each module has been tested independently, there is a good chance the switched control system will also perform well. Two important disadvantages must be noted. First, the overall behavior of the robot can become quite poor if the switching is itself a high-frequency event. The robot may be unstable in such cases, switching motion modes so rapidly as to dramatically devolve into behavior that is neither path-following nor obstacle avoiding. Another disadvantage of switched control is that the robot has no path-following bias when it is obstacle avoiding (and vice versa). Thus in cases where control *ought* to mix recommendations from among multiple modules, the switched control methodology fails.

In contrast, the much more complex *mixed parallel* model allows control at any given time to be shared between multiple modules. For example, the same robot could take the obstacle avoidance module's output at all times, convert it to a velocity vector, and combine it with the path-following module's output using vector addition. Then the output of the robot would never be due to a single module, but would result from the mathematical combination of both modules outputs. Mixed parallel control is more general than switched control, but by that token it is also a more challenging technique to use well. Whereas with switched control most poor behavior arises out of inopportune switching behavior, in mixed control the robot's behavior can be quite poor even more readily. Combining multiple recommendations mathematically does not guarantee an outcome that is globally superior, just as combining multiple vectors when deciding on a swerve direction to avoid an obstacle can result in the very poor decision of straight ahead. Thus great care must be taken in mixed parallel control implementations to fashion mixture formulas and individual module specifications that lead to effective mixed results.

Both the switched and mixed parallel architectures are popular in the behavior-based robotics community. Arkin [2] proposes the *motor-schema* architecture in which *behaviors* (i.e., modules in the above discussion) map sensor value vectors to motor value vectors. The output of the robot algorithm is generated, as in mixed parallel systems, using a linear combination of the individual behavior outputs. In contrast, Maes [103, 104] produces a switched parallel architecture by creating a *behavior network* in which a behavior is chosen discretely by comparing and updating activation levels for each behavior. The subsumption architecture of Brooks [45] is another example of a switched parallel architecture, although the active model is chosen via a suppression mechanism rather than activation level. For a further discussion, see [2].

One overall disadvantage of parallel control is that verification of robot performance can be extremely difficult. Because such systems often include truly parallel, multithreaded implementations, the intricacies of robot-environment interaction and sensor timing

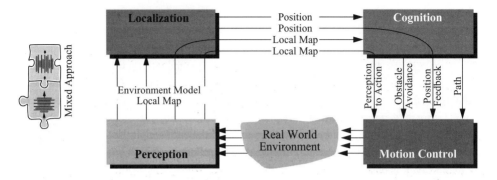

Figure 6.22
The basic architectural example used throughout this text.

required to properly represent all conceivable module-module interactions can be difficult or impossible to simulate. So, much testing in the parallel control community is performed empirically using physical robots.

An important advantage of parallel control is its biomimetic aspect. Complex organic organisms benefit from large degrees of true parallelism (e.g., the human eye), and one goal of the parallel control community is to understand this biologically common strategy and leverage it to advantage in robotics.

6.3.4   Case studies: tiered robot architectures

We have described temporal and control decompositions of robot architecture, with the common theme that the roboticist is always composing multiple modules together to make up that architecture. Let us turn again toward the overall mobile robot navigation task with this understanding in mind. Clearly, robot behaviors play an important role at the real-time levels of robot control, for example, path-following and obstacle avoidance. At higher temporal levels, more tactical tasks need to modulate the activation of behaviors, or modules, in order to achieve robot motion along the intended path. Higher still, a global planner could generate paths to provide tactical tasks with global foresight.

In chapter 1, we introduced a functional decomposition showing such modules of a mobile robot navigator from the perspective of information flow. The relevant figure is shown here again as figure 6.22.

In such a representation, the arcs represent aspects of real-time and non real-time competence. For instance, obstacle avoidance requires little input from the localization module and consists of fast decisions at the cognition level followed by execution in motion control. In contrast, PID position feedback loops bypass all high-level processing, tying the perception of encoder values directly to lowest-level PID control loops in motion control.

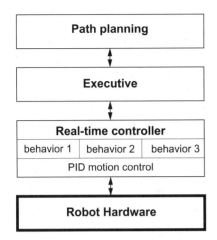

Figure 6.23
A general tiered mobile robot navigation architecture based on a temporal decomposition.

The trajectory of arcs through the four software modules is provides temporal information in such a representation.

Using the tools of this chapter, we can now present this same architecture from the perspective of a temporal decomposition of functionality. This is particularly useful because we wish to discuss the interaction of strategic, tactical, and real-time processes in a navigation system.

Figure 6.23 depicts a generic tiered architecture based on the approach of Pell and colleagues [120] used in designing an autonomous spacecraft, *Deep Space One*. This figure is similar to figure 6.19 in presenting a temporal decomposition of robot competence. However, the boundaries separating each module from adjacent modules are specific to robot navigation.

Path planning embodies strategic-level decision-making for the mobile robot. Path planning uses all available global information in non real time to identify the right sequence of local actions for the robot. At the other extreme, *real-time control* represents competences requiring high bandwidth and tight sensor-effector control loops. At its lowest level, this includes motor velocity PID loops. Above those, real-time control also includes low-level behaviors that may form a switch or mixed parallel architecture.

In between the path planner and real-time control tiers sits the *executive*, which is responsible for mediating the interface between planning and execution. The executive is responsible for managing the activation of behaviors based on information it receives from the planner. The executive is also responsible for recognizing failure, saving (placing the robot in a stable state), and even re-initiating the planner as necessary. It is the executive in

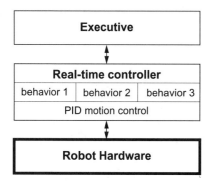

Figure 6.24
A two-tiered architecture for off-line planning.

this architecture that contains all tactical decision-making as well as frequent updates of the robot's short-term memory, as is the case for localization and mapping.

It is interesting to note the similarity between this general architecture, used in many specialized forms in mobile robotics today, and the architecture implemented by Shakey, one of the very first mobile robots, in 1969 [115]. Shakey had *LLA* (low-level actions) that formed the lowest architectural tier. The implementation of each LLA included the use of sensor values in a tight loop just as in today's behaviors. Above that, the middle architectural tier included the *ILA* (intermediate-level actions), which would activate and deactivate LLA as required based on perceptual feedback during execution. Finally, the topmost tier for Shakey was *STRIPS* (Stanford Research Institute Planning System), which provided global look ahead and planning, delivering a series of tasks to the intermediate executive layer for execution.

Although the general architecture shown in figure 6.23 is useful as a model for robot navigation, variant implementations in the robotics community can be quite different. Below, we present three particular versions of the general tiered architecture, describing for each version at least one real-world mobile robot implementation. For broader discussions of various robot architectures, see [26].

6.3.4.1 Off-line planning

Certainly the simplest possible integration of planning and execution is no integration at all. Consider figure 6.24, in which there are only two software tiers. In such navigation architectures, the executive does not have a planner at its disposal, but must contain a priori all relevant schemes for traveling to desired destinations.

The strategy of leaving out a planner altogether is of course extremely limiting. Moving such a robot to a new environment demands a new instantiation of the navigation system, and so this method is not useful as a general solution to the navigation problem. However such robotic systems do exist, and this method can be useful in two cases:

Static route-based applications. In mobile robot applications where the robot operates in a completely static environment using a route-based navigation system, it is conceivable that the number of discrete goal positions is so small that the environmental representation can directly contain paths to all desired goal points. For example, in factory or warehouse settings, a robot may travel a single looping route by following a buried guidewire. In such industrial applications, path-planning systems are sometimes altogether unnecessary when a precompiled set of route-based solutions can be easily generated by the robot programmers. The Chips mobile robot is an example of a museum robot that also uses this architecture (118). Chips operates in a unidirectional looping track defined by its colored landmarks. Furthermore, it has only twelve discrete locations at which it is allowed to stop. Due to the simplicity of this environmental model, Chips contains an executive layer that directly caches the path required to reach each goal location rather than a generic map with which a path planner could search for solution paths.

Extreme reliability demands. Not surprisingly, another reason to avoid on-line planning is to maximize system reliability. Since planning software can be the most sophisticated portion of a mobile robot's software system, and since in theory at least planning can take time exponential to the complexity of the problem, imposing hard temporal constraints on successful planning is difficult if not impossible. By computing all possible solutions off-line, the industrial mobile robot can trade versatility for effective constant-time planning (while sacrificing significant memory of course). A real-world example of off-line planning for this reason can be seen in the contingency plans designed for space shuttle flights. Instead of requiring astronauts to problem-solve on-line, thousands of conceivable issues are postulated on Earth, and complete conditional plans are designed and published in advance of the Shuttle flights. The fundamental goal is to provide an absolute upper limit on the amount of time that passes before the astronauts begin resolving the problem, sacrificing a great deal of ground time and paperwork to achieve this performance guarantee.

6.3.4.2 Episodic planning

The fundamental information-theoretic disadvantage of planning off-line is that, during run-time, the robot is sure to encounter perceptual inputs that provide information, and it would be rational to take this additional information into account during subsequent execution. Episodic planning is the most popular method in mobile robot navigation today because it solves this problem in a computationally tractable manner.

As shown in figure 6.25, the structure is three-tiered as in the general architecture of figure 6.23. The intuition behind the role of the planner is as follows. Planning is compu-

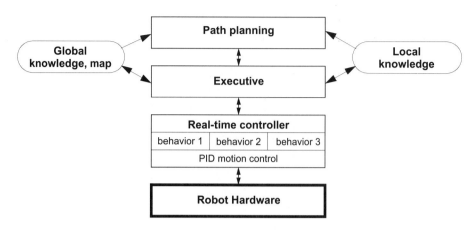

Figure 6.25
A three-tiered episodic planning architecture.

tationally intensive, and therefore planning too frequently would have serious disadvantages. But the executive is in an excellent position to identify when it has encountered enough information (e.g., through feature extraction) to warrant a significant change in strategic direction. At such points, the executive will invoke the planner to generate, for example, a new path to the goal.

Perhaps the most obvious condition that triggers replanning is detection of a blockage on the intended travel path. For example, in [129] the path-following behavior returns failure if it fails to make progress for a number of seconds. The executive receives this failure notification, modifies the short-term occupancy grid representation of the robot's surroundings, and launches the path planner in view of this change to the local environment map.

A common technique to delay planning until more information has been acquired is called *deferred planning*. This technique is particularly useful in mobile robots with dynamic maps that become more accurate as the robot moves. For example, the commercially available Cye robot can be given a set of goal locations. Using its grassfire breadth-first planning algorithm, this robot will plot a detailed path to the closest goal location only and will execute this plan. Upon reaching this goal location, its map will have changed based on the perceptual information extracted during motion. Only then will Cye's executive trigger the path planner to generate a path from its new location to the next goal location.

The robot Pygmalion implements an episodic planning architecture along with a more sophisticated strategy when encountering unforeseen obstacles in its way [36, 122]. When the lowest-level behavior fails to make progress, the executive attempts to find a way past the obstacle by turning the robot 90 degrees and trying again. This is valuable because the

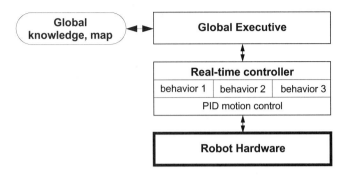

Figure 6.26
An integrated planning and execution architecture in which planning is nothing more than a real-time execution step (behavior).

robot is not kinematically symmetric, and so servoing through a particular obstacle course may be easier in one direction than the other.

Pygmalion's environment representation consists of a continuous geometric model as well as an abstract topological network for route planning. Thus, if repeated attempts to clear the obstacle fail, then the robot's executive will temporarily cut the topological connection between the two appropriate nodes and will launch the planner again, generating a new set of waypoints to the goal. Next, using recent laser rangefinding data as a type of local map (see figure 6.25), a geometric path planner will generate a path from the robot's current position to the next waypoint.

In summary, episodic planning architectures are extremely popular in the mobile robot research community. They combine the versatility of responding to environmental changes and new goals with the fast response of a tactical executive tier and behaviors that control real-time robot motion. As shown in figure 6.25, it is common in such systems to have both a short-term local map and a more strategic global map. Part of the executive's job in such dual representations is to decide when and if new information integrated into the local map is sufficiently nontransient to be copied into the global knowledge base.

6.3.4.3 Integrated planning and execution
Of course, the architecture of a commercial mobile robot must include more functionality than just navigation. But limiting this discussion to the question of *navigation* architectures leads to what may at first seem a degenerate solution.

The architecture shown in figure 6.26 may look similar to the off-line planning architecture of figure 6.24, but in fact it is significantly more advanced. In this case, the planner tier has disappeared because there is no longer a temporal decomposition between the executive and the planner. Planning is simply one small part of the executive's nominal cycle of activities.

The idea of speeding up planning to the point that its execution time is no longer significant may seem wishful. However, using specific algorithms in particular environments, such reductions in the cost of planning have been demonstrated. Consider the work of Stentz [139]. Stentz designed a mobile robot control architecture for a large off-road vehicle traveling over partially known terrain at high speeds. Using advanced caching techniques from computer science, Stentz optimized a grassfire path-planning algorithm called $D*$ so that global path planning would be possible *within* the basic control loop of the executive.

The result, depicted in figure 6.26, is an architecture in which the local and global representations are the same, and in which the executive has all global planning functionality required for the problem built in. The advantage of this approach is that the robot's actions at every cycle are guided by a global path planner, and are therefore optimal in view of all of the information the robot has gathered. Of course, the method is computationally challenging and will not be practical in more complex environments until processor speeds increase even further. It also has basic limits of applicability as the size of the environment increases, but this has not yet been a barrier when applying this method to real-world scenario sizes.

The somewhat recent success of an integrated planning and execution method, $D*$, underlines the fact that the designer of a robot navigation architecture must consider not only all aspects of the robot and its environmental task but must also consider the state of processor and memory technology. We expect that mobile robot architecture design is sure to remain an active area of innovation for years to come. All forms of technological progress, from robot sensor inventions to microprocessor speed increases, are likely to catalyze new revolutions in mobile robot architecture as previously unimaginable tactics become realities.

Bibliography

Books

[1]   Adams, M.D., *Sensor Modelling, Design and Data Processing for Autonomous Navigation*. World Scientific Series in Robotics and Intelligent Systems. Singapore, World Scientific Publishing Co. Ltd., 1999.

[2]   Arkin, R.C., *Behavior-Based Robotics*. Cambridge MIT Press, MA, 1998.

[3]   Bar-Shalom, Y., Li, X.-R., *Estimation and Tracking: Principles, Techniques, and Software*. Norwood, MA, Artech House, 1993.

[4]   Borenstein, J., Everet,t H.R., Feng, L., *Navigating Mobile Robots, Systems and Techniques*. Natick, MA, A.K. Peters, Ltd., 1996.

[5]   Borenstein, J., Everett, H.R., Feng, L., *Where Am I? Sensors and Methods for Mobile Robot Positioning*. Ann Arbor, University of Michigan. Available at http://www-personal.engin.umich.edu/~johannb/position.htm.

[6]   Breipohl, A.M., *Probabilistic Systems Analysis: An Introduction to Probabilistic Models, Decisions, and Applications of Random Processes*. New York, John Wiley & Sons, 1970.

[7]   Bundy, A. (editor), *Artificial Intelligence Techniques, a Comprehensive Catalogue*. New York, Springer-Verlag, 1997.

[8]   Canudas de Wit, C., Siciliano, B., and Bastin G. (editors), *Theory of Robot Control*. New York, Spinger-Verlag, 1996.

[9]   Carroll, R.J., Ruppert, D., *Transformation and Weighting in Regression*. New York, Chapman and Hall, 1988.

[10]   Cox, I.J., Wilfong, G.T. (editors), *Autonomous Robot Vehicles*. New York, Spinger-Verlag, 1990.

[11]   Craig, J.J., *Introduction to Robotics: Mechanics and Control*. 2nd edition. Boston, Addison-Wesley, 1989.

[12]   de Silva, C.W., *Control Sensors and Actuators*. Upper Saddle River, NJ, Prentice Hall, 1989.

[13]   Dietrich, C.F., *Uncertainty, Calibration and Probability*. Bristol, UK, Adam Hilger, 1991.

[14]   Draper, N.R., Smith, H., *Applied Regression Analysis*. 3rd edition. New York, John Wiley & Sons, 1988.

[15]   Everett, H.R., *Sensors for Mobile Robots, Theory and Applications*. New York, Natick, MA, A.K. Peters, Ltd., 1995.

[16] Faugeras, O., *Three-Dimensional Computer Vision, a Geometric Viewpoint*. Campridge MIT Press, MA, 1993.

[17] Genesereth, M.R., Nilsson, N.J., *Logical Foundations of Artificial Intelligence*. Palo Alto, CA, Morgan Kaufmann, 1987.

[18] Haralick, R.M., Shapiro, L.G., *Computer and Robot Vision, 1+2*. Boston, Addison-Wesley, 1993.

[19] Jones, J., Flynn, A., *Mobile Robots, Inspiration to Implementation*. Natick, MA, A.K. Peters, Ltd., 1993. [also available in German and French].

[20] Kortenkamp, D., Bonasso, R.P., Murphy, R.R. (editors), *Artificial Intelligence and Mobile Robots; Case Studies of Successful Robot Systems*. Cambridge, MA, AAAI Press / MIT Press, 1998.

[21] Latombe, J.-C., *Robot Motion Planning*. Norwood, MA, Kluwer Academic Publishers, 1991.

[22] Lee, D., *The Map-Building and Exploration Strategies of a Simple Sonar-Equipped Mobile Robot*. Cambridge, UK, Cambridge University Press, 1996.

[23] Leonard, J.E., Durrant-Whyte, H.F., *Directed Sonar Sensing for Mobile Robot Navigation*. Norwood, MA, Kluwer Academic Publishers, 1992.

[24] Manyika, J., Durrant-Whyte, H.F., *Data Fusion and Sensor Management: A Decentralized Information-Theoretic Approach*. Ellis Horwood, 1994.

[25] Mason, M., *Mechanics of Robotics Manipulation*. Cambridge, MA, MIT Press, 2001.

[26] Murphy, R.R., *Introduction to AI Robotics*. Cambridge, MA, MIT Press, 2000.

[27] Nourbakhsh, I., *Interleaving Planning and Execution for Autonomous Robots, Norwood, MA,* Kluwer Academic Publishers, 1997.

[28] Raibert, M.H., *Legged Robots That Balance*, Cambridge, MA, MIT Press, 1986.

[29] Ritter, G.X., Wilson, J.N., *Handbook of Computer Vision Algorithms in Image Algebra*. Boca Raton, FL, CRC Press, 1996.

[30] Russell, S., Norvig, P., *Artificial Intelligence, a Modern Approach*. Prentice Hall International, 1995.

[31] Schraft, R.-D., Schmierer, G., *Service Roboter. Natick, MA,* A.K. Peters, Ltd, 2000. [also available in German from Springer-Verlag].

[32] Sciavicco, L., Siciliano, B., *Modeling and Control of Robot Manipulators*. New York, McGraw-Hill, 1996.

[33] Todd, D.J, *Walking Machines, an Introduction to Legged Robots*. Kogan Page Ltd, 1985.

Papers

[34] Aho, A.V., "Algorithms for Finding Patterns in Strings," in J. van Leeuwen (editor), *Handbook of Theoretical Computer Science*, Cambridge, MA, MIT Press, 1990, Volume A, chapter 5, 255–300.

[35] Arras, K.O., Castellanos, J.A., Siegwart, R., "Feature-Based Multi-Hypothesis Localization and Tracking for Mobile Robots Using Geometric Constraints," in *Proceedings of the IEEE International Conference on Robotics and Automation (ICRA'2002)*, Washington, DC, May 11–15, 2002.

[36] Arras,K.O., Persson, J., Tomatis, N., Siegwart, R., "Real-Time Obstacle Avoidance for Polygonal Robots with a Reduced Dynamic Window," in *Proceedings of the IEEE International Conference on Robotics and Automation (ICRA 2002)*, Washington, DC, May 11–15, 2002.

[37] Arras, K.O., Siegwart, R.Y., "Feature Extraction and Scene Interpretation for Map-Based Navigation and Map Building," in *Proceedings of SPIE, Mobile Robotics XII*, Vol. 3210, 1997, 42–53,.

[38] Arras, K.O., Tomatis, N., "Improving Robustness and Precision in Mobile Robot Localization by Using Laser Range Finding and Monocular Vision," in *Proceedings of the Third European Workshop on Advanced Mobile Robots (Eurobot 99)*, Zurich, September 6–9, 1999.

[39] Astolfi, A., "Exponential Stabilization of a Mobile Robot," *in Proceedings of 3rd European Control Conference,* Rome, September 1995.

[40] Barnard, K., Cardei V., Funt, B., "A Comparison of Computational Color Constancy Algorithms." *IEEE Transactions in Image Processing.* 11: 972–984, 2002.

[41] Barron, J.L., Fleet, D.J., Beauchemin, S.S., "Performance of Optical Flow Techniques." *International Journal of Computer Vision*, 12:43–77, 1994.

[42] Batavia, P., Nourbakhsh, I., "Path Planning for the Cye Robot," *in Proceedings of the IEEE/RSJ International Conference on Intelligent Robots and Systems (IROS'00)*, Takamatsu, Japan, November, 2000.

[43] Borenstein, J., Koren, Y., "The Vector Field Histogram – Fast Obstacle Avoidance for Mobile Robots." *IEEE Journal of Robotics and Automation*, 7, 278–288, 1991.

[44] Brock, O., Khatib, O., "High-Speed Navigation Using the Global Dynamic Window Approach," *in Proceeding of the IEEE International Conference on Robotics and Automation*, Detroit, May 1999.

[45] Brooks, R., "A Robust Layered Control System for a Mobile Robot," *IEEE Transactions of Robotics and Automation*, RA-2:14–23, March 1986.

[46] Brown, H.B., Zeglin, G.Z., "The Bow Leg Hopping Robot", *in Proceedings of the IEEE International Conference on Robotics and Automation*, Leuwen, Belgium, May 1998.

[47] Bruce, J., Balch,T., and Veloso, M., "Fast and Inexpensive Color Image Segmentation for Interactive Robots," *in Proceedings of the IEEE/RSJ International Conference on Intelligent Robots and Systems (IROS'00)*, Takamatsu, Japan, October 31–November 5, 2000.

[48] Burgard,W., Cremers, A., Fox, D., Hahnel, D., Lakemeyer, G., Schulz, D., Steiner, W., Thrun, S., "Experiences with an Interactive Museum Tour-Guide Robot," *Artificial Intelligence*, 114, 1–53, 2000.

[49] Burgard, W., Derr, A., Fox, D., Cremers, A., "Integrating Global Position Estimation and Position Tracking for Mobile Robots: The Dynamic Markov Localization Approach," *in Proceedings of the 1998 IEEE/RSJ International Conference of Intelligent Robots and Systems (IROS'98)*, Victoria, B.C., Canada, October 1998.

[50] Burgard, W., Fox, D., Henning, D., "Fast Grid-Based Position Tracking for Mobile Robots," *in Proceedings of the 21th German Conference on Artificial Intelligence (KI97)*, Freiburg, Germany, Springer-Verlag, 1997.

[51] Burgard, W., Fox, D., Jans, H., Matenar, C., Thrun, S., "Sonar-Based Mapping of Large-Scale Mobile Robot Environments using EM," *in Proceedings of the International Conference on Machine Learning*, Bled, Slovenia, 1999.

[52]   Campion, G., Bastin, G., D'Andréa-Novel, B., "Structural Properties and Classifi-
       cation of Kinematic and Dynamic Models of Wheeled Mobile Robots." *IEEE Trans-
       actions on Robotics and Automation*, 12, No. 1, 47–62, 1996.

[53]   Canudas de Wit, C., Sordalen, O.J., "Exponential Stabilization of Mobile Robots
       with Nonholonomic Constraints." *IEEE Transactions on Robotics and Automation*,
       37, 1791–1797, 1993.

[54]   Caprari, G., Estier, T., Siegwart, R., "Fascination of Down Scaling–Alice the Sugar
       Cube Robot." *Journal of Micro-Mechatronics*, 1, 177–189, 2002.

[55]   Castellanos, J.A., Tardos, J.D., Schmidt, G., "Building a Global Map of the Envi-
       ronment of a Mobile Robot: The Importance of Correlations," *in Proceedings of the
       1997 IEEE Conference on Robotics and Automation*, Albuquerque, NM, April
       1997.

[56]   Chen, C.T., Quinn, R.D., "A Crash Avoidance System Based upon the Cockroach
       Escape Response Circuit," *in Proceedings of the IEEE International Conference on
       Robotics and Automation*, Albuquerque, NM, April 1997.

[57]   Chenavier, F., Crowley, J.L., "Position Estimation for a Mobile Robot Using Vision
       and Odometry," *in Proceedings of the IEEE International Conference on Robotics
       and Automation*, Nice, France, May 1992.

[58]   Chong, K.S., Kleeman, L., "Accurate Odometry and Error Modelling for a Mobile
       Robot," *in Proceedings of the IEEE International Conference on Robotics and Auto-
       mation*, Albuquerque, NM, April 1997.

[59]   Choset, H., Walker, S., Eiamsa-Ard, K., Burdick, J., "Sensor-Based Exploration:
       Incremental Construction of the Hierarchical Generalized Voronoi Graph." *The
       International Journal of Robotics Research,* 19, 126–148, 2000.

[60]   Cox, I.J., Leonard, J.J., "Modeling a Dynamic Environment Using a Bayesian Mul-
       tiple Hypothesis Approach." *Artificial Intelligence*, 66, 311–44, 1994.

[61]   Dowlingn, K., Guzikowski, R., Ladd, J., Pangels, H., Singh, S., Whittaker, W.L.,
       "NAVLAB: An Autonomous Navigation Testbed." *Technical report CMU-RI-TR-
       87-24, Robotics Institute*, Pittsburgh, Carnegie Mellon University, November 1987.

[62]   Dugan, B., "Vagabond: A Demonstration of Autonomous, Robust Outdoor Naviga-
       tion," *in Video Proceedings of the IEEE International Conference on Robotics and
       Automation*, Atlanta, GA, May 1993.

[63]   Elfes, A., "Sonar-Based Real World Mapping and Navigation," *in* [10].

[64]   Ens, J., Lawrence, P., "An Investigation of Methods for Determining Depth from
       Focus." *IEEE Transactions. on Pattern Analysis and Machine Intelligence*, 15: 97–
       108, 1993.

[65]   Espenschied, K. S., Quinn, R. D., "Biologically-Inspired Hexapod Robot Design
       and Simulation," *in AIAA Conference on Intelligent Robots in Field, Factory, Ser-
       vice and Space*, Houston, Texas, March 20–24, 1994.

[66]   Falcone, E., Gockley, R., Porter, E., Nourbakhsh, I., "The Personal Rover Project:
       The Comprehensive Design of a Domestic Personal Robot," *Robotics and Autono-
       mous Systems, Special Issue on Socially Interactive Robots,* 42, 245–258, 2003.

[67]   Feder, H.J.S., Slotin, J-J.E., "Real-Time Path Planning Using Harmonic Potentials
       in Dynamic Environments," in *Proceedings of the IEEE International Conference
       on Robotics and Automation*, Albuquerque, NM, April 1997.

[68] Fox, D., "KLD-Sampling: Adaptive Particle Filters and Mobile Robot Localization." *Advances in Neural Information Processing Systems 14*. MIT Press, 2001.

[69] Fox, D., Burgard,W., Thrun, S., "The Dynamic Window Approach to Collision Avoidance." *IEEE Robotics and Automation Magazine*, 4:23–33, 1997.

[70] Gander,W., Golub, G.H., Strebel, R., "Least-Squares Fitting of Circles and Ellipses." *BIT Numerical Mathematics*, vol. 34, no. 4, pp. 558–578, December 1994.

[71] Genesereth, M.R. "Deliberate Agents." *Technical Report Logic-87-2*. Stanford, CA, Stanford University, Logic Group, 1987.

[72] Golub, G., Kahan,W., "Calculating the Singular Values and Pseudo-Inverse of a Matrix." *Journal SIAM Numerical Analysis*, 2:205–223, 1965.

[73] Gutmann, J.S., Burgard, W., Fox, D., Konolige, K., "An Experimental Comparison of Localization Methods," *in Proceedings of the 1998 IEEE/RSJ International. Conference of Intelligent Robots and Systems* (IROS'98), Victoria, B.C., Canada, October 1998.

[74] Guttman, J.S., Konolige, K., "Incremental Mapping of Large Cyclic Environments," *in Proceedings of the IEEE International Symposium on Computational Intelligence in Robotics and Automation (CIRA)*, Monterey, November 1999.

[75] Hashimoto, S., "Humanoid Robots in Waseda University - Hadaly-2 and WABIAN," *in IARP First International Workshop on Humanoid and Human Friendly Robotics*, Tsukuba, Japan, October 1998.

[76] Heale, A., Kleeman, L.: "A Real Time DSP Sonar Echo Processor," *in Proceedings of the IEEE/RSJ International Conference on Intelligent Robots and Systems (IROS'00)*, Takamatsu, Japan, October 31–November 5, 2000.

[77] Horn, B.K.P., Schunck, B.G., "Determining Optical Flow," *Artificial Intelligence*, 17:185–203, 1981.

[78] Horswill, I., "Visual Collision Avoidance by Segmentation," *in Proceedings of IEEE International Conference on Robotics and Automation*, 902–909, 1995, IEEE Press, Munich, November 1994.

[79] Jacobs, R. and Canny, J., "Planning Smooth Paths for Mobile Robots," *in Proceeding. of the IEEE Conference on Robotics and Automation*, IEEE Press,1989, pp. 2–7.

[80] Jennings, J., Kirkwood-Watts, C., Tanis, C., "Distributed Map-making and Navigation in Dynamic Environments," *in Proceedings of the 1998 IEEE/RSJ Intl. Conference of Intelligent Robots and Systems (IROS'98)*, Victoria, B.C., Canada, October 1998.

[81] Jensfelt, P., Austin, D., Wijk, O., Andersson, M., "Feature Based Condensation for Mobile Robot Localization," *in Proceedings of the IEEE International Conference on Robotics and Automation*, San Francisco, May 24–28, 2000.

[82] Kamon, I., Rivlin, E., Rimon, E., "A New Range-Sensor Based Globally Convergent Navigation Algorithm for Mobile Robots," *in Proceedings of the IEEE International Conference on Robotics and Automation*, Minneapolis, April 1996.

[83] Kelly, A., "Pose Determination and Tracking in Image Mosaic Based Vehicle Position Estimation," *in Proceeding of the IEEE/RSJ International Conference on Intelligent Robots and Systems (IROS'00)*, Takamatsu, Japan, October 31–November 5, 2000.

[84] Khatib, M., Chatila, R., "An Extended Potential Field Approach for Mobile Robot Sensor-Based Motions," *in Proceedings of the Intelligent Autonomous Systems IAS-4*, IOS Press, Karlsruhe, Germany, March 1995, pp. 490–496.

[85] Khatib, M., Jaouni, H., Chatila, R., Laumod, J.P., "Dynamic Path Modification for Car-Like Nonholonomic Mobile Robots," *in Proceedings of IEEE International Conference on Robotics and Automation*, Albuquerque, NM, April 1997.

[86] Khatib, O., Quinlan, S., "Elastic Bands: Connecting, Path Planning and Control," *in Proceedings of IEEE International Conference on Robotics and Automation*, Atlanta, GA, May 1993.

[87] Ko, N.Y., Simmons, R., "The Lane-Curvature Method for Local Obstacle Avoidance," *in Proceedings of the 1998 IEEE/RSJ International Conference on Intelligent Robots and Systems (IROS'98)*, Victoria, B.C., Canada, October 1998.

[88] Koenig, S., Simmons, R., "Xavier: A Robot Navigation Architecture Based on Partially Observable Markov Decision Process Models," *in* [20]

[89] Konolige, K.,. "A Gradient Method for Realtime Robot Control," *in Proceedings of the IEEE/RSJ Conference on Intelligent Robots and Systems*, Takamatsu, Japan, 2000.

[90] Konolige, K., "Small Vision Systems: Hardware and Implementation," in *Proceedings of Eighth International Symposium on Robotics Research*, Hayama, Japan, October 1997.

[91] Koperski, K., Adhikary, J., Han, J., "Spatial Data Mining: Progress and Challenges Survey Paper,". *in Proceedings of the ACM SIGMOD Workshop on Research Issues on Data Mining and Knowledge Discovery*, Montreal, June 1996.

[92] Koren, Y., Borenstein, J., "High-Speed Obstacle Avoidance for Mobile Robotics," *in Proceedings of the IEEE Symposium on Intelligent Control*, Arlington, VA, August 1988, pp. 382-384.

[93] Koren, Y., Borenstein, J., "Real-Time Obstacle Avoidance for Fast Mobile Robots in Cluttered Environments," *in Proceedings of the IEEE International Conference on Robotics and Automation*, Los Alamitos, CA, May 1990.

[94] Kuipers, B., Byun, Y.-T., "A Robot Exploration and Mapping Strategy Based on a Semantic Hierarchy of Spatial Representations." *Journal of Robotics and Autonomous Systems*, 8:47–63, 1991.

[95] Lamon, P., Nourbakhsh, I., Jensen, B., Siegwar,t R., "Deriving and Matching Image Fingerprint Sequences for Mobile Robot Localization," *in Proceedings of the 2001 IEEE International Conference on Robotics and Automation*, Seoul, Korea, May 21–26, 2001.

[96] Latombe, J-C., Barraquand, J., "Robot Motion Planning: A Distributed Presentation Approach." *International Journal of Robotics Research*, 10: 628–649, 1991.

[97] Lauria, M., Estier, T., Siegwart, R.: "An Innovative Space Rover with Extended Climbing Abilities." *in Video Proceedings of the 2000 IEEE International Conference on Robotics and Automation*, San Francisco, May 24–28, 2000.

[98] Lazanas, A., Latombe, J.-C., "Landmark-Based Robot Navigation," *in Proceedings of the Tenth National Conference on AI*. San Jose, CA, July 1992.

[99] Lazanas, A. Latombe, J.C., "Motion Planning with Uncertainty: A Landmark Approach." *Artificial Intelligence*, 76:285–317, 1995.

[100] Lee, S.-O., Cho, Y.-J., Hwang-Bo, M., You, B.-J., Oh, S.-R.: "A Stabile Target-Tracking Control for Unicycle Mobile Robots," *in Proceedings of the 2000 IEEE/RSJ International Conference on Intelligent Robots and Systems*, Takamatsu, Japan, October 31–November 5, 2000.

[101] Lumelsky, V., Skewis, T., "Incorporating Range Sensing in the Robot Navigation Function." *IEEE Transactions on Systems, Man, and Cybernetics*, 20:1990, pp. 1058–1068.

[102] Lumelsky, V., Stepanov, A., "Path-Planning Strategies for a Point Mobile Automaton Moving Amidst Unknown Obstacles of Arbitrary Shape," in [10].

[103] Maes, P., "The Dynamics of Action Selection," *in Proceedings of the Eleventh International Joint Conference on Artificial Intelligence*, Detroit, 1989, pp. 991–997.

[104] Maes, P., "Situated Agents Can Have Goals," *Robotics and Autonomous Systems*, 6: 49–70. 1990.

[105] Martinelli, A., Siegwart, R., "Estimating the Odometry Error of a Mobile Robot during Navigation," *in Proceedings of the European Conference on Mobile Robots (ECMR 2003)*, Warsaw, September 4–6, 2003.

[106] Maybeck,P.S., "The Kalman Filter: An Introduction to Concepts," *in* [10].

[107] Minguez, J., Montano, L., "Nearness Diagram Navigation (ND): A New Real Time Collision Avoidance Approach," *in Proceedings of the IEEE/RSJ International Conference on Intelligent Robots and Systems*, Takamatsu, Japan, October 2000.

[108] Minguez, J., Montano, L., "Robot Navigation in Very Complex, Dense, and Cluttered Indoor / Outdoor Environments," *in Proceeding of International Federation of Automatic Control (IFAC2002)*, Barcelona, April 2002.

[109] Minguez, J., Montano, L., Khatib, O., "Reactive Collision Avoidance for Navigation with Dynamic Constraints," *in Proceedings of the 2002 IEEE/RSJ International Conference on Intelligent Robots and Systems*, 2002.

[110] Minguez, J., Montano, L., Simeon, T., Alami, R., "Global Nearness Diagram Navigation (GND)," *in Proceedings of the 2001 IEEE International Conference on Robotics and Automation*, 2001.

[111] Montano, L., Asensio, J.R., "Real-Time Robot Navigation in Unstructured Environments Using a 3D Laser Range Finder," *in Proceedings of the IEEE/RSJ International Conference on Intelligent Robot and Systems*, IROS 97, IEEE Press, Vol. 2. Grenoble, France, September 1997, pp. 526–532.

[112] Moravec, H. and Elfes, A.E., "High Resolution Maps from Wide Angle Sonar," *in Proceedings of the 1985 IEEE International Conference on Robotics and Automation*, IEEE Press, At.-Louis, MO, March 1985, pp. 116–121.

[113] Moutarlier, P., Chatila, R., "Stochastic Multisensory Data Fusion for Mobile Robot Location and Environment Modelling," *in Proceedings of the 5th International Symposium of Robotics Research*, Tokyo, 1989, pp. 207–216.

[114] Nayar, S.K., "Catadioptric Omnidirectional Camera." *IEEE CVPR*, pp. 482–488, 1997.

[115] Nilsson, N.J., "Shakey the Robot." *SRI, International, Technical Note*, Menlo Park, CA, 1984, No. 325.

[116] Nourbakhsh, I.R., "Dervish: An Office-Navigation Robot," *in* [20].

[117] Nourbakhsh, I.R., Andre. D., Tomasi, C., Genesereth, M.R., "Mobile Robot Obstacle Avoidance via Depth from Focus," *Robotics and Autonomous Systems*, 22:151–158, 1997.

[118] Nourbakhsh, I.R., Bobenage, J., Grange, S., Lutz, R., Meyer, R, Soto, A., "An Affective Mobile Educator with a Full-Time Job." *Artificial Intelligence*, 114:95–124, 1999.

[119] Nourbakhsh, I.R., Powers, R., Birchfield, S., "DERVISH, an Office-Navigation Robot." *AI Magazine*, 16:39–51, summer 1995.

[120] Pell, B., Bernard, D., Chien, S., Gat, E., Muscettola, N., Nayak, P., Wagner, M., Williams, B., "An Autonomous Spacecraft Agent Prototype." *Autonomous Robots*, No. 5, 1–27, 1998.

[121] Pentland, A.P., "A New Sense for Depth of Field." *IEEE Transactions on Pattern Analysis and Machine Intelligence (PAMI)*, 9:523–531, 1987.

[122] Philippsen, R., Siegwart, R., "Smooth and Efficient Obstacle Avoidance for a Tour Guide Robot," *in Proceedings of the IEEE International Conference on Robotics and Automation (ICRA 2003)*, Taipei, Taiwan, 2003.

[123] Pratt, J., Pratt, G., "Intuitive Control of a Planar Bipedal Walking Robot," *in Proceedings of the IEEE International Conference on Robotics and Automation (ICRA '98)*, Leuven, Belgium, May 16–21, 1998

[124] Raibert, M. H., Brown, H. B., Jr., Chepponis, M., "Experiments in balance with a 3D One-Legged Hopping Machine." *International Journal of Robotics Research*, 3:75–92, 1984.

[125] Ringrose, R., "Self-Stabilizing Running," *in Proceedings of the IEEE International Conference on Robotics and Automation (ICRA '97)*, Albuquerque, NM, April 1997.

[126] Rowe, A., Rosenberg, C., Nourbakhsh, I., "A Simple Low Cost Color Vision System," *in Proceedings of Tech Sketches for CVPR 2001*. Kuaii, Hawaii, December 2001.

[127] Rubner, Y., Tomasi, C., Guibas, L., "The Earth Mover's Distance as a Metric for Image Retrieval," *STAN-CS-TN-98-86, Stanford University*, 1998.

[128] Schlegel, C., "Fast Local Obstacle under Kinematic and Dynamic Constraints," *in Proceedings of the IEEE International Conference on Intelligent Robot and Systems (IROS 98)*, Victoria, B.C. Canada 1998, pp. 594–599.

[129] Schultz, A., Adams, W., "Continuous Localization Using Evidence Grids," *in Proceedings of the IEEE International Conference on Robotics and Automation (ICRA '98)*, May 16–21, 1998, Leuven, Belgium, pp.2833–2839 [also available as NCARAI Report AIC-96-007].

[130] Schweitzer, G., Werder, M., "ROBOTRAC – a Mobile Manipulator Platform for Rough Terrain," *in Proceedings of the International Symposium on Advanced Robot Technology (ISART)*, Tokyo, Japan, March, 1991.

[131] Shi, J., Malik, J., "Normalized Cuts and Image Segmentation." *IEEE Transactions on Pattern Analysis and Machine Intelligence (PAMI)*, 82:888–905, 2000.

[132] Siegwart R., et al., (2003) "Robox at Expo.02: A Large Scale Installation of Personal Robots." *Journal of Robotics and Autonomous Systems*, 42:203–222, 2003.

[133] Siegwart, R., Lamon, P., Estier, T., Lauria, M, Piguet, R., "Innovative Design for Wheeled Locomotion in Rough Terrain," *Journal of Robotics and Autonomous Systems*, 40:151–162, 2002.

[134] Simhon, S., Dudek, G., "A Global Topological Map Formed by Local Metric Maps," *in Proceedings of the 1998 IEEE/RSJ International Conference on Intelligent Robots and Systems (IROS'98)*, Victoria, B.C., Canada, October 1998.

[135] Simmons, R., "The Curvature Velocity Method for Local Obstacle Avoidance," *in Proceedings of the IEEE International Conference on Robotics and Automation*, Minneapolis, April 1996.

[136] Smith, R., Self, M., Cheeseman, P., "Estimating Uncertain Spatial Relationships in Robotics," *Autonomous Robot Vehicles, I. J.* Cox and G. T. Wilfong (editors), Springer-Verlag, 1990, pp. 167–193.

[137] Sordalen, O.J., Canudas de Wi,t C., "Exponential Control Law for a Mobile Robot: Extension to Path Following," *IEEE Transactions on Robotics and Automation*, 9:837–842, 1993.

[138] Steinmetz, B.M., Arbter, K., Brunner, B., Landzettel, K., "Autonomous Vision-Based Navigation of the Nanokhod Rover," *in Proceedings of i-SAIRAS 6th International Symposium on Artificial Intelligence, Robotics and Automation in Space*, Montreal, June 18–22, 2001.

[139] Stentz, A., "The Focussed D* Algorithm for Real-Time Replanning," in *Proceedings of IJCAI-95*, August 1995.

[140] Stevens, B.S., Clavel, R., Rey, L., "The DELTA Parallel Structured Robot, Yet More Performant through Direct Drive," *in Proceedings of the 23rd International Symposium on Industrial Robots*, Barcelona, October 1992, pp. 485–493.

[141] Takeda, H., Facchinetti, C., Latombe, J.C., "Planning the Motions of a Mobile Robot in a Sensory Uncertainty Field." *IEEE Transactions on Pattern Analysis and Machine Intelligence*, 16:1002–1017, 1994.

[142] Thrun, S., Burgard, W., Fox, D., "A Probabilistic Approach to Concurrent Mapping and Localization for Mobile Robots." *Autonomous Robots*, 31:1–25. 1998.

[143] Thrun, S., et al., "Monrovia: A Second Generation Museum Tour-Guide Robot," *in Proceedings of the IEEE International Conference on Robotics and Automation (ICRA'99)*, Detroit, May 1999.

[144] Thrun, S., Fox, D., Burgard, W. Dellaert, F., "Robust Monte Carlo Localization for Mobile Robots," *Artificial Intelligence*, 128:99–141, 2001.

[145] Thrun, S., Gutmann, J.-S., Fox, D., Burgard, W., Kuipers, B., "Integrating Topological and Metric Maps for Mobile Robot Navigation: A Statistical Approach," *in Proceedings of the National Conference on Artificial Intelligence (AAAI)*, 1998.

[146] Tomasi, C., Shi, J., "Image Deformations Are Better Than Optical Flow." *Mathematical and Computer Modelling*, 24:165–175, 1996.

[147] Tomatis, N., Nourbakhsh, I., Siegwart, R., "Hybrid Simultaneous Localization and Map Building: A Natural Integration of Topological and Metric." *Robotics and Autonomous Systems* 44, 3–14, 2003.

[148] Tzafestas, C.S., Tzafestas, S.G., "Recent Algorithms for Fuzzy and Neurofuzzy Path Planning and Navigation of Autonomous Mobile Robots," *Systems-Science*, 25:25–39, 1999.

[149] Ulrich, I., Borenstein, J., "VFH*: Local Obstacle Avoidance with Look-Ahead Verification," *in Proceedings of the IEEE International Conference on Robotics and Automation*, San Francisco, May 24–28, 2000.

[150] Ulrich, I., Borenstein, J., "VFH+: Reliable Obstacle Avoidance for Fast Mobile Robots," *in Proceedings of the International Conference on Robotics and Automation (ICRA'98)*, Leuven, Belgium, May 1998.

[151] Ulrich, I., Nourbakhsh, I., "Appearance-Based Obstacle Detection with Monocular Color Vision," *in the Proceedings of the AAAI National Conference on Artificial Intelligence*. Austin, TX. August 2000.

[152] Ulrich, I., Nourbakhsh, I., "Appearance-Based Place Recognition for Topological Localization," *in Proceedings of t he IEEE International Conference on Robotics and Automation*, San Francisco, pp. 1023–1029, April 2000.

[153] Vanualailai, J., Nakagiri, S., Ha, J-H., "Collision Avoidance in a Two-Point System via Liapunov's Second Method." *Mathematics and Simulation,* 39:125–141, 1995.

[154] Van Winnendael, M., Visenti G., Bertrand, R., Rieder, R., "Nanokhod Microrover Heading towards Mars," *in Proceedings of the Fifth International Symposium on Artificial Intelligence, Robotics and Automation in Space* (ESA SP-440), Noordwijk, Netherlands, pp. 69–76, 1999.

[155] Weiss, G., Wetzler, C., Puttkamer, E., "Keeping Track of Position and Orientation of Moving Indoor Systems by Correlation of Range-Finder Scans," *in Proceedings of the IEEE/RSJ International Conference on Intelligent Robots and Systems (IROS'94)*, Munich, pp.595–601, September 12-16, 1994.

[156] Wullschleger, F.H., Arra,s K.O., Vestli, S.J., "A Flexible Exploration Framework for Map Building," *in Proceedings of the Third European Workshop on Advanced Mobile Robots (Eurobot 99)*, Zurich, September 6-9, 1999.

[157] Yamauchi, B., Schultz, A., Adams, W., "Mobile Robot Exploration and Map-Building with Continuous Localization," *in Proceedings of the IEEE International Conference on Robotics and Automation (ICRA'98)*, Leuven, Belgium, May 1998.

[158] Zhang, Z., "A Flexible New Technique for Camera Calibration." *Microsoft Research Technical Report 98-71.*, December 1998
[see also http://research.microsoft.com/~zhang].

Referenced Webpages

[159] Fisher, R.B. (editor), "CVonline: On-line Compendium of Computer Vision," Available at www.dai.ed.ac.uk/CVonline/.

[160] The Intel Image Processing Library: http://developer.intel.com/software/products/perflib/ipl/.

[161] Source code release site: www.cs.cmu.edu/~jbruce/cmvision.

[162] Newton Labs website: www.newtonlabs.com.

[163] For probotics: http://www.personalrobots.com.

Interesting Internet Links to Mobile Robots

General homepages with mainly mobile robots

http://ranier.hq.nasa.gov/telerobotics_page/coolrobots.html
http://www-robotics.cs.umass.edu/robotics.html
http://www.ai.mit.edu/projects/mobile-robots/

http://www.ri.cmu.edu/project_lists/index.html
http://www.roboticsclub.org/links.html
http://www.activrobots.com/
http://asl.epfl.ch (at EPFL)
http://robotics.epfl.ch (at EPFL)
http://www.cs.cmu.edu/~illah/EDUTOY (at CMU)
http://www.cs.cmu.edu/~mercator/ (at CMU)

Homepages with mainly wheeled mobile robots
http://www.laas.fr/RIA/RIA.html
http://www.cs.cmu.edu/~illah/lab.html
http://www.cs.umd.edu/projects/amrl/amrl.html
http://www.cc.gatech.edu/ai/robot-lab/
http://www.engin.umich.edu/research/mrl/index.html

Homepages with walking and climbing robots
http://www.uwe.ac.uk/clawar/
http://www.fzi.de/divisions/ipt/
http://www.automation.hut.fi/
http://www.ai.mit.edu/projects/leglab/
http://asl.epfl.ch/
http://www.cs.cmu.edu/~personalrover/

Homepages for robots on the Web
http://telerobot.mech.uwa.edu.au/secn/links.html
http://queue.IEOR.Berkeley.EDU/~goldberg/art/telerobotics-links.html
http://www.cs.uni-bonn.de/~rhino/
http://www.cs.cmu.edu/~minerva/
http://telerobot.mech.uwa.edu.au
http://www.ieor.berkeley.edu/~goldberg/GC/www.html
http://pumapaint.rwu.edu/
http://mars.graham.com/wits/
http://www.cs.cmu.edu/~illah/SAGE/index.html
http://www.dislocation.net/
http://rr-vs.informatik.uni-ulm.de/rr/
http://www.eventscope.org/Eventscope/main.htm

Index